EBBING TI

A Final Fishy Tale

Dedication

This book is dedicated to those remaining fishermen around our coasts who have survived the worst the EU, assisted by the UK government, have wreaked to date. I sincerely hope they have the resilience to continue their way of life in this unequal fight and pray that one day their livelihood will be secure from political oppression.

CONTENTS

ACKNOWLEDGMENTS

Grateful thanks are due to my sister, Jan Palmer, Jilly Manser, Alana Parker, Ian Forbes and Rita Wharton, my dedicated, conscientious proofreaders. Jilly Swales, a stickler for punctuation, sadly passed away days before the completion of this book and will be missed by family and friends. Thanks to Capt. Martin Willis, Steve Johnson, Dave Winspear and Trevor Goodall for their invaluable help with Scarborough, Bridlington and Whitby boats and skippers names. Thanks to the staff at the Scarborough Public Library for their assistance with archive material and to Geoff Jefferson for his photographic assistance. Finally, my thanks as ever to Dave Mercer, Duncan Beal, Cathi, Clare and Christopher at YPS for their professional work and guidance in preparing this volume.

AUTHOR'S NOTES

I have attempted to keep this book light hearted and in the same humorous vein as the earlier volumes with tales of the hard working, hard drinking culture that was the Scarborough and Yorkshire fishing industry during my working life. But this, the final volume in the series, has been difficult to document, as some parts relate to the sad decline of the UK fleet. The earlier books depict the wonderful way of life I was born into and in which I made my career, tracked from a 1950's childhood through to the early 80's. Apart from real life humour at sea and ashore, readers will discover within this volume the insidious way in which this lifestyle has been taken away from fishermen by politicians, sacrificed to the alter of Europe by the government of Edward Heath.

CHAPTER 1

LIFE AND DEATH IN THE SKIES

The group were gathered close together on one side of the minibus at the end of the runway in excited anticipation, not knowing what to expect. The windows in the vehicle were slid open and the occupants vied to gain clear vantage for the coming display. They didn't have long to wait. A loud, throaty roar of engines sounded from the distant aircraft, which were suddenly hurtling in their direction at a huge rate of knots. The noise became even louder as the silver jets drew close. Despite being inside the bus, hands were cupped over otherwise unprotected ears as the sound grew to an unbearable crescendo. The speed of the two craft was incredible as they left the ground in close succession, adjacent to the open-mouthed, wide-eyed gathering. The red, twelve-seater bus rocked wildly from the slipstream and the watchers struggled to take in the scene unfolding before them. The 'Lightnings' didn't just leave the ground, the massive twin-engines powered the beasts almost vertically into the sky, flames belching from their over and under jet engines. In no time at all there was just the pinprick glow of exhausts to be seen by those in the front seats, then nothing. Only the distant sound of thunder gave any evidence of the planes' passing until the massive double explosion as the vanished jets passed through the sound barrier, accelerating to fifteen hundred miles an hour.

The little gathering was speechless, unable to find words sufficient to describe the recent show, which had been organised just for them. The reverie was broken when a confident voice at a window addressed the group inside. "We'll take you to the mess now ladies and gentlemen. We have some food and refreshments and a small acknowledgement of your efforts. I'm sure you won't be disappointed. Please follow us." The officer returned to his Land Rover and his driver slowly led the way to the accommodation block.

The visitors weren't disappointed. The evening programme at this RAF Station in South Yorkshire had been organised with military precision and was very special.

Following a splendid buffet and some generous measures from the mess bar, the Commanding Officer presented Colin Lawson, chairman of the Scarborough Sub Aqua Club with a shield depicting the base's insignia. He also handed over a polished wooden plaque on which were mounted three cannon shells, then finally the identification number, cut from the fuselage of a 'Lightning' jet fighter.

One of the downsides of the spectacular show was that I wasn't available to witness the demonstration, being at sea. The other negative was that the Station's hospitality was in appreciation to the members of the diving club for their recovery of the body of a 'Lightning' pilot from the sea in Scarborough's North Bay a few weeks earlier. Members from the club had also marked the wreckage of the plane to assist in the salvage of the broken aircraft, after I'd helped to locate the downed jet with the sonar on my new vessel, *Emulator.*

The fighter had been flying low over the bay, the pilot executing some spectacular manoeuvres when catastrophic engine failure caused the plane to ditch into the sea. The pilot had stayed with his aircraft until he was sure of avoiding the busy shoreline before ejecting, but sadly too late to survive the crash. The club's diving boat had been crossing the bay and the occupants, witnessing the ditching, quickly headed for the parachute, useless on the surface but still attached to the pilot. Sadly the man's body was broken and inert. They had been unable to save the flier's life. The fantastic visit to the airbase was the RAF's way of showing appreciation to the diving club for their involvement and I'd missed the occasion.

"Those were his," one of the deceased pilot's fellow officers said sadly as he pointed to the flying boots nailed to the ceiling. There were other pairs in close proximity, marking the passing of earlier fliers who'd courageously turned their toes up in the service of their country in these 'Cold War' times.

The story of the air display was being recounted, among other tales as we congregated in the clubhouse around the beer filled table not long after noon on Saturday, while planning our next expedition. The past twelve months had been memorable for the club members. We'd broken new ground with our expedition to the 'Well Bank' the previous summer, then the jet fighter episode was followed months later by the *Navena* incident. Some members had been instrumental in helping the insurers inspect the ship when *Emulator, Our Heritage* and *Cassamanda* had beached the stricken trawler after she'd been abandoned and was in danger of foundering.*

Our latest plan was to head southeast to Flamborough Head then on to the Dudgeon Lightship and beyond to the shallow, wreck-strewn grounds of the Humber approaches. Meanwhile, there would be a couple of weeks fishing to be done and we'd be sailing soon after midnight. There was a new problem on the horizon for British fishermen. The European Commission had deemed that all vessels fishing for whitefish, as well as adhering to the recent quota restrictions, must also tie up for eight consecutive days each month. The fact that we sailed in the early hours of Sunday and landed each Thursday morning, spending almost three days each week in port, made no difference.

Following a hunch, rather than steaming off to our usual hunting grounds seventy to ninety miles offshore, we'd sailed in the early hours and shot the trawl twelve miles from port, on grounds where we'd often taken good hauls in the past. A four-hour drag had yielded a reasonable haul of quality fish and we'd put the net down again, hoping for similar results. The lads on deck had picked up ten boxes of fish and were gutting this catch. We were on clear ground with no shipping close by, so I took the opportunity to put a light under the kettle then dropped down the cabin ladder

* See The Tide Turns.

to seek out a jar of coffee and a packet of biscuits. I was surprised to discover Colin Thompson, a Hull crewman, lying on the cabin floor unconscious. I almost tripped over his inert body. What had happened to him? How long had he been here? The man was supposed to be on deck with the others, processing the catch. He couldn't have been here for long, we'd only been trawling about three-quarters of an hour. I bent down and shook him but got no response. Patting his face two or three times I received an incoherent mumble. He was alive but 'spark out'.

I rushed up the ladders then out onto the deck where the other hands were gutting the catch. "What's wrong wi' t' big feller?" I yelled. "'E's flaked out on t' cabin floor. Ah thought 'e was dead."

Mick, spokesman for the trio of knife-wielding men said, "'e was feelin' lousy an' was 'ardly movin' so we told 'im to get turned in. We thought 'e'd feel better after t' next 'aul."

"'E could 'ave 'ad an 'eart attack. Why didn't yer tell me? Go below an' mek 'im comfortable," I called, then dashed to the wheelhouse to radio for assistance. It was lucky for the casualty that we were close to home and not at our normal offshore haunts. Calling the Coastguard on the VHF radio, I was soon patched through to a doctor who carefully asked for relevant details and symptoms.

On receiving this information the medic advised that the patient should be airlifted to hospital as soon as possible. The Coastguard would scramble a helicopter.

I reported our vessel's position to the shore station then went below to check the patient's condition. There seemed little change apart from the pillow and blanket now in place. Leaving Mick with the inert crewman, I returned to the wheelhouse. Sean and Gordon engaged the winch clutches and we commenced hauling the trawl. I took care of the aft trawl board, securing the ungainly object in position and unclipping the heavy G link. Polished chain that had recently been dragged along the seabed now rattled in the block above my head as the net came into view. The three of us scrambled the net onboard and were soon heading for home.

Shortly after returning to the wheelhouse I was responding to a radio call from the helicopter and could see the aircraft on the radar. In no time the big yellow bird was hovering above us, its spinning rotors generating a massive downdraft, creating white water around our vessel. An RAF crewman appeared at the open door and was lowered to our afterdeck to organise the operation. The next drop brought a doctor and a secure stretcher.

The medic was escorted to the casualty and the prone deckhand was given a thorough check over. To assist in his diagnosis, the crew, now back from the deck after stowing the fish below, were also questioned about their shipmate's immediate history. The doctor discovered that the Hull man had been pricked by a spike from a gurnard's dorsal fin during our previous voyage, shortly before we headed for home. Colin's two days ashore had been mostly spent sleeping and feeling lethargic. He'd returned to the boat hoping to feel better as the week progressed but his condition had worsened. With this additional information the doctor diagnosed septicaemia.

An oxygen mask was placed on the unconscious man's face and he was strapped into the stretcher but we were then faced with the difficult job of getting the immobile patient out of the cabin. The Hull man was over six feet tall and heavily built. The cabin hatch was only two feet square, offset on the port side with the exit up a vertical, iron ladder. Though we now had six fit men onboard and had the stretcher upright with lines attached from above, we faced an impossible task. We couldn't get the unconscious man from the cabin. I reported this to the pilot of the helicopter.

A Royal Navy Fishery Patrol Vessel was passing close to our position, heading north and on hearing my message her Commanding Officer quickly despatched a small boat with an officer and three ratings to assist in the evacuation. We had plenty of strong, willing helpers but even with the additional naval personnel, the hatch was so inaccessible that it was impossible to get sufficient bodies close enough to be of use.

"Why don't we take 'im out through t' cabin's emergency 'atch, straight on t' t' deck?" Mick suggested. "Mebbe we could use t' winch."

5

This was a great idea and the answer to our dilemma. We'd need a vertical lift but if we passed a wire from the trawl winch through a block on the mast above the hatch, we'd be able to take the casualty from the cabin with no trouble at all. It took only a few minutes to lead a wire to a point directly above the now open hatch and the stretcher was gently hauled vertically from the cabin to be laid on the deck. The chopper was signalled to approach and the now manoeuvrable human cargo was quickly transferred to the helicopter, escorted by the RAF crewman. I requested and was given permission to accompany the sick man to hospital, so leaving Mick and the remaining hands to take the boat back to Scarborough, I was lifted up to the chopper along with the doctor.

As we were assisted into the helicopter's cramped interior by the third flyer and pushed towards a seat, I was surprised to see a uniformed nurse already administering to the patient. The doctor took over the care of the patient and the attractive young redhead was fastened into the place at my side. During the short flight back, above the deafening noise of the engine, the lovely nurse turned in my direction shouting, "I don't know what I'm doing here, I'm terrified of flying, I won't even go on holiday by plane. When the helicopter landed in the hospital grounds, the doctor and I thought the patient was on board. We climbed inside, then the helicopter took off and we were flown out here."

The big crewman was efficiently moved to the hospital and minutes later I caught up. Sitting outside the pristine hospital ward I felt very conspicuous, hot and smelly, awaiting the diagnosis from the doctor, now assessing the sick fisherman. It was a couple of hours before septicaemia was confirmed, but the infection had been caught in time and our big shipmate was expected to make a full recovery. This wonderful news was also given to Colin's wife, who'd newly arrived, post-haste from Hull. Knowing the good news I took a taxi home to a very surprised Dotty, who wasn't expecting to see me for several days yet.

We sailed again at midnight and fortunately were not short-handed. Dave 'injection' Allison, a fair-haired, pale faced lad had offered to fill the vacant berth at short notice until our regular man recovered. Dave was a good hand and had been in several boats over the years. His nickname, by which he was universally known, was due to nothing more sinister than him being a diabetic and using a syringe to take his insulin.

We'd returned to the grounds we'd been working before the incident. The results from the brief time we'd spent earlier were promising. The tow we were doing was in a north/south line but as the coastline runs northwest/southeast, our distance from land at the southern end was about nine miles, moving out to approximately fourteen miles from shore at the northernmost part. On the second haul of the day, as the catch dropped from the codend, a large silver fish fought its way from under the mass to flap vigorously on the top of the pile. This was a magnificent wild salmon and must have weighed about 9 or 10 pounds. "That's mine," I called out before anyone else could lay claim to the fish and in due course the lovely creature lay on top of the ice below in the fish-room.

Late morning the following day, as we were heaving the trawl up, the same navy ship that had assisted us the previous day came steaming south again, still on patrol. This time we were in for an official visit. "*Emulator, Emulator,* this is the Royal Naval vessel on your port side. I notice you're hauling your trawl. I'm sending my small boat across to conduct an inspection. Please give my boarding party your full co-operation."

This sounded very formal. Until recently boardings had been rare and were usually friendly affairs. The inspections were quite cursory, though we had nothing to hide and the sailors invariably left with half a basket of fish for their evening meal. Now, with membership of the EEC, reductions in quotas and more intense policing, we no longer 'enjoyed' visits from the Royal Navy.

The boarding party arrived while we were stopped in the water with our net on the deck. Three men were put onboard and the small boat stood off to await the return of the sailors. The officer in charge came to the wheelhouse. With little in the way of greeting he said, "good morning skipper. Can I see your vessel's catch logbook?"

It was hard to believe this was the same man who yesterday had been helpful and obliging. The big, rectangular, blue book with gold lettering on the cover that had been requested was on the chart table, opened at the correct page. I'd just spent the past five minutes filling in the relevant columns, knowing he was coming. The book was the official catch recorder now carried by every vessel over fifteen metres in length. Each numbered page was in quadruplicate. The first three pages were carbon coated so when the white copy was completed the coloured sheets below received the same information. The bureaucracy was becoming mind-boggling. At the end of each day by law, we were required to record the number of boxes stowed below, species by species and the total estimated weight of each box had to be marked in the correct column. A twenty percent tolerance for error was permissible. Punitive fines were in place for non-compliance. This allowance would later be reduced to ten percent.

The top two sheets of the logbook were left with our fish-selling agent who, following the auction handed these, along with a copy of his sales ledger, to the Fisheries Inspectorate. The two amounts were then compared for accuracy before being forwarded to the Ministry of Fisheries and Food (MAFF) in London. Presumably this information was then directed to Brussels.

The officer asked me to sign the logbook, verifying its contents before copying the details meticulously into his notebook. Next he made his way to the deck where, producing an aluminium gauge from his shoulder bag, proceeded to measure the codend meshes. I knew he was wasting his time, as our netting was bigger than the required legal size. Nevertheless he pushed the wedge shaped measure through twenty different diamonds, calling out each reading to an assistant who'd joined him for this exercise and who jotted the number in the notebook. On completion of the exercise a calculator appeared from the official bag and the average size of the netting was tabulated.

He was unappreciative when I pointed out that as all twenty readings were over the legal limit, the sum total had to be greater than the legal requirement.

"I need an average figure," was all he'd say.

Next the officer wanted to see our catch, though I was keen to get our trawl back down as we were wasting time needlessly. The lads were still picking up the most recent haul from the deck, watched by the third matelot as I accompanied the official to the fish-room, along with his pencil-pushing assistant. The additional sailor appeared to have little to do other than observe the proceedings and chatted cheerily with the lads on deck as we passed. His hand gesture, directed at, and unseen by his superior warmed me to him immediately and I grinned, nodding in agreement with his sentiments.

The number of boxes in the hold must have been comparable with the recorded sum, so with regret, the unhappy chap looked at me and said, "Everything seems to be in order here skipper."

"Ah could 'ave told yer that 'alf an hour ago an' saved yer all this trouble," I replied with equal lack of humour.

His next retort was predictable. "I'm only doing my job."

As he stepped towards the ladder, 'Officer Jobsworth' spied my salmon on the ice. Stiff in rigor mortis, the superb fish, without a scale missing, looked like a bar of silver. Its beautifully formed tail was like a feather, in contrast to the farmed variety of the species where tails and fins are totally disfigured, having been chewed by the other fish in the pen. "What's that?" the lieutenant asked, more out of curiosity than from a professional perspective.

"It's a salmon," I replied. "It's goin' 'ome wi' me when we get in." I could equally have said, "it's a halibut, a mackerel or a kipper." The man would have been no wiser.

"Ah ha," he said, a sparkle coming to his eyes and as if by magic, the notebook reappeared. Pausing only briefly to raise and moisten his pencil the officer said, "Did you catch this fish inside or outside the twelve-mile limit?"

"Outside," I replied without hesitation, thinking that would put us outside the UK's territorial limit and his jurisdiction.

"Ah, then I must ask you to return it to the sea," he said, pleasure noticeable in his voice.

Crestfallen at my wrong choice of a line on a chart I replied, "alright then, we caught it inside o' twelve miles."

"You've already stated that you caught this fish outside the limit," he countered.

"Well ah thought that's what yer wanted me t' say. Ah thought yer were tryin' to 'elp me. We've been trawlin' north an' south, in an' out o' t' twelve-mile line. 'Ow do ah know where we caught it? The bloody thing's dead now anyway. What's the point o' dumpin' it?"

The verbal jousting continued. "I really must insist you return the fish to the sea, skipper. You're not allowed to have this salmon onboard."

This was news to me. I'd never heard of this regulation, though we seldom encountered these migratory fish. As I climbed the ladder back to the deck leaving the fish untouched on the ice, I turned and assured him, "Ah promise yer that the fish will eventually end up back in t' sea." I was thinking, via digestive then sewerage systems.

The officer wasn't satisfied with my dubious promise but realising my resolve, didn't seem prepared to confiscate the fish, so following me to the deck he gathered his dignity and his team then signalled the rubber boat. His parting shot as he climbed over the port side was, "you'll be hearing more about this matter skipper."

The trawl was already going over the starboard side as, for want of something better to say I replied, "no doubt ah will." This was another example of the change of attitude of the Fishery Patrol Vessels. Not too long ago we only saw the 'Grey Funnel Line' when they wanted fish for dinner. Now they were enemies, fulfilling Europe's political requirements, via an obsequious national government.

We fished on without incident for the remainder of the week and by early Thursday had enough fish below to ensure a reasonable wage and headed for home, but the boarding and the parting comment of the bureaucratic officer had stayed in my thoughts. With half a mile to go to the pier-end I eased the engine down and allowed *Emulator* to come to a stop, looking for a likely small boat to give assistance. I hadn't long to wait. Within minutes Bill 'Blondie' Wood came alongside in his little passenger boat, *Adventure* with a party of anglers on board. Bill was the head launcher of the lifeboat and was the last of the dozens of small boat operators who, post war made a living taking tourists on fishing trips and excursions in the bay. He also worked a couple of fleets of lobster pots, which he hauled three times a day. "What's up?" Blondie called, knowing we wouldn't have stopped unless we had a problem.

"Can yer tek this in fo' me?" I asked, holding the rigid silver creature by the gills. "T' bogeyman might be waitin' for us," I added by way of an explanation. "Put it in yer warehouse. Ah'll get it later."

Without question he reached up, taking the fish by the gills on the other side of its head and quickly wrapped the stiff salmon into sacking, which he normally used for covering and quietening any newly caught lobsters.

"See yer later," he said, engaging the engine of his flimsy little vessel. His hand unconsciously scratched his head below the peak of his cap and he gave a theatrical wink. His shout of, "save us a fry," as he moved off was totally expected.

Sure enough, as we pulled alongside the pier, the Fisheries Inspector was awaiting our arrival. I nodded in his direction in acknowledgement as I climbed the ladder to the quay. "'Ave yer been waitin' for us?" I asked innocently.

The balding, bespectacled inspector was a changed man since being compelled to enforce inequitable regulations. He'd gone from being a friendly, cheery chap who would pass the time of day with a chat to a warrant-carrying policeman who was no longer trusted. "Not specifically," he replied, "but I have had a report that you may have a salmon onboard, taken outside the twelve mile limit."

"Ah thought yer might 'ave," I replied. Truthfully I said, "it went back over t' side before we got t' 'arbour. Yer can search me boat from top t' bottom if yer want."

He declined the invitation, though happened to be in the vicinity when we eventually left the boat to go home, having landed the catch.

Later the same morning, following a bath, change of clothes and a visit to the Alliance office for our pay packets, I exchanged two haddocks and two lemon soles with Blondie for a large, silver fish.

I took the opportunity during the afternoon to visit our casualty, still in the hospital and due to be transferred to the Hull Royal Infirmary. Though still quite weak Colin was coherent and updated me on the events he could recall during the previous few days. He'd undergone intensive blood transfusions and had subsequently broken out in large, black skin blotches, though these had mostly disappeared now. In turn I told him of his unorthodox exit from the cabin, the nurse and the passage ashore.

Thanks to the prompt response of the Coastguard, RAF and the hospital staff, our shipmate had survived, though it had been touch and go for the first few hours. He remembered nothing of his time in the cabin or of his lift and ride in the helicopter, though vaguely recalled seeing a nurse hovering over him at some point. The fates had certainly been on his side and watching over him that day. If we'd been fishing further from land, as we usually were, we may have been out of range of the helicopter. If we'd been going further offshore he could have been in his bunk for at least another seven hours. Would he have died? If the big fella had managed to get into his bunk instead of collapsing on the cabin floor, we would almost certainly have allowed him to remain there for an extended period. That would have been fatal.

CHAPTER 2

A ROYAL TIME

I arrived home from the harbour one evening in February to be greeted by an excited Dotty who said, "You've had a phone call from Jimmy Saville. He's ringing you back in half an hour."

"You're kiddin'," I answered, knowing my wife could be mischievous, though unable to think why she'd say this other than if it were true. "Did 'e say what 'e wanted?"

This well-known television personality had originally been a presenter on the prime time television programme, 'Top of the Pops', playing the latest hit records from the charts. He'd later gone on to host his own show, 'Jim'll Fix It'. The format was that Jim helped to make wishes come true, mostly for younger viewers. I was extremely curious to know why he wanted to contact me.

The ringing phone, immediately following a hot bath, promised to ease my curiosity. The distinctive voice said, "I guess I'm talking to Fred." On confirmation he went on to inform me that he'd had a request from no less a person than HRH, the Prince of Wales. The heir to the throne was planning to visit the Yorkshire Coast later the following month and had expressed a desire to meet some fishermen from the area. Jimmy enquired if I was able to 'fix it' by producing four fishermen from Scarborough, four from Whitby and the same number from Bridlington.

My mind whirled. This would be no problem at all, quite the reverse in fact. I knew lots of men fishing from all these ports. My dilemma was that I would lose friends by being unable to provide additional places. In the brief conversation I assured the presenter that I could oblige. He wouldn't divulge where he'd acquired my name and contact details or why the future king would wish to meet a gang of rowdy trawler-men. The caller went on to say the venue was to be an Italian Restaurant in Redcar on Teesside, an hour's drive north. "Why there?" I asked. "Doesn't 'e want t' come t' Scarborough? It's closer an' much nicer."

Jimmy didn't know the answer. I was informed that I'd get more details through the post in due course from the Prince's personal equerry.

I replaced the receiver, confused. Was this a big hoax? The whole scenario was incongruous. My doubts were removed when the letter of invitation and instructions, printed on thick, cream paper, embossed with the royal coat of arms arrived while I was at sea. I subsequently gave some thought to those I'd like to take along and began discreetly asking the individuals if they'd be willing to participate. All said yes.

Though there were still several weeks before the big day, word had got out that we were to meet Prince Charles. "Yer could 'ave asked me," was a phrase I heard often and felt quite guilty explaining that I was strictly limited in the numbers I could take.

* * * * * *

"I think we've trawled some drugs up," Col Jenkinson, skipper of the new vessel, *Our Pride* said, half way through the next week. "There's a polythene bag with twenty five smaller plastic packs inside." He went on to describe the heavy parcel containing a brown coloured substance. "Jimmy thinks it's cannabis resin," he added. Jimmy was one of *Our Pride's* crew and was fairly street-wise. It was a safe bet that he'd be right. We were fishing about eighty miles to the north-northeast and were catching at a steady rate. Strangely, there were several Dutch beam trawlers fishing in the area. This wasn't a place where we caught any quantity of flatfish and were not seeing many now.

The weather remained fine and the latter part of the trip passed with little out of the ordinary. Along with several other vessels, *Our Pride* and *Emulator* landed moderate catches in time for Thursday's market. Later in the morning, following a few hours at home in bed I returned to the harbour to find the place a hive of activity. Police cars were parked prominently and a team of divers were operating in the harbour close to *Our Pride*. "There's bloody 'ell on," Col said when I caught up with him on the quayside. "A couple o' them buggers aboard my boat opened that pack an' 'ave been messin' about with it. Some of it's gone missin'." He went on to describe how he'd handed the parcel over to the authorities but two of the blocks had been removed. Clearly the drug squad officers were all too familiar with what was supposed to be in the package and had questioned the crew. One of the culprits, not realising the seriousness of the situation said they'd thrown the missing packets in the dock. Now police divers were searching the mud at the bottom of the harbour in zero visibility for the missing substance and were having no luck.

The missing packets were handed over by the culprits late in the morning when it became obvious that the police were not going away and were taking a hard line. There was still the threat of wasting police time but realising there was nothing sinister about the crewmen's actions the pair were given a severe rocket by the senior officer and no further action was taken.

* * * * * *

Dotty and I, as usual were in the Leeds Arms on Thursday evening to discover that Les, the long time landlord had lost none of his perverse nature. Bill, the barman and protégé of the host reported that during the week they'd had another visit from Alan Ayckbourn, the world-famous playwright. The writer, who lived close by, occasionally visited the hostelry with members of his cast.

The great man, who'd innovated and developed the revolutionary 'Theatre in the Round' in the town, would greet the host profusely. Les, true to form, would always be rude and surly in return. The landlord's attitude and his reluctance to open punctually, which should have coincided with the end of rehearsals, eventually wore the writer down. He and the theatre company stopped visiting the Leeds Arms. Alan Ayckbourn never forgot Les and his perversity however and realised he'd been presented with some wonderful material for his next play.

* * * * * *

We returned to the same grounds the following week on our own, to discover there were still a couple of Dutchmen in the area. Early on the third day at sea as the net emerged I thought we'd taken a good haul of fish. There were haddock and cod floating belly-up in the mouth of the net, but for some reason the codends wouldn't surface. There was something weighing the bag down, quite possibly a small stone or an old oil drum. As we pulled on the bellies the floating fish were forced down the sleeve till all were trapped in the thicker netting and it was a good haul. The catch just fitted inside the 'lifting rings' but part of the haul would be the, as yet unidentified heavy object. A dull thud sounded as the fish spilled to the deck but there was no sign of its cause, though the sight of a pound full of quality fish was pleasing to the eye. There'd be plenty of time to investigate the catch when the gear was back on the bottom.

I watched with interest through the open window as the fish were picked up into the wooden boxes. There were some fine quality cod scattered through the ten boxes filled so far. A tapping on the wheelhouse attracted my attention causing me to lean out and look down. Mick was holding a heavy, brown coloured polythene bag up to his chest. "Look what we've got 'ere Freddy," he said, grinning.

I didn't need telling what this was. The description Col had given me left me in no doubt that we'd also caught a bag of illegal substance. Before I could speak there was a further surprise. "There's another one 'ere," Sean called up excitedly, exposing an identical package from beneath a pile of small, undersized haddocks. Curious, I left the wheelhouse briefly, leaving the boat steering on autopilot and went onto the deck, taking possession of the newly excavated find. Though expecting the tightly sealed bag to be heavy, I was still surprised at its density. Each of the small blocks weighed one kilo. Twenty-five kilos was almost four stone. With Mick trailing behind lugging the other parcel I dragged mine to the pound at the stern, where our spare nets were stowed. I nestled the weighty object into a secure position leaving enough room for the second bag. With a serious expression on my face I turned to Mick who was my accepted second in command and said, "Fo' fucks sake Mick, don't let 'em touch these. Col was in a heap o' trouble last week with that stuff 'e'd caught. We could finish up in jail."

Though we stayed in the general area for another thirty-six hours, luckily we caught no more of the stuff and set off for home on Wednesday evening. As soon as we were in VHF range on the homeward passage and with a further three hours to steam, I contacted the watch-keeper in the lighthouse, asking the duty officer to notify the police that we had two parcels of illegal drugs onboard. I said I wanted to hand the bags in and we'd be in harbour at about 0600 hours. With an hour to go I contacted the shore base again to arrange for Dad and Eddie, our shore team to turn out and to gather a supply of empty boxes in readiness for landing. I wasn't prepared for the reception committee as we steamed through the piers.

Though it was still early morning, conspicuous around the harbour on all the piers, I could see uniformed officers. More officials were present as we came alongside the fish market. Two of their number hurried down the ladder before any of our complement could leave the boat and the lads were then prevented from going ashore. I was out of the wheelhouse like a shot. "Oy, leave 'em alone. The stuff yer lookin' for is aft on t' spare nets an' it 'asn't been touched."

To my surprise these men were customs officers, not policemen. "It must be a joint operation," I thought, chuckling to myself at the pun. I led the pair to the stern, pointing to the two polythene bags, wedged in the storage space. "Is that what yer lookin' fo'? Ah wasn't expectin' a confrontation."

The pair looked at each other and nodded. One gave a thumbs-up sign to a superior officer on the quayside and he in turn spoke into a radio. It was as if a safety valve had been released. The tension went out of the situation and the men's attitude changed dramatically. Taking possession of the drugs, one of the pair, notebook in hand, asked for the position where we'd caught the parcels. Mr Notebook then asked politely if I had any objection to his men making a cursory search of the *Emulator*. We had nothing to hide so I gave consent then left them to it. We had fish to land.

The Chief Customs Officer stepped forward to introduce himself as I reached the pier top, but then instinctively took a step back as either the sight of five days growth of beard or a not much shorter period without a shower offended his senses. Realising he'd little choice, the man stepped forward again, shaking my hand and expressing thanks for our public spiritedness. He said there would be a reward.

Keen to get our fish ashore I just said I wasn't expecting anything and anyone else would have done the same, though noticed no sum was stated during this brief encounter. The mention of a reward cheered up at least one of my crew who was sure he could have obtained a large sum of money for the contents of the parcels given the opportunity. His joy soon turned to dismay when he was informed that no one was going to benefit from drugs, even indirectly and any reward would go to the recently established, St Catherine's Hospice.

We were later to discover that our catch was only a small part of a four-ton cargo jettisoned offshore when the crew of the vessel carrying the substance realised they were being shadowed by a customs launch. The cargo was worth millions.

A few weeks later I was contacted by Customs and Excise and a date was agreed when we could meet for the formal presentation of a cheque as a reward for our honesty. The press would be on hand for publicity. I requested that the cheque be made out to the local hospice and contacted a lovely lady from the organisation, asking if she would like to come along to accept the donation.

The following Saturday, showered, clean-shaven and wearing some smart casual clothes I turned up at my vessel, berthed on the West Pier. Until I spoke to Mandy from the hospice, the customs officer and his assistant hadn't recognised me as the skipper of the *Emulator*. When the gold-braided officer realised I was the scruffy, smelly person he'd met previously, this time he didn't recoil in horror but shook my hand vigorously. He took great pleasure in handing over an envelope, which I accepted with thanks. I passed the envelope, unopened to the hospice representative.

With good grace the lady waited till the press had taken their photos and the party had left the pier before opening the sleeve. Handing back a letter of thanks that was addressed to me, the lady looked at the cheque. It was made out for the sum of £150. Following our unusual catch the newspapers reported that our two-pack haul had a street value of £70,000. No wonder the beam trawlers were fishing in the area. Catches of that stuff would be worth a fortune on the Amsterdam market.

Over the next few weeks I frequently wondered what would have happened if we'd caught the first parcel and not *Our Pride*. I'm sure the bags would have been opened out of mere curiosity. Events would have turned out differently for us if the contents had been tampered with.

* * * * * *

The big day of the royal visit finally arrived and along with Col from *Our Pride*, Bluey, my partner in *Independence* and John, a skipper and director in the Alliance agency, I travelled to the arranged location. Very foolishly, I'd volunteered to drive. The Whitby and Bridlington contingents had shrewdly arranged chauffeurs. It was shortly after noon when we arrived at the venue. The Prince of Wales was scheduled to arrive at 1245 hours. Crowds were thronging the streets waving patriotic union flags and with reporters and television crews also present we felt quite important. Showing our letter of invitation we were able to pass through the police security cordon in the street and presenting this same document to the personnel at the entrance to the restaurant, we gained access.

Inside the door we discovered at least twenty tables, of four people, all of whom we discovered had paid £20 for their place. Hovering uncertainly in the centre of the room and feeling conspicuous in full view of the waiting audience, we were spied by the restaurant owner and quickly ushered upstairs. My immediate thought was that we were being moved out of the way before the Prince arrived. This was dispelled when at the head of the stairs we met up with our colleagues from Brid' and Whitby and with them, three Redcar fishermen. One of the Whitby men, pointing to a magnificent seafood and meat buffet said, "Look at that lot." The spread, extending the full length of one wall was, literally a feast fit for a king.

We'd arrived at the location very early so still had some time to kill before the royal visitor arrival. "'Ave you lads ordered any drinks?" I asked after introductions and handshakes with the Redcar men.

"There dun't seem much chance o' that," Tom Cowling from Brid' answered. "That little Italian bloke's dashin' back an' forward like a fiddler's elbow. 'E ignored us when we asked 'im if we could 'ave a beer."

Half an hour passed and we were all feeling overdressed and uncomfortable in these unfamiliar surroundings and were in need of refreshments to slake our thirsts and lighten the atmosphere. The Italian owner, immaculately dressed and clearly anxious, was fussing with his final preparations and studiously ignoring the strange group gathered in his upstairs room. He was eventually confronted by one of the Whitby men while attempting to pass without eye contact. "'Ere mate, any chance o' some beer. Can yer get us fifteen pints?"

Now challenged, the dapper proprietor snapped, "you can 'ave nothing till da great man arrive. I want no drunken fishermen spoil dis day. You can 'ave drink when Prince come, and will you please keep a little more quiet?" The Italian stormed off full of importance. We were clearly not welcome in his establishment.

We continued clock watching and the appointed hour came and went with no sign of the Prince of Wales or any beer. After some dry coughing and mumbling the group of mariners were growing very restless and ten minutes later with still no royal appearance, the Italian was again asked to supply drinks. The man was flustered and realising he was facing a mutiny, condescended to allow each of us a glass of wine. This was a start, we all agreed, but what use was a little glass of wine to a thirsty fisherman. The glasses were soon empty and now there was no sign of the owner. The regal party was clearly running late and the owner would be downstairs hovering between the door and his eighty paying customers, all sitting with knives and forks poised and like us, becoming impatient.

"'E got t' wine from that little pantry over there," another of the Whitby men said, pointing. Ah bet there's some more in there." He looked down the stairs, making sure there was no sign of the worried owner then dashed to the beaded curtain screen, parting the strings of wooden baubles with both hands and sticking his head through the gap. Seconds later he withdrew his head and turned in our direction, a huge, crafty grin on his face. "There's bloody 'eaps o' booze in 'ere," he called out in a stage whisper, hiding his mouth behind a raised palm, then added, "an' they're all open."

Not waiting to elaborate further, the pathfinder disappeared through the screen. There was a general movement in his direction but I urged caution. "'Ang on lads, we can't all go at once. Jus a few at a time, then 'e won't notice if some of us are missin'." I pointed a finger towards the staircase to where we knew the twitchy owner would be stationed. As soon as possible without drawing attention, I too slipped behind the curtain. There were indeed lots of bottles of wine. The reds were standing opened on the table with the corks loosely replaced. There were also four silver buckets of ice, each containing two bottles of white. The ice, though now mostly melted had clearly done its job and the bottles were coated with fine globes of dew. In the centre of the table stood a large, very special bottle of wine. Leaning against this container was a card, hand-written in copperplate saying, 'HRH, The Prince of Wales'.

I knew very little about wine, but enough to know what 'Gran Reserva' meant and the bottle was clearly old.

"Shall we 'ave some o' that?" Arnold, one of the Whitby boys at my side asked.

I was horrified, not knowing if he was joking, until a daft grin spread across his face and he gave a cackling laugh.

"Yer'll finish up in t' Tower o' London if yer touch that," I replied, then pointing in the direction of the stairs added, "if t' Mafia don't get yer first."

"We'll 'ave some o' this then," he said, picking up a fresh bottle of red. There were already two empty bottles on the table and we weren't the last in the queue.

"T boss isn't going t' like this. I 'ope Charlie comes soon or there'll be bugger all left at this rate." I replied. "Good job there's safety in numbers."

It was about 1330 hours when the Prince finally arrived and there were more empty wine bottles to testify to his delay. We knew he was close when we heard cheering from the crowd outside. Then looking down the staircase I saw HRH and his party on the floor inside the main door where we had previously stood. The owner of the restaurant greeted the royal visitor and his entourage profusely. Next he turned to introduced his beautiful, raven-haired wife to the Prince. The lady must have been waiting in private quarters and had appeared for the first time with the arrival of the honoured guest.

"'E'll be ages yet," the Whitby trailblazer said, heading for another drink. "'E's got t' get round that lot down there before 'e comes up 'ere."

There was a murmur of agreement from our group but amazingly the Prince walked past the eighty, paying and now applauding guests with a regal wave and headed for the stairs.

"Bloody 'ell e's comin' up 'ere," I said, stating the obvious.

We moved away from the top of the stairs nearer the pantry as the missing Whitby man shot out, glass in hand, wondering what was happening.

Ignoring the gawping, now pleasantly mellow fishermen who were spoiling his day, the Italian with his stunning wife in company, guided the royal guest towards the splendid display of food. The centrepiece of the banquet was a beautiful, white marble statue of a nude Roman god, which the Italian pointed to and named. Though the piece was too heavy to lift easily, the owner made it clear that this work of art was a gift for the Prince and his wife, Princess Diana. The present was accepted with good grace but then after a cursory glance at the magnificent food, HRH noticed the group of uneasy fishermen at the rear of the room and immediately headed in our direction, much to the dismay of the owner.

The future King put us at ease immediately, shaking hands and speaking briefly to everyone. He asked knowledge-based questions of what type of vessels we operated, which species we caught and what areas we fished, and seemed to have a genuine interest in our answers and our way of life. I presented him with a folder of enlarged action photographs of fishing, showing bad weather at sea and deck loads of fish, which he seemed to find very interesting.

In turn he told us of his time at sea serving in the Royal Navy, where he spent time on small, wooden minesweepers that were renowned for being uncomfortable in heavy weather, rolling wickedly. He made us laugh when he said he was dreadfully seasick and had tried many remedies but the best cure he'd ever found was to sit under a tree. The restaurant's waiters were now dispensing the remaining bottles of the excellent red wine.

Soon it was time to eat the splendid food and a smart waiter escorted us to a table, laid up with fifteen place settings. A few feet away, a smaller table had been set for three; clearly for the smart Italian owner, his wife and the Prince. The royal visitor immediately vetoed this arrangement saying, "I've come to meet these people," and insisting that the tables were put together. The future King relocated several times during the meal, talking in turn to everyone. The special bottle of wine, which was opened under the guidance of the proprietor, was decanted into glasses and circulated. Prince Charles commented on the quality, though frankly I couldn't tell the difference now, having imbibed several glasses already.

His Royal Highness moved again and I found myself sitting to his right. On his left was the raven-haired beauty. The Prince was eating some very tasty smoked salmon and was also attempting to talk to the Italian lady. "I do enjoy salmon, don't you?" he asked politely.

The beautiful woman seemed flustered and appeared none too fluent in English. In a stilted voice she falteringly replied, "yes I like salmon," which appeared to end the conversation.

HRH turned in my direction and said, "I do like salmon, but I like them best when I've hooked one in the river. They're great sport." He then asked, "Have you ever hooked a salmon?"

It was at this point that I uttered the gaff that will remain with me for the rest of my days. In my best English I replied, "no Your Highness, I've never had a salmon on a rod. I caught one last week in my trawl net. One of your Mum's gunboats came along an' tried to take it off me."

The Prince coughed slightly as the sip of wine caught in his throat but he quickly recovered his composure. The heir to the throne never uttered a word of comment but the raised eyebrows spoke volumes.

When HRH had moved again to chat to some of the others, his equerry, a Lieutenant Colonel who'd been keeping in the background, crossed the room to say hello and introduce himself. This was the officer who'd corresponded with me to formalise the arrangements and had sent the invitation and instructions following the original phone call. The officer informed us that the visit was now running an hour and a half late but that when he'd reminded Charles of this fact, HRH had informed his secretary that he was in no hurry to move to his next engagement just yet.

Sadly, all too soon this special occasion did come to an end and about 1600 hours the royal visitor departed. The Whitby fisherman who'd first attempted to get drinks for all hands called out to the owner, "now can we 'ave fifteen pints o' bitter, landlord." As an afterthought he said, "an' bring a bottle o' 'Chivas Regal' an' some glasses."

The proprietor nodded and the drinks duly arrived, along with a bill. "Dat will be £57 sir, t'ank you."

A large cheer went up at the skipper's generosity, but this was short-lived. The poor man rocked on his chair and almost choked on the remains of his drink. Recovering from the shock he forlornly made the gesture of searching his pockets, eventually raising slightly over £18. His bacon was saved by a 'tarpaulin muster' by all present. The joint collection covered the bill and the embarrassment. Following this episode and another round of drinks it was agreed that we should travel to Whitby and continue the party there.

The Whitby men's driver was dutifully waiting outside the building but the Brid' chauffeur had become bored waiting, and had departed to the nearest pub for a beer. He was now less sober than his charges.

I very foolishly decided that I'd be able to take our group to the party, though I also rang Dotty, asking her to take a taxi to Whitby, from where she would be able to drive us back to Scarborough.

The party continued in Whitby for a while, where Dotty, having left Paula and Danny to look after little Sarah, joined us. My lovely wife, exceedingly tolerant with four very happy and somewhat inebriated fishermen onboard, drove back to Scarborough. On arrival it was agreed that perhaps we should just have maybe one more beer in the Leeds Arms to round off a perfect day, and what a day it had been for those who could remember it.

CHAPTER 3

HURRICANE

The cold wind was screaming from the west-northwest and must have been reaching force 10 to 12. I'd never experienced such awesome power. The sea was totally white, the spindrift flying high into the air and obscuring visibility. *Emulator's* deckhouse was vibrating as she forced her bluff bow into the swells. We were to the southeast of Flamborough Head, fifty miles from home, though only twenty-some miles from land and making for the shelter of Bridlington Bay. The seas were not huge, as the wind seemed to be flattening rather than building the waves. Had the gale been from the north it would have been a different story.

Incongruously, the wheelhouse was dry and warm and I was clad only in shirt and jeans and was wedged back in a comfy, hydraulic chair, my feet, in carpet slippers were firmly jammed against the steering wheel, helping to keep my position. The autopilot, clicking rapidly with every adjustment was holding our course steady in a way no helmsman could match. It was difficult to imagine how only a generation ago men would have coped with these conditions in their smaller boats and clearly, in the days of sail, this storm would have been a widow maker. The fishing smacks, if unable to anchor, would have been driven mercilessly downwind and offshore under bare poles until the growing seas swamped them.

My beautiful vessel with her broad beam and deep draft was, at three-quarter speed, taking this punishment in her stride. The heavy spray was constant across her open deck, lashing the wheelhouse and swilling against the windows. The whaleback and its wave-break were stopping any weight of solid water coming over her stem. The fish-room hatch was secured in place by six solid clamps and wouldn't yield despite the weather.

There hadn't been much in the trawl when we'd hauled after the storm had dramatically struck, and the lads had quickly cleared the fish down into the hold before securing the hatch. They were now below in their bunks, oblivious to the screaming maelstrom above.

Concentrating on the radar, I was as certain as I could be that no shipping was in close proximity and thought I'd drop down into the engine room to check the oil level in the big 'Kelvin' diesel and have a quick look round to ensure nothing untoward was occurring. This could be achieved within five minutes and I could press the red button on the autopilot again before the alarm sounded, waking the sleeping men below. Time spent in the engine room checking belts, bilges and gauges was never time wasted.

The fireproof, spring-loaded door, which also kept out most of the sound, snapped at my heels as I stepped across the ten-foot drop to the steel ladder opposite. The noise was deafening but I ignored the ear defenders hanging on the top rung, knowing I'd only be a few minutes in this sense numbing environment. The entire machinery space was brightly lit and I quickly went about my visual check. It was comforting to see only a small amount of water in the bilge and I briefly engaged the pump to remove these dregs. Glancing at the collection of drive belts at the fore-end of the main engine powering her electrics, water pump and steering, all was well.

Rag in hand I drew the dipstick from the sump, wiping the black oil from the long thin rod then quickly pushed the stick in and out to obtain an accurate reading. Half a gallon of new oil would bring the level back to full and I unscrewed the hot filler top, immediately inverting the flat top onto the floor plates. The two-inch hole, now exposed on the side of the crankcase was quickly plugged with a large plastic funnel, preventing hot flecks of oil flying up from within the machine. Filling a spouted tin jug from a five-gallon drum, I poured the golden liquid into the funnel in a steady stream.

Reaching for the brass filler cap, I swiftly pulled out the funnel and put back the stopper. This was a precarious operation, as the top was hot and was threaded. I'd dropped the cap into the bilge weeks earlier when scorched fingers were unable to engage the thread in time, resulting in the deployment of a wooden plug and a messy fishing operation under the engine.

Mission accomplished I stood upright and for the first time noticed an olive-green metal nut with part of a broken bolt still in place in the thread. The engine was painted olive-green so this fragment must be a part of the machine that had broken off. It took only seconds to spot that the hardened-steel bolt had been one of six on the timing shaft, connecting the fuel pump to the engine. This could have serious implications if any more were to sheer on this flange. I wasn't immediately concerned but would have to monitor the situation closely.

Twenty minutes later I dropped down the ladder again to discover my worst fears were justified. Another bolt had given way. The stress on the remaining bolts would be magnified and though we carried spares for almost every durable component onboard, this failure was unheard of and we had no bolts of this type. Returning to the wheelhouse I eased the engine to slow, which immediately alerted the men below and they were soon emerging from the cabin. "Get t' anchor ready," I instructed. "We 'ave a problem below an' I'm gonna 'ave t' stop t' engine."

The watertight door from the accommodation to the deck was hooked back and the horrendous weather outside was clear for them to see. Eyes were rolling as the lads began donning their oilskins in preparation for their work on deck. Though we had two anchors on board, one for'ard and one aft, we'd never needed to use a 'hook' before and both were firmly lashed to strong points away from the working areas.

The anchor under the whaleback was released and carried with difficulty across the rolling deck to the for'ard gallow. The stock was manoeuvred into place and the locking pin hammered home then lashed with heavy twine for good measure. The net was unshackled and the anchor attached in its place. The 5/8th alloy chain was worn but strong enough to hold the vessel if sufficient cable was deployed. With the hook hanging overboard, I slowly turned *Emulator* up into the wind and pulled the throttle to neutral. The force of the wind stopped her almost instantly and she began blowing downwind with her starboard, working side across the weather. I opened a forward facing window and looking to the winch man shouted, "leggo!"

There was a rattle of chain and I knew the anchor would quickly hit the bottom. This entire area was shallow and nowhere more than twenty fathoms. It was essential that the cable be allowed to run out unfettered before the brake was applied. "Let it run! Don't check it!" I bawled at the top of my voice, not sure the muffled character behind the winch could hear me. The thirty fathoms of chain ran out and as this was attached to the trawl warp, this thick wire also began to flow off the winch and over the side as *Emulator* blew down wind at speed. "Keep it goin'," I encouraged. "Don't stop till yer get t' 'undred fathom mark." I hoped there'd be sufficient spring in the cable at that point to arrest her passage without putting undue stress on the chain.

The ten and twenty-five fathom marks ran quickly through the top block then, inexplicably as if in slow motion, I watched the winch man screw up the brake, stopping the flow of wire as the forty-fathom mark shot out. "Don't stop it yet!" I screamed, my head almost out of the window in my anxiety to be heard, but I was too late. He looked in my direction as the wire drew taught as a bowstring, briefly slewing the heavy vessel's starboard bow into the wind then with a sudden jerk, the tension left the cable. The chain had parted.

I was dumbstruck at the stupidity of this action that had lost us not only part of our fishing bridle but one of our anchors too. "Yer might as well pull it back now," I shouted, as he looked askance in my direction. "It's fuckin' parted."

The wire and remaining chain, both highly polished from the abrasive rocky seabed were soon recovered onto the winch and I wasn't about to deploy our remaining hook yet. While *Emulator* blew rapidly eastwards, the growing waves cascading across her rolling deck, Mick and I went below and I stopped the engine. I pointed to the damaged joint and was relieved to see four bolts still in place. The pair of us scoured the various storage spaces and raked through the boxes of spanners for any suitable nuts and bolts. Collectively we found a half dozen useful pieces of varying thicknesses and lengths. I selected the two nearest to the required size and though rusty these were not seized. In a few minutes we again had six bolts in place. I was hopeful these would do the trick and now sweating profusely from the build up of heat from the hot engine, I pressed the button. The machine fired into life and the lights, powered from batteries, which were draining from lack of charge, brightened significantly. We were back in business.

There was no abatement in the weather yet. Usually extreme winds tend to whip across the country quickly but this one was persisting. Altering to our original course, and plotting our position on the chart from the 'Decca' navigator, I was amazed to discover we'd blown several miles out to sea and modified our course accordingly. The lads headed for the mess-deck for a smoke and a yarn and five minutes later Sean handed me a steaming mug of coffee. I was still sweating from the heat of the engine room.

I was checking the shaft regularly now and all was well for the first couple of hours. I was pleased to hear Col onboard *Our Pride*, calling from the harbour on the MF radio, asking for our position and a progress report.

On hearing of our difficulty he offered to sail and escort us home but I hoped this wouldn't be necessary. Col promised to keep regular radio schedules till he was sure we were out of trouble.

We were making reasonable progress even at half speed and before too long Flamborough Head appeared on the twelve-mile range on the radar. The wind had moderated slightly and we were benefitting from the lee of the land when one of the replacement bolts gave way. Not waiting for further damage, the engine was quickly stopped and the next strongest bolt, now cleaned and greased was fastened in place and nipped up. The passage resumed but the remaining spare bolts were thinner so we were sure to have trouble again before long. At least we were close to land now and couldn't blow ashore with the strong off land wind. The second anchor was shackled up and ready for letting go.

The sea flattened as we gained Flamborough Head and the wind had dropped to gale force but we'd lost two more bolts. Another stop and these were replaced but our supply of spares was dwindling and the remaining pair thin. These were used at the north end of Filey Bay and now we were out of bolts. We were on a wing and a prayer but no longer in danger. I was reluctant to ask Col for help and while I'd been a skipper I'd never needed assistance from the RNLI. We seemed to be crawling to the northwest and Mick soon reported another bolt had gone. With no spares, we were down to five. Another bolt went with three miles to go, then one of the green studs at two miles. I pulled the throttle to neutral a quarter of a mile from the pier-end and went below for a final inspection. Only two bolts remained in place and the flange was looking very vulnerable and was unlikely to get us to the harbour. If the two halves separated, the timing of the fuel injected into the engine would be lost, so with reluctance I stopped the machine. Racking my brains, I wondered how we could keep these two matching parts together.

I remembered an incident on my first vessel *Pioneer*, when we'd made a temporary repair on the winch shaft by lashing both parts together with rope, enabling us to recover our gear. It was worth a try. With Mick's help we secured the four exposed pairs of holes with as many turns of twine as the orifices would allow, then gingerly started the engine once more. The shaft was turning.

I hurried to the wheelhouse and at slow speed pointed *Emulator* towards the port entrance. The wind was only force five or six now and she behaved faultlessly as we made the harbour. Our ropes were thrown to the waiting pierman and with a final gentle burst astern taking the way off her, not waiting to ensure she was properly secured I dashed below and stopped the engine. We'd made it. There were strands of broken twine scattered across the engine plates and the flange had begun to twist out of position as the stress on the remaining bolts finally told, but it didn't matter now. We were home.

Chapter 4

A Winter Dive

It was almost December and as I strode up the hill from the harbour I noticed my Mother sweeping the step outside her house. I called out, "Hiya Mum. It's your birthday this weekend, are yer plannin' anythin' special?"

"Oh hullo Freddy," she replied, looking up as I approached. "Yes we're going to the Crescent for Sunday lunch. I've booked for all the family."

"Oh Mum," I said disappointed, "yer know we go t' sea on Sundays. Why don't you 'ave it on Sat'day night? That'd be better for us, then we can still sail next mornin'. I'd be 'appy t' pay for it."

"I want to go to the Crescent on Sunday. If you want to go to sea that's up to you," Mum replied matter-of-factly.

This was mother at her most stubborn and I knew better than to argue, though felt miffed that I'd have to alter our fishing routine to suit the occasion. My crew thought it highly amusing early on Saturday evening when they rang for sailing information and I had to say to each in turn, "we can't go t' sea tomorrow. My Mum won't let me."

We sailed at midnight on Sunday and fished through till Thursday night. There was only one more week to work now then we'd finish for the Christmas period. The time went fast, as December always seems to, and seven days later I found myself sitting in the Sub Aqua Club with some diver pals. We were reliving the summer expedition out on the 'Well Bank' where we'd dived several wrecks and discovered a submarine. This vessel was lying on its side with the thin plated conning tower detached and crumpled on the seabed. The hatch to the interior of the craft was open but almost the entire working space within the vessel had filled with silt, allowing no room for access. The hull of the craft appeared intact until we'd reached her stem where strangely an explosion appeared to have blown open the extreme tip of the sub's bows, revealing her forward torpedo tubes, but the space was so confined there was no way into this part of the vessel either. The wreck was not large and it had taken little time and effort to cover the length of the small sub' on both sides. The corpse of a dead porpoise lay tight alongside the hull and had given a scare to those who first encountered the body. Close by the mammal, a cluster of the marine growth, 'deadmens fingers', fallen from the wreck looked just like the real thing, adding to the eeriness.

One of her propeller blades lay on the seabed close to the two still attached to the boss. There was no evidence of lost trawling gear having caused this savage break and it was highly unlikely that a wire could have inflicted this damage. The thickness of metal at the point of severance was substantial. Speculation had been rife on the passage home. How had the blade been severed? Was the propeller still turning when the vessel hit the bottom? Had the piece snapped off on contact? Possibly. Had the crew been trapped inside and attempted to use the engine? Had they escaped through the open hatch? We didn't know the nationality of the mysterious craft, though it was probably German. Club members had the charted positions of several U boat wrecks off the Yorkshire Coast from both wars. These enthusiasts had dived on them all.

Pete, a club stalwart and joint author of 'Shipwrecks of the Yorkshire Coast' had subsequently done some research on our find and discovered she was *HMS C29*, a British submarine lost in World War 1. She had been commanded by Lt W R Schofield and had been targeting German U boats. The Hun was engaged in economic warfare and had sent hundreds of British trawlers to the bottom, including a large part of the Scarborough fleet. These little steam vessels were not deemed worthy of a torpedo and were boarded and scuttled with explosive charges in their engine rooms.

Their crews were usually allowed to take to the small boat though occasionally skippers were taken captive.

Research into the circumstances of the loss revealed that the submarine was being towed, submerged by the trawler, *Ariadne*, a decoy, when enemy U boats were known to be in the area. She was supposed to surface, surprise and sink the German vessels. This had worked on at least one previous occasion but then, on 29th August 1915 the *C29* had been inadvertently towed into a British minefield and lost. This explained the shattered stem.

The conversation turned to *UB 107* that lay on the seabed only three-quarters of a mile from Flamborough Head. This U boat, also from the Great War was stuck in the wreck of the merchant ship *Malvina*. Both ships were lost with all hands, so the circumstances of their coming together will never be known. Records show that *UB 107*, commanded by Kapitanluetnant Von Prittwitz, sailed from Zeebrugge on 26th July 1918 with thirty-seven officers and men, bound for the East Coast of England. *Malvina* is recorded as being torpedoed off Flamborough Head on 2nd August 1918 with the loss of her crew of fourteen.

According to the 'Loss list'* from World War 1, an armed yacht, *Vanessa*, in company with three requisitioned trawlers is credited with sinking *UB 107* north of Whitby on 27th July 1918. Oil was seen on the surface and these four vessels stayed on site in poor weather overnight. A headless corpse in German uniform was found on the surface the following day. Divers failed to find the wreck.

The U boat, identified by her number, etched on the propeller, must have survived this encounter and made her way to Flamborough. Had the steamer's crew seen the U boat on the surface and rammed her with the loss of both ships? Had the U boat hit the wreck of the *Malvina* while submerged? No one will ever know, but more than fifty men lost their lives when these vessels came together.

UB 107's periscope is now housed in the Sub Aqua Club. I'd been one of the relay team of divers that had hacksawed the steel tube from its position on the seabed.

* Also see 'U Boats Destroyed' by Paul Kemp.

"Is there any vis' at the Well Bank at this time of year?" someone asked.

A murmur of interest sounded within the group at this leading question.

"It'd be reasonable," I replied, still not sensing what the questioner had in mind. "Yer'd maybe get ten or twelve feet, max', ah'd guess. That's better than we get inshore in summer sometimes," I added.

"I've found a photo of the inside of the conning tower on this type of sub," another of the lads said. "The bell is hanging just inside the hatch, near the ladder."

This information seemed to inject even more excitement into the group. "We've all got dry suits. Why can't we go out there during this coming holiday?" the speaker added quickly.

"No reason at all really," I stupidly answered, judgement clouded by several pints of beer. "We could go t' day after Boxing Day. If we sailed on t' evenin', we could be there before breakfast, but we'd only get one slack water in daylight. There's less than eight hours o' light so it'd be a one dive trip if we went."

This proposed scenario seemed to find unanimous favour and plans were made to sail on the evening of the 27th, subject to weather. "This isn't the best dive trip you've been involved in," I told myself as we left the clubhouse. "Pray fo' bad weather."

Bad weather came, but not in the form of wind or waves. It snowed heavily overnight between Christmas Day and Boxing Day in the north east of England and a three-inch covering lay on the ground when I awoke on Boxing Day morning. It was the day of the Fishermen and Firemen's comic football match on the beach, with its usual crazy goings on. I'd been refereeing the game for several years now but would it have to be cancelled today? I hoped not. There'd never been a cancellation before.

Phone conversations with the two other key players and organisers, Billy Blades and Barry McNally, who both lived in the 'Bottom End', confirmed my own thoughts that the match should go ahead so with a couple of other early birds, I went to the beach to erect the goalposts.

The pitch looked very strange, the top half coated white where the snow was undisturbed and the lower half smooth, wet sand, where the high tide had left its mark, melting the white covering. This brown/white line ran between the goal posts, which were standing in barrels filled with a mixture of sand and snow for support. Our decision to go ahead with the match was vindicated from the players' perspective when the rabble arrived at the Foreshore, having followed the lively 'Comic Band' in parade from the town centre. No one complained at all about the conditions, though few would feel the cold, such was the amount of alcohol imbibed prior to the kick off.

The Mayor kicked off the proceedings, coating himself in snow in the process then quickly ran through the powder to the safety of the promenade. It wasn't possible to guarantee the welfare of the dignitary once the chaos had commenced.

The game progressed with the usual mayhem, though most of the combat took place on the lower end of the pitch near the sea with occasional splashing at the water's edge. It was extremely amusing when the ball was at the top end of the pitch when clouds of loose snow were propelled into the air when the ball was kicked. There were dozens of snowballs hurled between teams and a few faces rubbed in the powdery surface during unofficial scrums to gain ball possession.

Half time was shortened, allowing only enough time for a quick beer and toilet before proceedings recommenced, in the hope the few dozen hardy folk watching from the pavement beyond the railings, wouldn't drift away.

More madness, snowballing and splashing took place in the second half but despite the bitter cold, all too soon, the game was drawing to a close for another year. Skilled moves, tough tackles and 'no-holds-barred' play had only been interrupted when a combatant lost his hat, conceding a free kick. Miraculously, again none of the gladiators had incurred any serious injury, apart from the odd bruising. Several would struggle to walk tomorrow. Considering these lads had been on tour, drinking in houses and illegally in pubs since before sunrise, then consumed a bottle of beer at half time, their resilience was amazing. The players were certainly not feeling cold, unlike the spectators who, though well muffled had begun to move off.

I waited till the play was at the far end of the pitch away from the lifeboat station and pier when there was less chance of my being scragged and thrown into the sea, before blowing the whistle, bringing the contest to a finish. A couple of new players were promptly grabbed, held by arms and legs then carried into the freezing sea to be dropped. The teams quickly made their way to the lifeboat station for the presentations.

A small crowd of spectators had gathered in front of the lifeboat where Jimmy Saville, who had a place on Scarborough's South Cliff, overlooking the sea, was standing on the boat carriage, preparing to award the trophies to the team captains. The original, battered old gold-painted cup was presented to the winning team along with a bottle of rum. Incongruously a big, shining silver trophy was handed to the losers plus, a half bottle of whisky. Jimmy presented the 'Man of the Match' trophy and spoke for a couple of minutes about the good work of the charity, which gave meat and grocery vouchers to a significant number of old folk from the 'Bottom End' to redeem in local shops.

As soon as the speaker had finished and the crowd began moving away, I rushed along the seafront to watch the raft race. This was another manic event where the main requirement to enter was a lack of sanity. The water was not much above freezing and there was a fair chance, with the piratical behaviour of the crews and saboteurs that many competitors would end up swimming. A few years ago Danny, though only eleven, had been asked to participate in the Sub Aqua Club race around the harbour. Steve and Richard had built a raft, then enlisted the lad when they realised at the eleventh hour, that the minimum number of crew required to enter the race was three.

It was still extremely cold and I watched the closing stages of the competition with more than passing interest. I felt really sorry for Danny in his thin wetsuit as he paddled around the course with his buddies. There was a split in the fabric under his arm, which would remove any warmth the wetsuit may have had, and worse, would allow water in.

Despite being short-handed, the little raft was in the lead. I watched open-mouthed as a rogue diver approached the fragile craft with sabotage in mind. To my horror Danny raised his paddle and pole-axed the closing frogman with the edge of the blade. The would-be saboteur fell away, with a wound to the head. Minutes later the little craft hit the slipway: the club raft had won the race. The poor casualty had been taken to hospital by car, a wad of cloth held to his wound. I'd rushed to the frozen, tearful Danny and hurried him up the hill to home, teeth chattering. His Mum put him in a hot shower before peeling the light wetsuit from him.

An hour later, back at the clubhouse I met up with Steve and Richard and a warmer, happier Danny and listened to their story. Danny's body had been numb with cold due to the split in his suit till Richard had grabbed a floating plastic bag, stuffing the piece of jetsam in the gaping hole and psychologically cheering the lad instantly.

"It was me who told him to hit the diver with his paddle," Steve said, "but I meant with the flat of the blade. I didn't expect an attempted murder. He's OK though, just needed a few stitches."

It was the following afternoon when we assembled on the quayside where *Emulator* was berthed, her deck coated in snow. There was hardly a breath of wind so the weather gods had ignored my silent pleas for a gale. "Are yer sure yer want t' do this?" I asked the assembled party. "It'll be bloody cold out there."

Though there seemed some reluctance in the group now the moment had arrived, no one was prepared to voice their doubt. "Right! We'll start by shovelling t' snow off 'er decks," I instructed. "Then we'll get all t' kit aboard."

"We must be bloody crackers," I said to Pete and Steve, who were standing in the wheelhouse as *Emulator* steamed between the piers outward bound with a small inflatable RIB in tow.

The pair just grinned. They were keen to explore the submarine again.

Watches were shared through the long night as *Emulator* steamed slowly offshore. There was no rush; we'd be on location before dawn.

The sea looked grey and uninviting, though there was only a gentle swell as a watery sun reluctantly rose above the horizon, creating a glorious orange sky. Slack water was still a couple of hours away so there was plenty of time for breakfast and to locate the wreck. The target was only small, its beam not as wide as *Emulator's* and it was important to hit the spot with the shot line. There'd be no second chance if we missed the wreck and dived into the desert.

At 1000 hours after marking the wreck and dropping the heavy 'plonker' grapnel, I was one of eight divers wearing dry suits to hit the water, swimming towards the buoy. Two others remained on board, one to look after *Emulator,* the other to drive the RIB and recover the gear from the surfaced divers. This pair would dive on our return. There was no tide at all as we finned towards the buoy. The exposed flesh around my facemask was numb but worse still, I could feel a trickle of cold water penetrating my suit at the chest dump-valve.

There was little order as the bunch of frogmen hauled their way down the line and it was impossible to locate or identify my buddy. Torches were switched on as the gloom deepened and the sandy bottom came into view but there was no immediate sign of the wreck. I'd missed the sub with the shot. The expedition was going to be a total failure and it was my fault.

The visibility wasn't as good as I'd hoped and no more than six to eight feet. Torches were directed ahead but there was no shadow of shipwreck looming in the multiple scatter of light. Someone, probably Pete indicated by sign that one person stay at the bottom of the shot rope holding a torch, while others fanned out in an arc, swimming the extent of their own torch beams. I was now shivering with the quantity of seawater in my suit and couldn't concentrate on what I was supposed to be doing, but swam away from the rope, making sure I could still see the signal light over my shoulder.

Shining my torch in an arc into the dark desert with others on both sides, I saw nothing but sand, bits of weed and the occasional brown crab but now didn't care whether we found the wreck or not. I just wanted to get back on board *Emulator,* out of this non-dry suit and into the warm galley. Turning round I headed for the dim beacon, teeth chattering so much I could hardly clench the rubber mouthpiece. Others were returning with the same results and were shaking heads and waving palms of hands in a negative sign. I looked at Pete and he indicated upwards with a jerking thumb. Eight divers were back on the line, running the slack rope through their hands as we began the ascent. With so much weight on the line we were initially moving along the seabed until those in front began to leave the bottom. Only a few feet into our ascent and with the bottom of my suit filled with water, I was assuring myself I'd soon be on the surface. Then, a couple of torches pointed downwards illuminating the wreck of the submarine. We'd all swum over the top of the elusive vessel during our decent. Divers immediately left the line, dropping the few feet to the top of the old sub's pressure hull. "Bugger," I thought. "It'll be at least another ten minutes now before I can head to the surface." At least we'd used up some bottom time in the desert. My hands were totally numb now despite the neoprene gloves.

The other divers were obviously not affected by the cold to the same extent. I saw a pair enthusiastically shining torches into the open hatch, then as I neared the stern another was securing a line to the broken propeller blade, preparing to send the heavy lump to the surface. At the other end of the short cord his buddy was unrolling a yellow lifting bag. Soon he'd inflate the tapered sack from the air hose clipped to his belt and linked to his air bottles. The half filled bag, like a miniature hot-air balloon would surge upwards carrying the blade. The compressed air in the bag would expand as the pressure of the water reduced until the bag was completely full, then excess air would spill from the open neck of the sack as the apparatus hit the surface.

I didn't care about any of this activity. All I wanted was to stop the uncontrollable shivering and get out of the water. The next ten minutes were an eternity and it was with massive relief that we headed for the shot, now attached to the bows of the wreck. I'd never been so cold in my life and the lower part of my suit was now filled with seawater. I'd managed some brief relief by peeing in the suit. Usually bladder control is essential with a dry suit but on this occasion it seemed pointless. Initially the spreading warmth was a wonderful sensation but the liquid soon mixed with the seawater and cooled.

It was impossible to unfasten my gear on the surface and I could only link my arm through the loop of rope on the side of the RIB while the boatman unclipped my torch and weight belt then unbuckled the twin bottles. Other willing hands dragged me over the sponson and I lay on the broken propeller blade in the bottom of the little craft, virtually helpless. Someone removed my fins, allowing me to sit up on the side of the boat. Pushing my mask up to my forehead I looked around at the others in the boat. I could hardly speak such was the cold. I stuttered, "Ah'mmm ffuuuckin' fffreeezin."

No one else had been troubled with leaking dry suits, so though cold, they were not hypothermic as I was. Then Steve spoke. "I nearly died down there," he said quietly. "Me regulator froze up and I couldn't breath. It was while you were all out in t' desert looking for t' wreck. It was me that was hanging on to t' line shining me torch. If I hadn't had me buddy hose, I'd have been a gonner. There was no one t' share air with."

This life-threatening revelation stunned everyone and even briefly distracted me from my own discomfort. It was only recently that divers had been carrying buddy regulators as a way of sharing air in emergency situations. Prior to this, air was shared by passing a single working mouthpiece to and fro. Had this still been the case Steve wouldn't have survived.

I was aided back onboard and headed for the galley, ignoring the pile of gear in the small boat, leaving others to trans-ship the kit back on to *Emulator*. I asked the man in the wheelhouse to unzip my suit and with shaking hands peeled off the useless membrane. The woollen thermal vest and leggings were saturated and I discarded these also. The soggy garments were kicked into a pile and, shaking uncontrollably, I headed for the cabin, desperate to get dry and dressed.

Still cold, but with a hot drink warming my shaking hands and improving rapidly, I entered the wheelhouse. The second wave of divers was already in the water, having been dropped close to the buoy by a competent hand. Looking out of the window I saw a group observing the broken propeller blade. There was no hint of green on the metal so the cast must have been almost pure bronze.

No other artefacts came up from the wreck, despite the photographic evidence offering the bell, so an hour later, with the buoy recovered and RIB fastened on the stern, we were homeward bound and I wasn't sorry. I made a promise to myself that if I ever dived again in the North Sea in winter, it would be by compunction on fouled propellers, not for perverse pleasure.

Chapter 5

Cold

It was a new year and we were faced with further drastic quota cuts. When would this stupidity end? There was plenty of fish to be caught.

The streets were white over with a coating of frost that appeared as snow when I walked to the harbour shortly after midnight. There were icicles hanging from the eaves of houses as I cautiously trod down the hill. The bitter cold, penetrated the soles of my shoes, numbing my feet. Arriving on the pier I could see the galley light was lit but condensation from the singing kettle inside had steamed the glass to opaque. The iron ladders burned my hands as I cautiously manoeuvred from quayside to the *Emulator's* slippery deck. "It's bloody parky," I commented to the lads sitting round the galley table. "I don't think ah've ever known it so cold." I wasn't including my recent diving experience.

Mutterings of agreement from the three men were followed almost immediately by a brief whirring from the starter motor and dimming of lights. A dull click was heard as the starter motor disengaged again. Mick must be below, attempting to start the engine. Normally the powerful batteries would turn the motor at sufficient speed to fire the main engine into life, but not this morning. The cold had penetrated the engine room, weakening the batteries on a day when more power than usual was required to make the beast work. I went down the ladders to stand on the polished aluminium plates, watching as Mick stood alongside the small, silver-painted 'Lister' generator, holding the starting handle. "She doesn't want it this mornin'," he said grimly.

With the compression off, he engaged the handle, cranking furiously then dropped the first of the two levers on the cylinder tops. The little engine coughed then fired. He dropped the second lever and the engine rattled loudly, bursting into life. The dim lights suddenly glowed brightly as power surged from the alternator to the batteries.

Back at the main engine he squirted a shot of 'Easystart' spray into the air intake and pressed the button again. The lights dimmed again as the starter motor whirred a second time but with more promise and this time the engine fired into life with a loud clatter. The ether spray wasn't good for engines and we used it sparingly but sometimes this was an essential accessory. With the big engine running smoothly and producing its own power, Mick moved over to stop the little generator. This compact 22 horsepower machine was worth its weight in gold during the winter months when the starter batteries struggled to turn over the big 'Kelvin'.

In the freezing wheelhouse, I took off my jacket and donned the thick, dirty, fur-lined, three-quarter coat, which had been a permanent fixture onboard since the vessel was new. This wasn't a garment for social occasions or a fashion statement but the coat was warm and I wasn't going to a ball.

There was no sign of the pierman to let our ropes go and who could blame him. He'd be much warmer in his little office at the pier-end though his absence brought a volley of cursing from the whaleback, where 'Gogga' was flapping his arms vigorously across his chest, attempting to keep some feeling in his fingers. Young Sean was ashore, his gloved-hands vainly attempting to loosen the frozen head rope. A handy lump-hammer was thrown ashore by Mick and the young lad heartily beat the stiff knot into submission.

The piermen's hut looked cosy as we steamed through the harbour entrance. The sole occupant, George Simpson, boiler suited with cheese-cutter cap perched jauntily on the back of his head raised a steaming mug aloft as if to say 'cheers' as we passed. George, and his pal, Stan Wilson were invaluable assets to the trawling fleet, splicing wires of all sizes when not on duty. Their workshop, a converted bait shed was well rigged, with a solid wooden bench and a couple of vices bolted in place. A selection of shiny marlinspikes with both chiselled and pointed ends were in a rack above the bench. A large metal hook was fixed into the ceiling to keep the wire straight as the splicer worked the individual strands into place.

Outside on the concrete road, painted white marks denote ten, fifteen, twenty and twenty-five fathom distances, which the pair used to measure the wires prior to splicing. The two men charged a set fee per splice on a sliding scale based on wire size, though this was a small cost compared with the service provided. Their bills were never questioned and had they charged double, the pair would have lost no trade. Fish was always available from the boats for the wire workers and willingly given, though the pair would never take more than required for their own use. Their little store was filled with coils of wire and a notebook on the shelf recorded all the dimensions each skipper required for his fishing rig. One or both men would often turn out at short notice during antisocial hours in answer to a telephone request when a boat had parted a warp or encountered a wreck. These stalwarts made the art of wire splicing look easy and could form perfect eyes in the thickest and most difficult of steel cable, though not without an occasional curse at the stiffer, heavy duty varieties. I'd spliced wire occasionally but could never make the neat job these men invariably achieved in one-tenth of the time and without bloodletting from pointed, renegade strands.

The only other vessel at sea was *Our Pride*. Col, who was a fellow director of the 'Alliance Fish Company' must have had greater success in starting his engine as he'd been at sea for half an hour already. After setting the autopilot to a course of north-northeast, I called him up on the VHF radio. "Are yer on Col? It's bloody cold this mornin'. Where are yer bound?" I asked, as ever forgetting to say 'over', which was a constant source of irritation to him.

The radio speaker crackled and Col's voice came booming over the airwaves. "Yeh I'm gettin' yer. Yer right, it's as cold as it gets. We're 'eadin' northeast," he said cagily. "Where are you bound? Over."

His answer told me nothing, as well he knew. This was the approximate course we took most of the time. "We're off back t' where we finished up last week," I answered just as cautiously. We were the only two vessels at sea and no one else was liable to be listening so I elaborated. "We were at t' Outside 'Ole an' got a touch o' cod."

Satisfied with my candour he said, "we're off t' Ground Edge." This would take him a little over four hours. After a brief conversation about our respective weekends ashore we discussed the latest round of quotas announced by EEC. Cod, our staple diet had been cut drastically, despite the promises by our politicians that any quotas set by the Commission wouldn't affect British fishermen. How hollow was this promise now?

"There's only us abidin' by t' bloody rules anyway," Col grumbled, echoing the thoughts of UK fishermen everywhere.

"Ah know," I agreed, "t' crazy thing is that t' daft buggers 'ave increased t' 'addock quota an' we aren't seein' that many of 'em. They'll be puttin' whiting on quota next," I joked. These predators were to be found everywhere in abundance and were not valuable.

Following more dialogue about the injustice and stupidity of the regime rigidly enforced by people who didn't know a clam from a kipper, Col ended the exchange saying, "I'll 'ear yer after t' midnight forecast on t' big set."

We were to steam for sixteen hours into Scottish waters to an area where several deep, narrow trenches running north-south plumbed to depths in excess of a hundred fathoms and where we'd had good fishing previously. The wheelhouse was still cold and for the first time ever I regretted not installing a heater, always believing gas fires caused drowsiness. Now I was hunched in the chair wrapped in the thick coat, apart from occasional trips to the galley for coffee and I was pleased when my two hour stint ended and I called Sean to take over. Though only young, he was already proving to be a reliable, willing hand. He arrived in the wheelhouse minutes after being called, hot drink in hand and was pleased to receive my still warm, watch coat. There was nothing to report other than our position on the chart and he would update this frequently before calling Mick.

Now coatless, I popped onto the deck for a quick pee over the side of the boat before going below. The vapour from my breath underlined the temperature, blowing away on the freezing, easterly breeze as I stood shivering. Overhead, the display of stars on this black, clear night was unbelievable, though it was far too cold to hang about admiring the show. A thin film of ice remained on the deck, which was unusual. The tempering effect of the sea usually melted any residual frost that had formed in the harbour.

Shortly after eight o'clock the cabin lights were turned on and a call of, "breakfast fo' them that wants it," was announced by Sid. I was cosy and warm in a sleeping bag in my bunk but rolled out, pulling on gansey, sea-boot socks and slippers. At the top of the cabin ladder I looked aft to discover the steel door at the back of the accommodation had been closed to keep in the warmth. This door was usually hooked back unless the weather was really bad. "It isn't gettin' any warmer out there," Sid observed as he pulled a steaming tray of bacon from the oven. "It's like bein' back at Iceland," he said. "I saw plenty of ice on t' ships there."

"It can't be that bad," I said and went up the wheelhouse steps. It was daylight now, but the sun had yet to make an appearance. Gogga was wearing the watch coat, though it was considerably warmer now with the outside door closed and the engine exhaust emitting heat behind the panelling in the alleyway.

"Ah've never seen owt like this before," the watch keeper said, looking in my direction wide-eyed, then pointing out of the window. Revealed with the coming of daylight was a scene from the arctic. The shelter-deck was coated in ice. The topping lift rope, which hauled the landing pole into place, was three times its normal thickness. Even the thin halyard on the foremast had grown to the thickness of my wrist. The ship's little bell hanging on the front of the wheelhouse between two windows had swollen and become a huge ice bell. Incongruously, horizontal icicles, six to eight inches in length were clinging to the railings. The light breeze from the east was creating a swell and the spray from the waves was freezing as the droplets came in contact with the boat. I'd heard of 'black ice' before and tales of trawlers capsizing from loss of stability when they became top heavy, but I never thought I'd experience the phenomena in the North Sea.

I spent a few minutes establishing that *Emulator*'s rolling period had not changed significantly. The rolling time from port over to starboard then back to port was the major indicator of a vessel's stability. *Emulator* was a stiff ship. If anything, at times she was too lively but with a rolling time of five seconds there was no detectable difference in her equilibrium. We were in no danger at present. If our circumstances changed we could always turn round and with a following wind we'd create no spray and the build-up of ice would stop immediately. "What are we gonna do?" was the question when I returned to the galley for breakfast.

"We'll keep goin' fo' now," I replied, looking at the huge fry up in front of me and not at the speaker. "We aren't in any trouble." I stayed in the wheelhouse for the remainder of the passage apart from a quick visit to the deck to check that the winch wasn't iced up. The machine was hidden out of view under the whaleback. There was no freezing to be seen here. I was content that things were not getting any worse.

It was dark again when I eased the engine down to shoot the trawl and I watched through the window as the four muffled figures gingerly and reluctantly made their way onto the deck. The trawl, neatly stowed in the pound along the starboard side was stiff but loosened up following a few cracks with the deck shovel and the ice fell easily from the lifting wire as the trawl doors were heaved outboard.

With the trawl in the water I called, "tell 'em two-fifty aft," to Sean, standing by the fore gallow. He relayed the message to the men at the winch. This length of warp was almost the full capacity of the drums. Only one of the holes was deeper and we bottomed that one with the full two hundred and seventy-five fathoms of wire.

As soon as the trawl was down the four men hurried back indoors, all blowing loudly on their hands and shedding the extra layers of clothing they'd donned. It would take four hours to trawl the length of this hole so, following a splendid beef dinner with trimmings, which we enjoyed while Sid manned the wheelhouse, the lads turned in. I illuminated all the upper-deck lights to monitor the ice situation, though this ruined my night vision so I was compelled to rely on the radar to detect encroaching shipping.

"There isn't another ship t' be seen," I commented as the four sat round the cabin table drinking coffee and smoking, prior to hauling.

"There's no bugger else as daft as us," one of the four replied. "Are you really that 'ard up?"

I returned to the wheelhouse but his words had got to me. "It isn't a matter of money." I thought, analysing my motives as the winch slowly cranked the gear back to the surface. It's the challenge of making a living despite the elements. The hanging blocks in both gallows were struggling to turn with the cold as the wires were dragged through the gaping apertures. Three of the four men had returned to the accommodation to keep warm for the next ten minutes, leaving one of their number to guide the wires evenly back onto the drums. With the twenty fathom mark inboard, the trio reluctantly returned to their positions. The doors surfaced, were unclipped then chains and thin wires hauled in until finally the mouth of the trawl was alongside. I looked to windward waiting for the 'bag' to float. This was the part of the operation that never lost its thrill. Until hauling time we never knew what was waiting for us in the net. The sounder sometimes gave clues and lifted expectations but at this depth it was difficult to detect fish and I'd seen nothing of any substance to excite me.

The codend surfaced slowly and looked like a wet sock. "Was it wo'th it?" came a disappointed call from the deck, and though not aimed directly at me, was intended for my ears.

"Gimee some chips an' ah'll eat it," came a further quip.

The bag, when lifted in and emptied contained no more than two or three boxes of fish. We could have caught more fishing on the doorstep a few miles from the harbour. There was certainly no point in going back over the same ground. "Lift t' wing-ends in," I called out. "We'll shift back in t' sou'west." Though taking the dangling parts of the net aboard, I deliberately avoided saying, "lift t' doors in," because then they'd know we were going home. Expectations would rise and it would be difficult to change my mind. I'd keep all options open.

The half past midnight forecast was for the easterly wind to freshen and a prediction of mild to moderate icing was given for the northern North Sea. Tuning in the MF radio, I called to Col in *Our Pride* but received no reply. I tried again but the airwaves remained silent. If Col was still at sea, he would almost certainly have answered, unless otherwise engaged. I suspected he'd returned to port and decided that's where we were going.

Sean came into the wheelhouse when the small quantity of fish had been stowed below and I headed down into the alleyway, looking into the galley as I headed for the cabin. Sid was facing in my direction. "Yer can try too 'ard sometimes skipper. Yer can't beat the elements all the time."

The steam home was downhill and comfortable. The watches came and went, as did the daylight and it was almost dark again when, half an hour from home we lifted the doors inboard. I radioed to the lighthouse watch-keeper, requesting him to ring my home to ask Dotty to bring my camera down to the harbour. *Emulator* was still shrouded in ice but it wouldn't last long and I wanted to record her in this condition. I might never see a sight like this again. It was now late on Monday afternoon. We'd been at sea for nearly forty hours for no reward and were pleased to be home. Tomorrow was another day.

CHAPTER 6

SCREW FULL

Winter had long gone and late spring found us fishing at the 'Potholes', seventy miles to the north-northeast of Scarborough. The weather was glorious. We'd been fishing steadily away in the deep trench and getting quantities of monkfish and lemon sole along with the haddock and cod, but there was so little wind I was concerned we'd get our trawl in the propeller. The lads were being ultra careful and so far we'd kept out of trouble. Several other vessels were showing on the radar within a six-mile radius and everyone in the area was in VHF contact and occasionally in sight. Two of the blips on the screen were easily identifiable as the Bridlington pair trawling team, *Enchanter* and *Pilot Us* whose echoes, close together and moving in unison with a trawl between them were distinctive.

The fish from our recent haul had been put below and I was idly looking out of the starboard window awaiting the arrival of the next watch-keeper, when a sudden movement on the deck caught my eye. A beautifully marked song thrush was hopping around amongst the weed and shells where the net had been. It wasn't uncommon to see shore birds out at sea, especially during spring and autumn when they're migrating and the creatures are sometimes blown out to sea with strong offshore winds or lost in bad visibility. Ornithologists would delight at the close up availability of birds hardly ever seen on shore. Small warblers seldom survived their landing on boats, possibly due to the consumption of salt and their tiny speckled bodies are sadly but unceremoniously consigned to the deep. Some nights, huge flocks of noisy starlings eerily fill the masts and aerials like a scene from a Hitchcock thriller. Last week we'd had a shrike onboard; a bird I'd never seen before. Now I kept a camera on board and I'd taken a photograph of the colourful creature, enabling identification on my return home.

I was drawn from my reverie when Kevin, Sean's younger brother came into the wheelhouse holding a steaming mug in one hand and a sandwich big enough to choke a horse in the other. Kevin had been with us several months now, replacing Gogga and he was a powerful, headstrong young man with a contrasting temperament to his brother. Informing him of the tow I wanted him to follow and the callout time, I went below to join the others in the galley for a sandwich and a drink before turning in. Coffee was to be avoided if I was to get any sleep.

Sean and Mick were seated at the table while Sid hovered at the worktop near the sink with the makings of our next meal. He'd already laid out a tray of cold, fried fish, the leftovers from breakfast and I slapped an inch-thick piece of woof between two slices of bread, lifting the top layer and applying salt and vinegar as an afterthought.

Mick, as usual was fighting his way through a plateful, sweating profusely as he concentrated on the task in hand. Short and stocky in stature, Mick had been part of *Emulator's* crew since the boat was new, having transferred from *Independence*. He was an extremely reliable hand and skilled net mender and had on occasion taken the boat to sea in my absence with good results.

Leaving the three in the galley I made for the cabin. Sid would potter in his domain for ages, wiping surfaces, polishing the copper gas pipes and reading the previous week's newspapers he'd brought from home. He hardly slept during daylight hours but still had no problem turning out during the hours of darkness. Mick would follow me below on completion of his meal while young Sean would sneak off onto the deck to smoke a quick, illicit cigarette, knowing I disapproved of his habit. Walking up the steps from the galley I noticed the lively little thrush had made its way into the doorway, seeking warmth. I shooed the fearless feathered friend back onto the deck again, hopefully preventing someone from standing on the little creature.

Lying in my bunk, clad in shirt, jeans and stocking feet in case of urgent callout, I only managed to read a few pages of the current thriller before heavy eyelids compelled me to turn off the reading light. Then as ever, the two hours below passed in a flash. We were being summoned from our beds by Kevin switching the cabin lights on and gruffly calling, "aye aye, 'aulin' time. T' kettle's boilin'. Let's 'ave yer."

Back in the wheelhouse with coffee in hand and awaiting the winch-men heading for'ard I looked out the window to ensure all was clear on the deck below. The scattered brown and cream feathers in the net area didn't register at first, then I realised there were two small legs among the strewn plumage. This was all that remained of our little visitor.

I ran down the steps to the alleyway where the lads were donning oilskins yelling, "what 'ave yer done t' that poor little thrush?" at a startled Kevin.

His obvious confusion and protests of innocence at the carnage convinced me he hadn't been the assassin and I returned to the wheelhouse perplexed. This was inexplicable. Nothing mechanical had been running on the deck in my absence to destroy the bird.

The men would be heading for the winch any minute and I opened the nearest front window to allow communications. The riddle of the dead thrush was solved immediately as I spied a large hawk sitting atop the whaleback, pruning its talons with hooked beak and looking in my direction as if awaiting the next course.

Fascinated with this newcomer, a totally different type of bird to anything I'd seen close up before, my eyes were glued to the raptor, which didn't even startle when Mick and Sean walked for'ard, below its location. I eased the engine and engaged the winch clutch before advancing the throttle back to half speed. The fearless bird stood its ground despite the sound of the winch motor and revolving drums and I watched entranced. "Short mark," yelled Sid from the side deck, announcing ten fathoms of wire to come before the doors appeared. I dragged my eyes away from the spectacle to pay attention to the work in hand. The bang of the for'ard trawl door on the metal cladding put paid to our visitor's stay and after an initial frenzied flap, the predator circled the boat once to get its bearings then headed westwards.

Again with great caution we managed to avoid any coming together of net and prop' and after emptying the trawl and getting the gear off the boat's side it was with relief we began paying out the cables. Five minutes later our trawl was back on the bottom. Someone close by hadn't been quite so lucky, as I discovered when Mick Laws, skipper of *Pilot Us,* called on the radio with gushing flattery. "*Emulator, Emulator*, Freddy my favourite friend ever. Are yer receiving me mate, over?" He clearly wanted something.

Looking into the radar I could see their echoes two miles to the west and glancing up could see the blue and red boats in the middle distance. They weren't trawling. The symmetry of the vessels was wrong.

Entering into the humour I clicked the transmitter on and off a few times as I answered and replied, "'ello! Ah think that was you Mick. Yer very broken up." He and everyone else in range on the frequency would hear my intermittent and virtually undecipherable message.

"Naw! Come on Freddy, stop messin' about. Ah know that's you. 'Ave yer still got yer divin' gear aboard, my pal?"

So that was it. He'd got a fouled propeller and needed someone to clear the obstruction. It would take Frank and his crew in the *Enchanter* at least fifteen hours to tow his partner back to port then have the propeller cleared. They'd lose a minimum of a day and a half by the time they returned to the grounds.

"Yer, ah'm listenin' an' ahm guessin' yer've got a screw full, Mr Laws."

"Yer not wrong mate. There's not a lot in there, but we're knackered with it. Can yer come an' clear it for us?"

"Ah think ah might be able to 'elp yer," I replied seriously. "Ah'll sort summat out an' get back t' yer." Having just shot our trawl, it would be nearly five hours before we'd haul again unless a seabed fastener hastened the process. At that point we could be quite some distance from the pair. Reluctant to haul again so soon I summoned Mick from his gutting operations on the deck and explained the situation. "Can you take over in 'ere while I get kitted up and ready t' jump overboard? Yer can tow close past t' *Pilot Us* then put t' rudder 'ard over t' starboard an' I'll jump over t' port quarter, clear o' t' warps and t' propeller."

"Ah can manage that OK," he affirmed and quickly hung his blood splattered apron on a hook in the alleyway, kicked off his boots and returned to settle in the chair and acquaint himself with the plotter.

The *Enchanter* could have come for me and taken me back to the casualty but we were at our closest point of approach now and it wouldn't be much of a diversion to reach their position. Dragging my dive-bag from the steerage locker at the back of the cabin, I returned for the weight belt and twin aluminium cylinders, refilled following the winter diving trip. This was a leisurely kit up. We were trawling at three knots and were still a mile and a half from the stopped vessels. I was fully prepared and ready to go as *Emulator* approached the disabled *Pilot Us*. As ever when two vessels pass in close proximity, both crews were on deck to wave and shout humorous comments and occasionally throw missiles such as eggs, potatoes or small fish.

Sitting on the bulwarks aft side of the propeller, legs outboard and fins waggling in space I called, "'ard over," to the helmsman who'd somehow managed to get his head and shoulders out of the portside window. Mick moved the tiller at his side and the boat's heading changed as she went to starboard and the wires at the stern swivelled from the towing point and moved across the stern to the starboard quarter. I projected myself from the boat's side making sure the air bottles didn't catch the bulwarks and plunged into the crystal clear water. The wire warps were clearly visible cutting through the surface and leading down into the depths. Turning, I could see most of the length of *Emulator's* keel. The vortex from the propeller, powered through the nozzle looked amazing. I surfaced to see the full stern of my boat moving away and the angled wires back in the middle of the transom.

Turning to the nearby boat I gave a wave then, head down finned the short distance to the red boat's side. A couple of honed knives were lowered in a bucket on a light line and I grabbed one. Five minutes later the offending netting was free. It would probably take an hour or more for the crew to repair my ruthless slashing but *Pilot Us* was no longer immobile.

The wooden fish-room ladder had been lowered overboard and secured to the inboard bulwarks. I held onto one of the lower rungs while divesting the heavy bottles, which I hitched onto the line previously holding the bucket. Contorting to remove the chunky black rubber fins without sacrificing them to the depths, though gaining a mouthful of salt water in the process, these were also sent up. It was exceptional to experience no swell in the North Sea. Had she been rolling it would have been much more difficult to get from the water. Breathless and coughing from the intake of water I kicked my legs towards the bottom rung of the ladder and ascended the vessel's side.

The vision that met my eyes as I reached deck level will stay in my memory forever and caused another paroxysm of coughing as the last vestige of seawater caught the back of my throat. Mick Laws was standing on the deck in his underpants, in garb so farcical it must have taken a great deal of thought to improvise. Hitched to his feet were a pair of rubber 'pancakes', spares for the footrope of his trawl gear. Around his waist, on a piece of line hung random sized shackles, swivels and bits of chain, hitched in a big bow at the front. On his back was strapped a thirty-two pound, 'Propane Gas' cylinder with a hose leading from the regulator to his mouth. Covering his nose and eyes and somehow fastened at the back of his head was the black visor from his radar screen, used for daylight viewing. A pair of gutting gloves on his hands were held aloft, one holding a gutting knife. Spitting out the hose and with a grin a mile wide Mick said, "What took yer so long? Ah was just about t' come an' give yer an 'and."

I was speechless for a minute, even briefly thinking he was serious, but he wasn't. It was his show of relief and thanks for the time saved. "If on'y I 'ad a camera," was all I could say.

"Ah'm gonna get in t' this divin' lark. It's bloody useful," he said more seriously. "There's summat t' be said for it."

A few months later Mick Laws was a fully trained diver and had acquired his own equipment.

I was handed a mug of tea by one of the hands and sat on the fish-room hatch as Mick tentatively put the engine into gear. Almost immediately he was steaming after the *Emulator*, his partner vessel keeping company on our port side. I watched as the lads on deck stretched out the damaged trawl in readiness for mending and I felt a little guilty at the lack of care I'd taken in freeing the twisted netting.

"Yer've med a right mess o' this bugger," one of the lads said, without malice. "We'll be a bloody week mendin' this. Yer could at least fill some needles instead o' sittin' on yer arse doin' nowt."

I grinned back; knowing they were joking and replied, "we 'ave our needles filled ready, an' yer must be bloody slow menders. Our lads 'd 'ave that little 'ole patched up in ten minutes."

The interaction was soon over as the two boats came gently together, cushioned by fenders on both craft but the calling started up again between the two crews as my diving gear was passed back across to *Emulator*. Noticing that the men on deck were sending the remaining baskets of fish below, someone on board *Pilot Us* shouted, "ain't yer finished puttin' that little bit o' fish away yet? We would 'ave 'ad that bit put t' bed an hour ago."

"Yer've never caught this much," came back the swift repost from Mick, again leaning out of the wheelhouse window.

Our next haul was poor and as there were several boats in the area we took the trawl ends aboard, steaming southeast for an hour to the 'Compass' area, so called from the large compass rose that overlaid this location on the Admiralty Chart. There was an extensive area of hard ground to choose from, spread over many miles where we'd had good fishing in the past. I was hopeful of some good haddock fishing in the coming dark.

The night proved reasonably productive and both Mick and Sean as watch-keepers, were rewarded with good hauls, though there were substantial amounts of immature haddock to discard; many more than we were saving. A large flock of cackling fulmars, flapping along the surface followed us throughout our operations, devouring every edible thing that was hosed through the gaping scupper door. Importantly, a slight southwesterly breeze, which came with the dusk, had removed the threat of net and propeller coming together. There'd be no haddocks in the daylight, so as the sun rose in a cloudless sky I directed *Emulator* east-southeast, towing across soft, unproductive ground before turning her ninety degrees to starboard to maintain the thirty-seven fathom contour. We were heading towards some small, hard rises in the seabed, two to three fathoms high, each eight to ten minutes trawling time to cross. On our port side and only a short distance away, the ground shoaled to a mere twenty fathoms, forming the northwestern corner of the Dogger Bank.

The pale blue screen of the coloured sounder began recording a huge, distinctive, vertical red streak, this, the first of many. These could only be sandeels. These small silver darts, some as long as eight inches were the food of all species and were caught in vast quantities by the Danes at this time of year in fine mesh, mid-water trawls. These prolific catchers also directed their efforts seasonally at sprat, pout and juvenile herring and in the process slaughtered large quantities of immature haddock, whiting and cod. Each of the many vessels in this fleet of industrial fishers landed hundreds of tons at a time into the dozens of fishmeal plants scattered around the Danish ports. The quota set by the EEC for sandeels was one million tonnes annually, though how this was measured and what controls were in place to monitor the percentage of other species was doubtful. Fortunately there were no Danes working here at present, though reports from other vessels indicated a large fleet working at the southwest corner of the Dogger, some sixty miles from this location.

We continued to trawl through the huge streaks, all of which were suspended cigar shaped in mid-water, beyond the reach of our trawl's headline, apart from one large blob on the bottom. I surmised this to be a shoal of sandeels leaving the seabed and hoped there would be something worthwhile feeding on this mass.

The thought of industrial fishers cast my mind back to the previous winter when the skipper of a Danish 'shit-catcher', one of several working in the wreck strewn waters between Flamborough Head and the River Humber had broken the airwaves. The call of, "hello Coastguard, hello Coastguard. We need urgent assistance," on channel 16 caused everyone in hearing distance to pay attention.

The message received an immediate official response. "Vessel calling for assistance; please go to channel 67 and pass your vessel's name and the nature of your problem."

The skipper quickly changed frequency, along with thirty or forty other interested parties, all keen to know the problem that had caused this skipper to panic. Announcing the name of his vessel the man swiftly, in excellent accented English went on the say, "we are being towed backwards by a submarine."

The response of the duty officer was initially one of concern and he replied that he was unaware of any naval exercises in the area and said he would contact the Royal Navy immediately, then asked for further details. "Can you give me your current position and depth of water please, skipper?"

The Dane gave a position roughly twenty miles from land in a depth of eighteen fathoms saying he was going backwards at about three knots.

There was a pause in the communications for a couple of minutes while the now sceptical officer plotted this position. When the Coastguard transmitted again the speaker's voice was less official and he was clearly finding difficulty keeping his tone serious. "There is a wreck on my chart near that location sir. Has your position changed since we've been communicating? I don't think there is any possibility of a submarine operating in that depth of water sir."

The distressed and now irate fisherman's voice grew louder. "I am being towed backw---" then his voice faded to nothing when the realisation of his true situation sunk in. He'd been towing his net close to the bottom before a strong tide and had caught a wreck. Now stopped, the strong tide was flowing past his vessel giving an appearance of going backwards. Working their gear in mid-water, these vessels seldom encountered tidal effects as their speed through the water was constant. It was only speed over the ground that varied with the tidal effect. Everyone who fished on the bottom was well aware of the influence of the tide and tried to avoid excessive time towing into the stream and covering little ground.

Fifteen minutes later the Dane again contacted the Coastguard, sombrely thanking the shore-station for their assistance, confirming the officer's analysis and reporting a badly damaged lower trawl section.

The airwaves back on the working channel were alive with witty comments at the hilarity of the situation. It had been a slow day before this amusing interlude. No one had ever seen or heard of a submarine operating off our coast in peacetime. Someone pointed out in fairness to the skipper that there was virtually no tidal movement or rise and fall on the Danish coast or in the Baltic. I couldn't imagine a harbour where the tide didn't go in and out. I was to discover this for myself before too long.

Passing over the last piece of ground and into the desert the big 'feed' marks thinned out to nothing. Allowing what I thought was sufficient distance I turned *Emulator* as fast as the trailing gear would allow, intending to head back on a reciprocal course. She seemed sluggish, or was I in too much of a hurry to get her round. The warps took an age to reopen but eventually she was back on course and heading in the required direction. The gigantic marks were still suspended out of range but strangely the red blob had remained on the bottom in the middle of all this activity. Maybe this wasn't a sandeel mark I was looking at. Could it be cod? Were we looking at a bonanza here? It was time to find out. There was still an hour to go before we were due to haul but I boiled the kettle, making the usual requirements then called the lads from below. "Aye aye! We're gonna 'ave a look at it. Ah think we might be towin' a sausage." My description of a net full of fish added speed to their step and the usual half hour for a cuppa and cigarette for the smokers was shortened to twenty minutes.

Emulator lay across the wind and I looked keenly to windward hoping to see a surge as the bag blew out of the water. There was certainly something of value in the codends when the net surfaced and it was clearly big cod but not in the quantity I was hoping for. "It's a payable 'aul but not what I was expectin'," I shouted to the men at the gallows as they were leading the quarter ropes to the winch.

"Yer just wanted a shorter watch. Yer've flogged t' clock," a sceptical Sid yelled back.

I looked again at the fish in the net as the ropes tensioned and the ground gear began to break the surface. As the trawl's belly drew closer I noticed there were a few cod floating belly up and being pecked at by the fulmars in the water beyond the codend. "There must be an 'ole in t' lower bellies! Quick as yer can lads. She's busted. We're losin' fish."

The footrope dropped to the deck and I joined the four men, first pulling the headline then the body of the net in as fast as we could. A couple more cod floated free as we drew the bag closer but the momentum of our pulling forced the remaining fish down below the hole into the codend and we lost no more. A small split about two feet in length in the orange netting of the lower section of the trawl where the sleeve joined the thicker, green twine of the codend came over the boat's side. "We've lost a bloody big 'aul o' fish," I said grimly and needlessly.

The tight bag was lifted inboard and emptied into the fish pound. Around 120 stone in weight and almost every fish was a big cod. All were dead, bloated bellies filled with sandeels and more of the silver eels spewing from gaping mouths. The net must have been full before I'd made the hurried turn at the southwestern end of the tow. That was why she was so sluggish to get round and I hadn't realised the fact. The strain on the net must have been enormous as the trawl, stiff with fish, creased in the turn and the weakest point gave way, spilling a mother-lode. What had we lost?

We stretched out the damaged part of the trawl and looked at the small hole. This would take less than five minutes to mend but this minor damage, in a critical section of the net had lost us a fortune. "There'll be some left down there for us," I stated with some assurance as the repair was addressed. We strengthened other parts in the sensitive area that looked chafed and slightly worn, in addition to the repair. "It won't bloody well bust again," I declared as the codends were thrown over the side. "We won't be towin' long this time," I added.

With the gear down *Emulator* again dragged her trawl across the bumpy ground and I identified the cigar shaped sandeel marks but the chunky mark on the bottom was now in several smaller pieces. Had we broken up this huge ball of fish? If these were cod, still showing red on the sounder, there were plenty available for us yet.

The recent haul of big fish took little time to clear and stow below and the first of the oilskin-clad crew were soon entering the accommodation from the deck. "Kettle's boilin'. Yer've time for a quick sandwich an' a drink then we'll be pullin' it up again," I called down from the wheelhouse.

There was no mistake this time. From the vantage of the wheelhouse I could see the bubbles of a huge haul, deep in the water. The net burst to the surface like a submarine surging from the depths. "Bingo!" I yelled, praying the netting would hold. This was a massive haul. Rushing to the deck I assisted in getting the mouth of the trawl onboard. This was achieved with difficulty due to the weight of fish but luckily the weather was fine. Within minutes the ground gear and headline were onboard and several turns had been taken around the entire net overboard with a heavy rope, which was then secured to a strong point inboard.

The air in the swim bladders of the fish had expanded, blowing the bag to the surface. This was quickly dissipating and the haul was already semi-buoyant. With the air gone we would soon have deadweight on our hands, but that didn't matter now, we had control of the situation and the gear was safe. The 'pork line' connecting to the codend would allow us to bail the catch onto the deck in a controlled manner. Had we not acted quickly enough, ten or more tons of fish would have torn our net from its frame and both fish and net would have been lost.

This had happened previously when we'd caught a huge haul of dogfish in the Yorkshire Hole, a deep trench off the Humber estuary. Dogfish, with no swim bladder are deadweight when caught. The weather had been fresh with a short swell in the water and we hadn't been able to get the ground gear onto the deck at all. Each time the boat rolled, the footrope was dragged back over the side. Worse, we had no full-length pork line connected to the codend, only a short length of rope half way up the bellies. There was no way of taking the weight off the net. A small tear began in the centre of the belly of the net and with each consecutive roll the split grew. In vain we tried to secure the ground gear. In less than five minutes the majority of the trawl had unzipped from its strong edges and the net, full of fish sank to the bottom, leaving just the frame of our gear remaining. The footrope had come onboard easily then, with hardly any netting remaining. We'd chopped off this useless residue and in half an hour had put another trawl in place. Then, fixing a full-length pork line and making only short tows we'd still managed to catch 900 stone of 'dogs' in a few brief tows, getting a big market in Grimsby for the catch. *

That wasn't going to happen today. We might yet lose the catch if the strain becomes too much and the netting splits, but the main fabric of the gear was secure.

Mick began to heave gently on the pork line, hauling the codend to the surface, allowing the remainder of the catch to run down the sleeve. Sean reached over the side and forced the iron hook into the strop around the bag and Kevin, on the winch lifted the first bag aboard. We took three similar sized bags and there was still a mass of fish remaining in the water but we'd eased the pressure on the netting. If we were to take the mass of fish on board, much of it would deteriorate in the sun and wind before we could gut, wash and get it below and the quality would reduce dramatically.

The weather was fine and the boat hardly rolling, so I decided to take the chance of clearing what we had on deck before taking more fish onboard. At the back of my mind I could hear my old skipper, Tom Pashby saying, "it's never ours till it's on t' deck lads," but I was going to take the risk.

The fish took nearly two hours to clear then we took another four bags onboard. The weight eased further and I was now more confident of retaining the entire haul. Another two hours gained clear decks again and once more we repeated the process. Still there was fish hanging overboard. "There can't be much more. We'll tek what's left," I instructed. "It'll on'y be a lift or so." I was mistaken. There were three more bags overboard before the net

* At the time of writing, due to environmentalist pressure it is forbidden to land <u>any</u> dogfish, though these fish never survive being caught in a trawl and are only a by-catch, not a targeted species.

was empty. We set off for home with a big deck cargo still to gut and with *Emulator* distinctly down by the head, belly to ground. It was late afternoon now and the sun had lost its heat so the remains of the huge haul wouldn't spoil. We had a nine-hour steam to home ahead of us and this fish would be below in the chilled fish-room long before then.

The two hundred and fifty boxes of fish, mostly cod with tails extending over the ends of the boxes, looked spectacular laid out on the market, glistening with fresh ice, rigid in rigor mortis. The earlier catch of haddocks and flats looked small in comparison.

My previous vessel *Independence* had been in harbour all the past week with a mechanical problem and was due to sail. On seeing the superb catch we'd landed, her skipper, Bluey, my former crewman and now business partner came along, asking where we'd been.

Reluctant to release the exact position of the 'mark' even to my partner and hoping to get another sample from this ground, I told him the rough area we'd taken the fish from and he sailed, determined to find the hot spot.

* * * * * *

As ever Thursday night found us in the Leeds Arms meeting up with our regular group of friends. The pub was quite busy and Les, true to form, was chatting up a couple of attractive girls at the end of the counter close to the wall, while ignoring his customers. Drinks were impossible to get and most of the customers in his pub now had low, or empty glasses as the landlord hovered close to the females, wanting to join in their conversation, rather than serve the waiting clientele.

Tommy, standing next to us and also without a drink said, "I'll get his attention." Tommy Clark was a member of the diving club and one of the lifeboat crew. "What's t' phone number o' this place?" he enquired. In front of him on the counter and about the size of half a brick was one of the new 'mobile phones'.

"It's 61699" I replied. The pub's number was one of half a dozen contacts etched on my mind. I looked at this new piece of technology with interest. I'd heard of these gismos and seen them on TV but hadn't seen one of these amazing pieces of kit close up. We were soon to have them on our boats.

Picking up the machine Tommy prefixed the number I'd given him with the Scarborough code then pressed 'send'. All eyes turned towards the unsuspecting barman, still hovering near the pair of ladies. This was either going to be very funny or disastrous.

The phone, attached to the wall close to the pair began to ring, startling the females. Seizing the opportunity to get closer to his quarry, Les reached for the handset. Leaning on the counter facing in the girls' direction, in a very pretentious voice the host purred, "hellooo, Leeds Arms."

Tommy, in contrast to the silky voice on the line flatly said, "is there any chance of a drink at this end o' t' bar Les?"

As if stung, the barman spun round, his countenance changing from the pleasant smile to one of thunder. The huge roar of laughter when he realised he was the butt of a big joke that everyone was in on made matters worse. Even the ladies were grinning. Les slammed the phone back into its cradle and steadfastly refused even to look in our direction for the next five minutes, choosing instead to wash and polish glasses that were already gleaming. The two girls departed, still giggling. We did eventually get served when the dust had settled but only after several minutes of painful waiting. In despair of ever getting served again, poor Tommy left for the 'Britannia'.

I was back in the Leeds Arms at the weekend to meet up with the usual Saturday afternoon group for more good-humoured banter. It wasn't wise to bite or react to any adverse comments, as any reaction was immediately exploited, though not maliciously.

These were real fun sessions, and today was no exception but it was almost three o'clock. Les had called last orders and I was contemplating heading home. Syd, George, Jack and Col had already left and Bob was supping the dregs from his glass, ready to make tracks.

On bar stools at the counter, Frankie Thorpe was with an old friend he hadn't seen for years, and whom he'd met earlier in the day. The pair had clearly enjoyed an extended session round the pubs and continued to relive their mutual experiences. Both were quite animated and pleasantly intoxicated. Frank, who lived at the top of the hill, below St Mary's Church, was a pleasant man with an infectious grin. He'd been a talented footballer when younger, and though Frank hadn't followed a career at sea, most of his pals were fishermen.

The door opened briskly causing heads to turn and Carol, Frank's wife burst into the little bar. "There you are. I've been looking all over for you. Where have you been?"

Carol was not in any sense a large woman, but was well built and powerful.

Frank had clearly misread the signs in his wife's demeanour or his inebriated state made him braver than was wise.

His answer to her question went unheard by anyone else in the room but was clearly not the response Carol wanted to hear. Pulling back her right hand she threw a punch that any boxer would have been proud to deliver and Frank left the stool and hit the deck in one movement. His unconscious body lay on the floor. The victor, without another word turned and headed for the door, stepping on her husband's chest en route.

It was a few minutes before Frank came round and was able to sit up. "What happened?" he asked, still concussed and rubbing his swollen jaw.

"Your lass came in and hit yer," Les was pleased to report.

"What with?" Frank asked, still groggy.

"Just her fist. I think you're fighting a bit above your weight there," Les observed with a huge smirk.

I walked into the house quite soberly and was careful not to say anything to invite Dotty's displeasure. The forecast was stormy at sea and I wasn't going to face the same conditions at home. Frank was.

* * * * * *

Despite the weather prediction we sailed at midnight, heading back to the Klondyke, where we'd taken the huge catch the previous week. I was hoping to take more from the area, but was to be disappointed. Bluey had found the location of our bonanza and taken what fish remained on the ground. *Independence* was on her way home with a bellyful of cod.

Bluey was doing very well in my old boat. Maybe it was time we built a new one for him. I made a mental note to discuss this with him next time we met up.

We managed only a few modest hauls then retreated before the building storm. I arrived home to hear from Danny that he and his pal Billy had collected ten Alliance fish boxes from the beach. These cases were quite expensive so I'd always encouraged him to round up any strays, promising to pay him ten pence for each one he returned to the pier. I was delighted with his efforts and willingly paid him one pound.

Next morning on the fish pier I met up with our net mender, Eddie. He informed me that the market prices were good and we should do well for the small amount we'd landed. Then, with a chuckle he asked, "are you paying your Danny t' collect boxes from t' sands?"

"Ah certainly am," I said, proudly. "'E an' young Billy collected ten yesterday. I gave 'em a quid las' night."

"Ah'm not surprised 'e got so many," Eddie said, laughing again. "Billy was chuckin' 'em into t' sea 'alf way down t' pier an' your Danny was gatherin' 'em up as they washed ashore."

"The little buggers," I said, also laughing. "Jus' wait 'til ah get 'ome." I had to admire his enterprise, but it wasn't going to happen again.

* * * * * *

The crew of the Bridlington vessel *Pickering*, operating out of Scarborough, had refused to sail. They were convinced their boat was haunted. Skipper, Derek 'Sooty' Gates was unable to persuade his men otherwise, but had some sympathy with them.

There certainly were strange things happening on board the boat. Electrical instruments switched themselves on and off and the engine randomly revved up and eased down without human assistance. The boat felt cold. The story quickly became elaborated and was featured in the local press and radio, then broadcast across the Yorkshire region.

"You need an exorcist," someone who'd recently been to the cinema suggested jokingly. "Get a vicar down to say a prayer on board. That should do it."

Though not a believer in such things, the stocky, tousle haired, swarthy skipper thought it was worth a try if it would get him back to sea.

Accepting an offer from a priest who'd heard the story on the radio and claimed he had experience in these matters, Derek arranged to meet the man onboard *Pickering* at the weekend. Strange to relate, the priest did sense a presence and said he'd put the disturbed spirit at ease. The vessel encountered no more problems, though Sooty took a great deal of ribbing for weeks about strange spirits he'd encountered, though these were probably from bottles.

Some months later a television production company, having heard the story, came along wanting to film for a programme relating to the presence onboard *Pickering*. The skipper turned down a £500 offer to shoot onboard his vessel, not wanting to invite the return of the unwanted spirit. Following Sooty's refusal, I was one of several skippers who were asked if our vessels could be used for the re-enactment for the same fee. To a man we said, "No." No one believed in the supernatural of course, but weren't taking any chances either.

* * * * * *

Discussions with Bluey proved fruitful and we both felt confident that we could build and service the loan on our new vessel. There were exciting times ahead, despite the worry of this year's quota cuts. I'd begun making enquiries to various boatyards, seeking prices and possible delivery dates. The yards that had built

Independence and *Emulator* were no longer in business so we'd have to cast our net wider. This time our new vessel would be built of steel. An added bonus was that Malcolm, Bluey's right-hand man, was keen to buy his share of *Independence*.

There was bad news from the Town Hall where the local Council, in their wisdom had decided to close and demolish the block of six fish merchants' premises on the West Pier, located near the beach. These traders were the bulk of the buyers at the auction and not all would find new premises. This would affect not only fishermen's earnings, but would affect the ice factory and even the little teashop where the fish workers bought their snacks and drinks. The 'temporary' car park, soon to replace the structure would be a major source of income for the Council for years to come.*

The block containing the fish market was also to be demolished but this was due to the fabric of the building becoming unsafe. At least this structure would be replaced.

---

*   Later the Council would also remove the bait sheds and fishermen's stores for 'temporary' parking.

CHAPTER 7

DUDGEON BOUND

The trawl was on deck and the sparse amount of fish in the pound meant a change of territory. "Lift t' wing-ends in," I called from the window then looked at the chart for inspiration. Where could we move to that wasn't too far away and where no one had tried recently?

A bang then a shout brought me from my deliberations and I looked out of the window to the deck again. Kenny, a recent recruit standing near the Gilson winch was holding his gloved hand. A finger was missing from the glove. Others stood round concerned, asking if he was OK.

"What's 'appened?" I called out.

Kenny, clearly shocked, eased off the glove and held up his hand to show a ragged bloody mess where his finger had been severed.

"Oh shit!" I said for want of something sensible to say.

I called the coastguard for helicopter assistance then went on deck to examine the wound. There was little I could do apart from gently bandage his hand then support the arm in a sling.

"Don't forget this," one of the lads said, passing Kenny a plastic bag containing his finger end buried in ice as he was about to be lifted off in a harness.

Kenny walked onto the pier early on Thursday morning to collect his sea gear while we were mending the trawl, his hand heavily bandaged. Asking the question we all wanted an answer to, Mick called up to the casualty. "Did they stitch yer finger end back on?"

"Naw, they couldn't do it?" Kenny replied. "They said it 'ad frostbite."

* * * * * *

It was now midsummer and the long awaited annual diving trip was under threat from the weather. I'd been monitoring the forecasts throughout the week while at sea and on Wednesday night heard the announcer say, "Forth, Tyne, Dogger, southwesterly, four or five, perhaps six. German Bight, Humber, southwesterly, four or five." That strength of wind wouldn't be a problem for fishing but it would be no fun diving out on the Dogger or Well Banks. The swell would build with every mile of reach and seventy miles offshore it would be uncomfortable or unworkable taking the inflatable craft alongside a rolling trawler when loaded with divers and equipment.

I pored over the charts and realised that if we sailed in a southerly direction there were dozens of wrecks to choose from off the shallow Humber estuary. Though some of these were twenty to thirty miles off, they were close enough to shore to allow the trip to take place and there would probably be less wind in this region. I announced this to the waiting duo on the quayside on Thursday morning when Pete and club chairman, Colin stood waiting for a 'yea' or 'nay' prior to going to work. There was a fair draught of wind blowing and the pair looked glum as we pulled alongside the quay but the frowns turned to smiles when I gave a thumbs-up sign in their direction and shouted, "we're in business." Once on the pier I briefly explained my idea, as the lads on deck topped the landing gear and opened the fish-room hatch ready for discharging our catch.

We'd organised our summer diving trip for several years now and had discovered and identified previously unknown wrecks, recovering some wonderful brass trophies including bells, lamps, portholes and shell-cases. We'd been to the Nor'west Rough, Dogger Bank and the Inner and Outer Well Bank in the past but we'd never explored to the south, thinking the shallow water, offshore from the big river would be murky. Now this was the only option available if we were to go ahead with the trip and we'd take it.

Word was passed to the other members of the expedition during the day and it was an excited, though slightly apprehensive crew that manned *Emulator* as she sailed through the piers that evening. The sailing time allowed us about an hour once on site to locate, mark and buoy the chosen wreck, then to kit up before slack water. We'd opted to tow the new, high-powered rigid inflatable craft that the diving club had recently acquired. This new boat was larger than the previous vessel and couldn't be lifted onboard, though would handle most weather with ease. A dozen pairs of eyes were mesmerised watching the lively little craft plane in *Emulator's* wake at the end of the long towrope. Most of the voyage complement were standing aft, supping cans of beer. On earlier trips we'd taken small kegs of beer but cans proved easier and less temperamental and the new, draught-flow tins were a revolution. The ale was supplemented by thick wads of ham, cheese or corned beef sandwiches from the galley's endless production line. Colin, who enjoyed cooking, had opted to take on the dual role of diver/cook for this trip and had brought some wonderful pre-cooked dishes that were now stored below in the ice pound.

The sun had gone and the bell buoy light was flashing clearly on the Brigg end as Filey Bay was revealed from behind the protruding cliff. The red hue over the low lying back land promised a 'shepherd's delight'. I hoped there'd be no 'sailors warning' with the dawn. The cliffs grew in size as we headed southeast towards the towering Flamborough Head, its iridescent light also flashing in the gathering gloom. The divers had teamed up in pairs ensuring experience was combined with enthusiasm and drawn lots for the night watches. As ever, I'd be on call below when required.

Waiting till we'd reached a position with the magnificent chalky headland a mile to starboard, the course was altered to south southeast, towards the Dudgeon Lightship, some fifty miles distant, I left the first duo in control. The after-deck was uninhabited now, as I discovered when stepping out of the door for a final inspection. The towrope was bouncing reassuringly and in the dark distance a V of milky phosphorescence gave further evidence that all was well with our little charge.

Below, in the darkened cabin I discovered bodies everywhere. Not only were five of the six bunks filled, there were prone figures on camp beds on the floor and inert bodies on seat lockers and any horizontal surface capable of holding a curled up body. Though my bunk was empty, an unidentified sleeper was almost blocking the access, zipped tightly in a sleeping bag on the cushioned locker adjacent. Kicking off shoes I gingerly manoeuvred myself through the slight gap into my 'hole in the wall' and crashed out.

There were no calls for advice on close-quarter shipping movements during the night. Over the years the lads had developed a clear grasp of the boat's autopilot steering and plotter and most were familiar with the rule of the road at sea, so I surfaced to a cold, grey morning, having been summoned by Steve, the diver who'd survived the near death experience over the Christmas holiday. He'd drawn the sleep-robbing, dawn watch. Steve handed me a welcome mug of coffee as I settled in the wheelhouse chair and began taking in the surroundings and familiarising myself with traffic on the radar then getting acquainted with the vessel's position, speed and course. The sea merged with the sky and the sun was nowhere to be seen. Coupled with this, the cool wind was generating a three to five foot swell making the thought of diving distinctly uninviting. It was pleasing to see the RIB still following faithfully behind, unaffected by the swell.

Switching on the sonar, I waited until the mechanical hoist in the fo'c'sle had lowered the transducer below *Emulator's* keel then heard the steady ping, ping as the signal searched in a stepped arc ahead of our direction of travel. We were looking for the wreck of the 1261 ton, *Fireglow,* a collier mined in December 1941. Over recent years we'd accumulated a catalogue of many wrecks, mostly thanks to Pete's enquiries to the Hydrographic Department of the Royal Navy. The depth, approximate location and size of this sunken coal carrier made her a choice objective. In this shallow water the bigger ships would be dispersed over a wide area to allow safe navigation but we were hopeful this smaller vessel might be more intact.

The wreck took no finding at all, in fact there were several targets in the proximity of *Fireglow's* location; the sonar's beam echoing back from steel plate. This was a tangible reminder of E boat successes in these narrow waterways between shallow sandbanks. All hands had been roused and Steve and his watch mate had prepared the four-foot 'plonker' grapnel with chain and fifteen fathoms of line, attached to a plastic oil drum.

Sitting two fathoms proud on the bottom, its edges in a scour due to the fast running tide in this region, the wreck showed bright red on the coloured screen. I was confident of finding and hitting this target almost at will, so took a leisurely 360 degree turn and dodged dead slow into the failing tide. "Stand-by," I called from the window to the men standing aft, muffled in the cold dawn. The pair, already on alert and balancing the heavy weight on the stern, almost shoved the grapnel over the side at my call. These lads were used to diving in deeper water where wrecks were harder to hit and they were on a 'hair trigger'.

"Leggo," I called on the second run as the wreck stood crimson and solid on the sounder. I watched fascinated as the plonker was depicted on the fast-moving screen, dropping into the mass on the seabed. "Bingo," I called out but the riggers had already disappeared to grab a coffee with their mates on the mess-deck.

Down tide, with the engine in neutral and no shipping close, I joined them. Half a dozen men crowded round the table and a couple were standing, filling the little space below the wheelhouse. The remaining mug in the rack was lifted and a brew of instant coffee, filled from the singing kettle was passed in my direction. There was a distinct lack of enthusiasm among the troops, not surprising in the prevailing conditions.

"Who's gonna be first in?" I asked, encouraging the reluctant crew. "It's a brand new wreck. There'll be all sorts o' stuff down there, jus' waitin' t' be collected."

One or two averted their gaze but Dick Sellars, the Ebberston village blacksmith, a solid, reliable club man said to Steve, "are we gonna give it go?"

Not wanting to disappoint, his dive partner nodded, saying, "aye OK then, why not?" and the pair manoeuvred their way to the deck through the reticent crowd. Quickly kitting up despite *Emulator's* antics, fifteen minutes later the pals sat poised on the boat's starboard side, swaying in harmony with the motion of the vessel, despite the heavy cylinders on their backs. Goody bags and powerful torches were secured to their weight belts. With a little shunt astern '*Emmy*' was brought to a stop beside the green surface marker. Only a gentle wake trailed from the oil drum buoy, indicating slack water was imminent. The trailing RIB had been drawn to the port side, away from the action.

"Go now," I called and the buddies, each with a hand on their mask, dropped into the water together as the boat rolled in their favour, shortening the drop.

On the surface they finned towards the buoy then without hesitating rolled forward to descend down the line into the depths. There was little sign of enthusiasm from those watching from the deck, apart from Colin who was standing outboard, feet in the scuppers holding on to *Emulator's* side, awaiting the opportunity to drop into the gyrating inflatable. Clad in dry suit and an oilskin jacket, he was taking no chances of being wet or cold. Once onboard, Colin started the engine and dodged slowly towards the buoy, tying onto the line to await the divers' return. *Emulator* was positioned down what little remained of the tide. A couple of spotters were keeping lookout from the deck in case the pair surfaced away from the buoy. In this swell they could easily be missed even a short distance from the boat, as only heads would be visible between the waves. Inflatable 'surface markers buoys' would soon be available to enhance divers' ability to attract attention.

Less than twenty minutes later the pair resurfaced. This was disappointing. If the dive site or conditions had been good these lads could have stayed down another ten to fifteen minutes in these shallow waters. This was ominous. Had we had a wasted journey?

"They've got summat," Pete observed. "They've both passed full goody bags into the RIB."

As I watched, individual weight belts and twin bottles were unbuckled then hauled into the boat by Colin. Holding the grab ropes on the sides of the craft, with a quick duck underwater and kick of fins each in turn propelled their torso onto the sponson then swivelled legs inboard. The craft headed slowly towards the mother ship and as she drew close, Steve fumbled in his bag. With a huge grin on his face he held aloft the ship's bell. Dick, using both hands raised a sack full of lobsters.

There was an immediate scramble towards the kitbags and bottles, stacked in the fish pound, as everyone rushed for their gear, not pausing to help the two pioneers back aboard. The pair, without kit scaled nimbly up the matrix of tyres lashed on the boat's side. I stood with a short length of rope, ready to haul their gear and goodies to the deck.

"It's crawlin' wi' lobsters down there," Dick said, as he unhitched the pieces of equipment. "They're giants an' not frightened at all. They're just walkin' about waitin' t' be picked up."

Back on board, the pair shared their knowledge of the site with their friends. It transpired we had grappled into the bows of the wreck and the bell, with *Fireglow* etched boldly on its front, had been recovered from a lamp room under the fo'c'sle of the ship and not near the anchor windless where it should have been mounted. The good news was there appeared to be several brass and copper lamps in the room also, though not easily accessible.

It was dead slack when the next six divers entered the water and the wind appeared to be falling away with the tide. With no current running the half-dozen swimmers had no trouble reaching the line and soon there was only a mass of bubbles on the surface to mark where they'd been. It would be half an hour before the group in the water would be back up. Now, with Steve in the wheelhouse and Dick in the RIB, Colin and I, along with the remaining pair began a leisurely assembly of our gear then donned suits. I was back to using a wetsuit after my dire experience of dry suit diving.

On their arrival back on *Emulator* the returning frogmen were ecstatic. All had lobsters, some had lamp glasses and there were other bits of brass to be passed around, identified and admired. With Pete in the wheelhouse steering and the buoy lying slightly astern, we remaining four divers dropped into the water. The tide had turned now and we drifted slowly down onto the bobbing drum. Holding onto the rope, Colin and I followed the first pair down the line. In the shallow water it was no time at all before we saw the railings on the foredeck of *Fireglow* then the straight vertical line of the wreck's stem, leading down to the seabed. There was no point in looking for the bell, so we dropped down behind the foredeck to the port side where the lamp locker was situated. We found ourselves on the seabed and I looked at my depth gauge. It read a mere twenty metres. It was immediately obvious that the little cubicle on the portside of the ship was full of sand and silt. There were a few feet of what must have been a top shelf exposed just inside the door, and this was probably where the bell had been located. Shining my torch into the inner reaches while trying, without success to avoid disturbing silt, I could see parts of lamps, half-buried in the sand, inaccessible in the narrow space. The trinkets in reach had already been claimed.

We began to fin in the direction of the midship section and could see the occasional flashing of the torches from the other divers, so the visibility wasn't too bad. The water was a little grey but some natural light was penetrating from the surface. There were pieces of coal strewn everywhere. This ship was not only coal powered, she carried this mineral as cargo. *Fireglow* was one of a type known in the coastal trade as 'flatirons', due to their low profile and fold-down masts and funnels, enabling the ships to pass under the bridges of the River Thames. She had been just one of the scores of ships supplying the endless needs of the capital's power stations.

Colin grabbed a lobster from under a broken iron plate so I unhooked my bag and opened the small meshed container wide, allowed the crustacean to be shoved in, tail first. The claws were waving vigorously but found nothing to grab till they were bagged. A thumb and forefinger OK sign from Colin and we moved further down the wreck, soon coming to her bridge. Half a minute later I spotted a large lobster's tail protruding from under some ship's plate. Knowing the creature couldn't nip me from this direction I grabbed beyond the tail and holding the hard shell of the carapace pulled the animal from its hiding place, holding the black, tail-flapping shellfish aloft. Colin, receptive to my requirements opened his sack and the beast was slotted in.

There was no sign of the steering wheel or telegraph in the wheelhouse area though the collapsed roof hid most of the contents. The remains of an early radio transmitter/receiver were visible through what had been a door space. We continued our way towards the stern, conscious of being propelled by the new tide. From the bridge aft, the ship was badly smashed up, perfect lobster territory and working as a team we quickly added to our catch. Air was needed in our lifejackets now to compensate for the extra weight we were carrying. In no time we'd reached the after section of the wrecked ship but here she was quite sand-warped and hardly distinguishable. There was no sign of her collapsible funnel. The tide was running stronger now and carrying our bags of shellfish we could feel its drag. Colin pointed a finger towards the bows and I nodded, giving an OK. I looked at my watch. We'd been twenty-five minutes already and it had passed swiftly. We turned and began to make our way back to the shot rope. It helped to keep low, sheltering from the unseen force of the tide while pulling our way along the broken ship with any handhold in reach.

It's always a good feeling to grab hold of the rope leading to the surface and this time it was especially comforting. With this tide running and swell on the surface we could be quickly swept away. Making our way up the rope, I looked at my watch again. It had taken five minutes to get to this point and I was breathing heavily. The needle on my contents gauge was not quite into the red so I still had plenty of air for my ascent. We could see the other divers above us and could hear the reassuring throb of the outboard motor close by. Hand over hand up the rope we went, forcing ourselves to go slowly, hanging horizontally on the line like flags in a wind. Our bags of lobsters were dangling below us, clipped to the metal rings of our lifejackets. There was severe carnage taking place in my sack judging by the crunching of shell, audible above my now slowing breathing.

The pair ahead had now surfaced and left the rope. They'd be drifting with the tide now while discharging their kit and catch. They'd have no trouble. One of the pair, Gordon, was a fearless, tough diver with a ruthless reputation. I could recall on a previous trip while out on the Dogger Bank, he was physically grabbing hold of big cod, sticking his air hose into their rectums and giving the fish a shot of air, forcing the poor creatures unwillingly to the surface, to be collected by the surprised boatman.

Reaching the top of the shot rope, I was surprised to discover that we weren't on the surface. The pair ahead of us must have encountered the same experience. The green oil drum was cavorting wildly a few feet below the waves, suspended in the running tide, our combined weight dragging the container down. I pointed upwards and getting a nod, let go of the rope. The box shaped container surfaced, as did my buddy and I. The oil drum appeared to be leaving us at speed if the wake it was creating was to be believed but in reality the buoy was anchored and we were drifting away from its position on the tide.

Turning, it was good to see three men in the RIB waving and waiting for an OK from our end. This was quickly given and we both inflated our lifejackets fully from the reserves of air, drifting in relative comfort now, pending their arrival and our pick up. Minutes later we were back alongside the mother ship ready to off load our numerous pieces of kit and lobsters.

Onboard *Emulator*, the lads having shed their diving suits were relaxing on deck. The swell was dying now and the sky lighter. A distinct clatter was audible above the boat's engine noise; this emanating from the small, portable compressor vibrating on the foredeck recharging the spent air cylinders. Willing hands helped decant the boat and assist us back aboard. Our goody bags were taken and carefully emptied; the lobsters lifted out individually and kept apart, claws to be secured with strong rubber bands.

It was too late for some of the creatures that had been crushed within the confines of the goody bag by the claws of bigger animals. These broken lobsters and severed pincers were tipped onto the deck, soon to join other broken limbs and tails in a basket. These would be cooked as soon as Colin had finished serving breakfast and would form part of the midday meal.

The live lobsters were lowered below to the chilled fish-room then placed into three boxes; water-soaked bags covering each. This was a fine haul and would help to subsidise the expedition.

The tide was running like a millrace by the time we'd recovered the buoy and plonker but with these back onboard everyone could relax. The weather was now fine and tales of underwater exploits were being exchanged while the team waited to be fed. No one had seen any quantity of fish on the wreck apart from a few striped bream and an odd ling, so there'd be no sport with the rods on this wreck. A couple of the lads wearing ear defenders continued to refill the empty air bottles from the rattling compressor on the foredeck, its intake hose fastened in the rigging ten feet above the machine to avoid drawing in contaminated air.

We'd plenty of time now to find our next target. It would be nearly five hours before the next slack water. Phut bang, phut bang, phut, bang. The sonar was locked onto and bouncing back from something solid. This wasn't a target like *Fireglow*, which gave a firm enough echo. This must be something big and intact. We were in fifteen fathoms of water and heading to the west. The target was still eight hundred metres away but banging crisply. "This is summat good," I said to Pete, at my shoulder.

"It says 'unknown' on the print out," he replied, having pored over the computer information avidly since learning that we were heading to the Humber region. The target was dead ahead and *Emulator* was moving towards the object at half speed. Steaming across the strong tide we would have been offset from the wreck at a slower pace. There was no rush to grapple into this objective. I just wanted to get a precise fix with the navigator so the wreck could be located at will when the tide eased. The red mark, when it appeared on the screen surprised us both, standing over four fathoms high and almost square in shape. Speculation was rife for the next few hours as to what this lump of ship was. The wreck could be intact and in this depth and slightly off the shipping lanes, there was no reason why it shouldn't be.

Pete and his buddy were in the first wave and there was no reluctance now from anyone to get in the water. Half a dozen bodies dropped from *Emulator's* side in a variety of entries, marked for style by those watching. One nameless diver had forgotten to don his weight belt in the rush to kit up and was jeered by the spectators. He was compelled to hold on to the line till the missing item was delivered via the RIB. His enthusiastic buddy, not wanting to miss out on the opportunity of being one of the first on the new wreck, had submerged and would be waiting on the bottom of the shot rope for his mate.

Now on the second dive and going a little deeper, which wasn't the usual format for repeat dives, the explorers wouldn't stay down as long, but would still take the maximum bottom time allowed by the decompression tables. A few of the more progressive divers were using new wrist computers, which took the calculating element from the process. These machines gave readings of duration of dive, present depth, deepest decent during the dive and also indicated any decompression time required before surfacing. Those using this latest technology seemed to get more bottom time. I'd be getting one of these machines soon.

It wasn't long before the first batch were decompressing, three metres below the semi-submerged surface marker. There was virtually no tide running and the jumble of bodies was clearly visible on the line. Curious for news, I was waiting in the RIB with Steve when the first pair surfaced and easily finned the few feet to our position. An excited Pete spat out his mouthpiece and louder than intended yelled, "it's a bloody sailing ship."

Once onboard the rubber craft, he reported that the wreck was an iron hulled ship, sitting bolt upright on the seabed. He'd been to the stern of the ship on the seabed looking for the propeller but instead had discovered a long rudder, with no gap where the screw, had there been one, would be found. Though the masts had gone from her deck, there was no sign of any superstructure and conclusively, there were deadeyes and wooden blocks scattered around the ship's deck. These would be made from lignum vitae. This very dense, strong wood was so heavy the material had negative buoyancy. To further his case, as if this was necessary, he produced a deadeye from his bag. These oval shaped wooden units, with three holes formed through the middle were carved from single pieces of wood and pairs of these were used to tension ships' rigging prior to the invention of bottle-screws. The lovely black form was a superb trophy and had shared the bag with a single lobster. The lack of access in the intact hull gave little habitat for crustaceans.

The water was clearer than on our previous dive as we, the second team, discovered when descending to the deck of the old ship. The sun was near its zenith and the natural light was penetrating down to the wreck. She was indeed sat upright and her walled sides leading to the seabed descended out of sight, as I found when shining my torch in the direction of the bottom. No wonder she was a good sonar target.

The holds were filled with silt and there seemed nothing on the ship to confirm her identity. We finned along the centre of the vessel towards the bows, hoping for the bell. The fore end of the ship dipped and came to a point where a bracket had once held the bowsprit. There was no sign of a bell but there was a short length of weed covered rope, knotted around this iron band. This was a bad sign. Drawing the slack section of the material through a gloved hand caused a small cloud of silt to spoil the visibility close to the site. This also allowed us to identify the rope as synthetic. The line had been deliberately hitched in this location and could mean only one thing; the wreck had been dived before, and this had been the divers' shot rope. What a disappointment. I thought we were on a virgin wreck but someone had been here before us. Did they find a bell or any other form of identification? We'd never know. There was small solace in a couple of good lobsters bagged on the way back to the line, but the prospect of a unique dive had been dashed.

Lunch was a feast of lobster, eaten alfresco with coffee or tea and for those wanting something stronger, beer. Divers sat perched around the deck breaking large claws with the handles of diving knives or crushing and peeling open huge, curled tails, from broken lobsters. With bread and butter, salt and vinegar and chopped salad trimmings, this was a glorious feast. Again there was time for relaxing and many of the temporary crew hit the sack, resting in preparation for an early evening dip.

The third dive of the day revealed the remains of another war loss. This victim had been carrying military vehicles amongst her cargo. These now appeared as skeletons with most of their shell plating corroded away. She was a broken old wreck and more than half her length was engulfed by a huge sand dune. These giant ripples are in a constant state of movement and this bank was soon to consume the wreck entirely. Maybe, many years in the future this sub-aqua desert would yield up this time capsule for other generations of adventurers. Again there was no identification to be found and only an old porthole came up as a trophy, but the visible parts of the wreck did give us another good bag of lobsters.

The weather was perfect now and another delicious meal of soup, chilli con carne with rice then apple pie and cream to follow was taken alfresco. The warm, pleasant evening allowed the full complement to remain on the foredeck for a relaxing interlude of beer and good humour. Discussions took place about the following day's prospects. A fine forecast gave the option of moving offshore about twenty-five miles to the northeast where the readout offered some interesting choices, including two sites only a few miles apart, both 'unknown' wrecks, one of 345 feet in length. This was chosen as our target and the course was set. Watches began at 2200 hours and we dodged very slowly in the required direction for most of the night. There was little traffic around and the watch-keepers had an easy time. The wind and sea remained benign and there was a bonus in the form of an extra couple of hours in bed for everyone. According to the tidal predictions, slack water occurred an hour later today and in this new location further offshore, slack was an additional hour after the previous dive site. The wreck took no locating and the enthusiasm was now boundless, everyone wanting to be first in the water.

The sounder showed a clearly defined large wreck, which appeared to be lying in a north-south direction. I was in the first group with my buddy and sitting next to me on the gunwale waiting for the signal to go were little Jimmy Butler and his pal Alan, both from Mansfield. These two were guests on the trip, a trip that could have been filled twice over. Jim was an extremely affable character with a terrific sense of humour and just slotted into place whenever he turned up at the diving club.

The shout, "go" came from above and six frogmen fell into the water in planned and unplanned entries, all surfacing only feet from the oil drum, which was riding high in the motionless water. Not sure who was with whom, we all grabbed the rope and began the race down the line to explore the unknown shipwreck. This was the classic diving joke in real life, 'hit the bottom and scatter'.

My reaction to this new dive site after locating my buddy was again one of disappointment. Though huge, the ship was totally upside down. There was scant likelihood of trophies for anyone here. The only good news was the ship, which was sitting on a gravel bottom in thirty-five metres of crystal clear water, had begun to break up and the disintegrating hull should be a natural habitat for lobsters. Not only this, there was an abundance of cod swimming around the ship. These fish quickly moved off the wreck but remained in view out in the blue periphery. The shimmering mass would soon move back to the iron reef when we'd finished our dive and would be sport for the anglers onboard.

Colin and I worked together collecting lobsters as we headed towards the stern. The iron propeller, with two rusting blades pointing skywards and a matching pair, partially buried, was massive. The steam powered engine that had swung this huge screw must have been a slow revving machine with lots of horsepower. A couple of divers were examining the stern gear closely as we approached. One was measuring his length against an upright blade, stretching with fingers towards the tip, though not quite reaching but giving perspective to the size of the prop. Now his suit was stained with rust from the decaying piece.

Turning round, we headed for the bows, some distance away. There was no chance of getting lost on this wreck with such clear water and a keel running down the centreline. We swam past the shot rope with confidence, heading for the stem but could find no visible inlet to reveal the secrets this ship held. Though breaking up, she seemed to be double-bottomed and where the plating had corroded, the inner skin was intact. Her bulwarks on both sides were completely embedded in the gravel leaving no opportunity to shine torches into any hollows. The stem was no different and there was no sign of hawse-pipes for her cables, unless they too were buried. She was probably from an age when anchors were stowed on fo'c'sle heads and deployed from a cathead. It was around the bows that we found the third pair from our group, vainly scanning the seabed on both sides of the ship, perhaps hoping the bell had somehow been thrown clear. An OK sign from Jimmy then an unorthodox shrug signalled zero results.

The waiting boatmen, desperate for information were also disappointed as we gave them the situation report and our bags of lobsters. These lads had been banking on a super dive. Were they prepared to take the chance of me finding the other wreck in the area quickly?

Yes they were. The transfer of gear and personnel took place then we headed in the direction of the second wreck with the RIB following, as we made best speed towards our goal.

"There it is," I called out joyfully twenty minutes later as the first echoes came back from the sonar. With the engine going at slow speed we approached the wreck. There was no time for error and fortunately minutes later a small red blob appeared on the sounder screen. At the same instant I yelled, "leggo" to the men at the back of the boat.

The plonker dropped into the sea and relieved, I put *Emulator's* rudder to starboard in a slow circle. The second wave of divers were sitting on her side ready by the time we'd completed the loop and all dropped into the water as I stopped alongside the bobbing buoy. We'd taken only half an hour to find, mark and put six divers onto the wreck. How slick was that? There was hardly any tide running and I fervently hoped we'd hit this small wreck. At least the water was clear enough to allow room for error.

My self-congratulation was soon forgotten when a voice at my side said, "I think I've got a bit of a problem." I turned to see Jimmy with a pained expression on his face.

He was holding his chest and said," I think I might have a bend."

"Oh fuck!" was my instant reply. This was every diver's worst nightmare. Decompression sickness could strike indiscriminately, even when every precaution had been taken. Pete would know what to do but he was still in the water. We'd certainly need a helicopter. We were too far offshore to get the casualty to a hospital in a hurry and not just any hospital would do. There were few hyperbaric units on the East Coast. Hull and Great Yarmouth were the nearest possibilities but first we'd need the chopper.

Jimmy wasn't panicking and when assured I'd get some medical assistance, went back on deck to lay quietly on the fishing gear on the starboard side with his feet elevated. I contacted the Coastguards on the 2182 distress frequency.

In my best radio voice I called, "Humber Coastguard, Humber Coastguard, this is the fishing vessel *Emulator* on 2182. Are you receiving Sir? Over."

A confident, reassuring voice answered the call immediately. "*Emulator, Emulator, Emulator*, this is Humber Coastguard receiving you. Please tune to a working channel."

The operative suggested a new frequency and I quickly retuned. I could have continued on the distress channel but didn't want to draw attention to the situation. The curious would still eavesdrop on the communication.

"Good morning Sir, how can I help you?" came the voice again when communications were re-established.

"Good morning to you Sir. I have a diver on board with suspected decompression sickness. Could you possibly organise a helicopter to airlift him ashore?"

There was the briefest of pauses then the operative said, "I'm sorry Sir. I thought you said you were a fishing vessel."

It took less than a minute to explain that *Emulator* was a fishing vessel, but that we were out for the weekend with a group of divers, I took this opportunity to give him our position in latitude and longitude. He was sure to have a direction finder checking the bearing of our signal and this information would reassure him my call wasn't a hoax. I went on to explain that we still had divers in the water so I was unable to shorten the distance to any designated port until their return to the vessel.

The status of the casualty and his symptoms were described and I was rewarded with the operative's assurance he was scrambling Rescue Helicopter 128 from RAF Leconfield and the aircraft should be with us in approximately thirty minutes. This was wonderful news. Even if we had the chance to head for shore, we'd make no more than four miles in this time.

The divers began to surface, euphoric at having found an intact trawler yielding several interesting trinkets but their enthusiasm was soon dampened with the news of Jim's problem. Back on board they gathered round the casualty, attempting to amuse him and engage him with tales of their recent dip and their finds from the wreck.

"This is t' third time I've needed an 'elicopter in t' past couple o' years," I confided in the casualty, attempting to make light conversation. I went on to explain about Colin and Kenny, distracting him from his dilemma.

"They'll be inviting you to their Christmas parties before long," Jimmy replied with an attempted smile.

The chopper appeared on the radar on the twelve-mile range, intermittently at first but the signal quickly hardened and grew brighter as the aircraft drew nearer the screen's centre. "E's 'ere," I called out to the cluster of people on the deck and heads swivelled in the direction of my pointing arm. The speck in the sky three miles away grew quickly, as did the noise from the machine's rotors. A new voice came clearly over the airwaves. *"Emulator, Emulator, Emulator, this is Rescue Helicopter 128. I have you visual Sir. Do you receive? Over."*

Handset poised, anticipating the call and still in my best Queen's English I replied, "128, this is *Emulator*, receiving you loud and clear. I have you visual also Sir."

The pilot asked for up to date information on the casualty then instructed me to steer with the wind on the starboard bow, though this was only a gentle southwest breeze. I turned the autopilot to 180 degrees then went to the doorway to watch proceedings. I could hear the radio and would be able to return quickly to address any requirements the pilot may need. A minute later there was a deafening clatter overhead and the vessel was engulfed in a tremendous downdraft as the chopper hovered above us. An airman appeared at the open door attached to the thin wire cable and with stretcher and bag attached, began his descent. Seconds later he was suspended in mid air using his arms to signal another crewman in the doorway. He in turn directed the pilot, who had no visual of the events below. This was amazing teamwork and something I hadn't been aware of until my previous experience with the RAF's rescue squadron.

The divers, with the exception of Pete, kept out of the way on the starboard side while the dangling serviceman hovered above *Emulator's* after deck. "Don't touch me," the flier called, as our man moved in to steady him.

With feet firmly on the deck the airman unclipped himself and his cargo, waving the chopper away with another hand signal. "You'd have got a massive belt of electric shock," he explained. "I was alive with static electricity." Our visitor removed his helmet, revealing a head of blond hair, probably longer than regulation length.

With a ready smile and in a confident manner, the young man faced the welcome committee, now gathering around him. "Hello fellers," he said cheerily. "Where's the casualty?"

Leaving the stretcher on the stern a delegation took the flier for'ard to where Jimmy lay on the fishing gear, feet still elevated. His concerned pal, Alan was sitting by Jim's head in quiet conversation.

"Hello there. What have you been doing?" the visitor asked of the prone diver in his easy demeanour.

Jim explained how he'd developed chest pains shortly after his arrival back onboard, despite following all the necessary precautions and enjoying a relaxed, incident free dive. "I think I've got a bend," he said quietly.

"Ok, well, I think the best thing we can do is to take you off and get you to a chamber. If you do have decompression sickness they'll soon sort you out." His confident manner gave Jim a visible lift and the little man smiled for the first time since his symptoms had appeared.

The stretcher was brought from the stern and placed on the deck and the casualty helped into place by willing volunteers. He shuffled slightly to get comfortable. Cane flaps and canvas straps were fastened across various parts of his anatomy, securing Jimmy into position. More hands lifted the stretcher onto the net and the young airman, speaking into his hand-held radio summoned his aircraft.

The big yellow bird was drawing close, the downdraft visible on the water when, above the noise, Pete called out loudly to the waiting serviceman, "do you lads like lobster?"

"Of course, who doesn't like lobster?" came the swift reply.

"We've got loads of 'em. Do you want a few?" Pete asked.

With an affirmative response and the chopper drawing ever nearer the diver dashed across the deck and reached into the sack covered basket, returning with three large lobsters heaped, unresisting in his hands. "You should get a good meal from these," he said, attempting to hand over the crustaceans.

"Woh! Wait a minute. What am I supposed to do with those?" the shocked airman replied, his palms extended and for the first time unsure of his situation. "I need to put them in something."

Despite a hurried search, nothing suitable was forthcoming. "Can't you fasten them on with the straps on your stretcher," someone suggested, joking.

"Splendid idea," came back the reply and the flier, confidence returned, hurriedly unfastened three of the many retaining bands and refixed each to incorporate a lobster. The casualty looked on open-mouthed and disbelieving. A live lobster nestled between his shins and a second lay on his thighs, claws resting on his groin. A third was sitting on his chest, eyeball to eyeball with Jimmy, pincers near his throat. The casualty looked most uncomfortable. Despite the elastic bands securing the lobsters' claws the little fellow's mind was no longer on his ailment.

"Do you mind turning that one round, please? he asked. I'd rather look at its tail."

Jimmy left *Emulator* bound for a decompression chamber in Great Yarmouth with suggestions of crushed nuts and cheap vasectomies ringing in his ears, though the sound of the rotors quickly drowned the shouting. His pal Alan looked on disconsolate, knowing he would be driving home alone.

While assembled, I took the opportunity to ask the group what they wanted to do now. The only choices being to return home or finish the expedition as planned. There was a stony silence, no one wanting to upset Alan, who had been unable to accompany his buddy, and who probably wanted to get ashore as soon as possible to drive to his mate's destination. Eyes turned to the stocky, quiet man for a decision.

"Well Jim wouldn't want us to go back, would he? There's nothing to be gained by heading home now. He's going to be in a chamber anyway," came the response along with an attempted grin. "There's still some diving to be done."

Though a more subdued atmosphere hung over the vessel now, we set off to look for another dive site. The sun was shining and bodies lay around the deck in various states of undress as *Emulator* dodged slowly towards the next dive site. Sitting back in the comfortable seat with slipper clad feet braced on the steering wheel, I was mulling over the recent events, wondering what could have triggered Jimmy's ailment and considering what, if anything could have been done differently. My reverie was broken with the arrival of Colin bearing a cup of coffee and a chunky cheese and ham sandwich. "Well Fred, what a going on," he said. This was Colin's stock phrase for anything out of the ordinary. We were discussing recent events when, looking at the sounder and pointing, he said, "that's not a wreck is it?"

My eyes shot to the sounder, a place I'd normally be scanning constantly. "It bloody well is," I replied grabbing the throttle and easing the lever back to dead slow. The distinct, raised object, about a fathom and a half high above the sandy bottom was unmistakable. A minute at least had passed since the mark had been traced but the track on the plotter screen had recorded our passage and it was no trouble to reverse our course, running over the line on the display until we found the wreck again. This was an interesting scenario. We'd found a small wreck, possibly a fishing vessel that wasn't showing on the chart.

It was early afternoon when the first team dropped from *Emulator's* side to descend into the depths and I manned the RIB with Colin, eagerly awaiting their return. We were both quite surprised when Dick surfaced long before his expected time, spat his regulator out and with a huge grin said, "it's a tanker."

"It can't be a very big un," I replied, confused. "It doesn't stand up very 'igh on t' sounder."

"It's a road tanker," he said, laughing loudly. "It must 'ave fell off t' back of a ferry or summat." He handed up his air bottle and weight belt then heaved himself onboard. Continuing, he explained that there was no driver's cab, just the trailer section but there was no identification or number-plate. "It's been down there fo' years. It's well rusted an' decayin'," he added.

The others in the party surfaced not long after, bored after swimming round a road tanker several times. They were not quite as amused as Dick at this discovery, knowing they'd wasted one of their few remaining dives. Hearing the news, the second wave were disinclined to explore the new find and opted to miss this dip, thus giving them more bottom time on the early evening dive, when the absorbed gas in their bodies had dissipated. I concurred with this decision but now we needed a quality wreck to end the voyage on a high note.

The unidentified wreck, dispersed and scattered over a wide area this yielded several brass trinkets and full bags of lobsters, but everyone who dived this wreck reported seeing a strange, incongruous plastic cable. The long, clear plastic sleeve, containing a bundle of small, differently coloured wires was strewn around the wreck.

Pete asked the question as I stepped from the RIB. "What was all that plastic tubing? There was loads of it."

"It's seismic cable," I stated with authority, though this was supposition. There had been substantial oil and gas exploration throughout the Southern North Sea in recent years. Converted stern trawlers were towing these two-mile long cables over huge areas. The ships fired detonators every few minutes, recording the echoes from deep within the earth's crust, prospecting for subterranean mineral deposits. These cables, with their complex, exploding tailpieces cost a fortune.

Had the skipper of the vessel caught the wreck while turning? Had he moved from his designated area into these shallows while avoiding bad weather, rather than recover the cable? Was he still in a job? All these speculations were made along with others as we steamed on a northerly course for Flamborough Head, still towing the faithful RIB on the line astern. The crew, full of food again, were relaxing around the deck holding gin and tonics in plastic glasses or supping from cans of ale. Most would hit the sack soon after dark.

It was shortly after 0200 hours with Flamborough Light flashing reassuringly a mile to port when I altered our heading to northwest: only fourteen miles to home now. It seemed ages since we'd passed this headland going in the opposite direction.

Dawn was breaking though it would be a while yet before the sun made an appearance. Three miles from Scarborough and a good head of steam on the kettle, all hands were called. They'd have time to wake up and have a drink before getting their kit together ready for going ashore.

The first of the cobles were sailing to haul their pots as *Emulator* slowly entered the harbour mouth and friendly waves were exchanged with the passing crews. With plenty of hands to handle ropes we were soon tied alongside and our landing gear topped ready to land the compressor, diving bottles and our catch. Colin departed in the RIB to secure the little craft back on her berth in the outer harbour. A couple of willing bodies dropped below to send up the boxes of lobsters. Along with Pete and a few others, I climbed the ladders to the pier top.

The first three boxes of shellfish were being unhooked when two coble men passed, heading towards their boat, pulling a cart holding boxes of bait. Spying the large lobsters the pair stopped to examine our catch more closely. Misreading the situation I said, "What about them then? They're proper lobsters. We've another seven boxes t' come up yet."

The first man's face reddened and he snarled, "Yer've no business tekin' them, they're t' breedin' stock."

"Yer want it all," the other man said angrily.

Quite taken aback by these normally friendly fishermen's outburst I couldn't think of a reply that would placate them. These lobsters had come from more than sixty miles away and wouldn't affect their livelihood at all but there was no point in prolonging the confrontation. It occurred to me that if this pair had caught these lobsters they wouldn't have been thrown back. "Breedin' stock's always t' stuff that other people catch," I muttered under my breath, then heard the first of the pair speak again.

"We on'y got ten lobsters out o' four 'undred pots yesterd'y," he stated with passion. "Yer tekin' t' bread out of our mouths."

A few more men stopped to express their dissatisfaction before going about their business and I knew I was in trouble. No doubt the matter would be aired more vocally at the bar of the Lord Nelson on their return from sea. I made a mental note to avoid this pub when I was next home. Iron hook in hand I began to drag the cases of offending animals away two at a time, intending to hide the boxes under a fish cover pending the arrival of Terry our salesman. I'd almost completed the task when Dickie Elliott and his partner, Ernie came along, also transporting bait. Before I had chance to hide the evidence Dick spied the remaining pair of boxes and I awaited another tirade but, in true Dickie Elliott style, instead of criticising and without even stopping he said, "well it's nice to know there's still plenty around somewhere."

This was a refreshing change of opinion but typical of the man. Dick always had a positive outlook on life and looked for the best in everyone. His son David, an old school pal had chosen not to go to sea and a few months earlier Dick, wanting to pass on his wealth of fishing ground knowledge had said, "let me 'ave your Danny fo' a couple o' years. Ah'll teach 'im all ah know."

This was a wonderful gesture. Few men willingly passed on their knowledge but sadly it wasn't one Danny would comply with. He wanted to work on trawlers when he was older.

And it was true what the potters were saying, there were very few lobsters on the inshore grounds to be caught at present. It was the season when the creatures were holed up changing their carapace. Each year in early summer the animals shed their hard crust, growing a new, larger coat. While this new shell hardened the lobsters were vulnerable pray and stayed hidden within any protection they could find. Soon they'd be abundant, out from their shelter and would be hungry following their compulsory fast. Then the potters would have their annual bonanza, but at present lobsters were scarce and it had been tactless of me to wave this heap under their noses.

Alan England drove off alone with a wave, heading for Great Yarmouth. No one was to know we'd never see him again and that very sadly, in less than two years the big, affable, friendly man would be taken with bowel cancer.

Saying goodbye to the divers who were loading up their vehicles, retrieved from nearby streets, I went below to stop the engine and stow my bottles and kitbag away. We'd be sailing again in a few hours but there was time to make my way up the hill home for a bath, a couple of hours kip then to wake Dotty and the bairns before having breakfast and heading back to the harbour to sail.

We took ice and food aboard then let the ropes go, taking *Emulator* back to sea once more to pursue her real job, but for weeks after I thought about this huge untapped resource. If anyone were to rig up properly with large pots and a boat capable of getting to these inaccessible grounds, there'd be a good living to be made.

* * * * * *

A few months later, having completed the preliminary paperwork and approved some scale drawings of a well laid out working vessel, Bluey and I signed a contract to build a new steel vessel in a yard in Truro, Cornwall. She was to be an inch short of sixty feet and 100 gross registered tons. On signing, we paid a cheque for ten percent of her cost to the yard's Managing Director, Patrick Bray. The company, 'Steelship' was currently constructing a vessel and having read the reports of this craft and seen photos, we were confident of getting a fine ship. She was to cost £450,000 but we'd get some government grant towards the build and a 'ship mortgage' from the 'Department of Trade and Industry' for fifty percent of her cost. We were also given a written guarantee by Patrick that if for any reason we didn't get our vessel within a year of commencement, we'd get our money back. This was something

I'd never experienced before and though I hoped this wouldn't be necessary, the offer was quite reassuring. Her keel was to be laid in a few weeks, at which point a further twenty percent was payable.

Bluey and I would have to give some thought to a name for the new craft and now, due to the introduction of a new regulation, we'd have to purchase a license to operate the vessel.

CHAPTER 8

THE ZINC WRECK

The powers that be had proclaimed yet another cut in the quota, to be implemented in the New Year. The situation was becoming serious. Cod was plentiful and unavoidable. Perversely the huge, unwarranted haddock increase of the previous year had not only been taken back, the quota had been reduced by more than half. If this were not bad enough, we now had a whiting quota to adhere to. If it weren't so drastic, this would be laughable. These were fish that fed on the young of all others and swam in huge predatory shoals, amongst which few other species were to be found. What was the point of putting a quota on these?

We'd been stuck in harbour for three days now as the latest of a series of gales blew through. This was an unusually long spell but we were certainly in the best place. The northerly storm had reached force ten or more, causing structural damage to buildings ashore and several vessels to part their mooring lines in the harbour. There'd also been some serious problems at sea including the loss of the five hundred ton German cargo vessel *Renate S*, which had gone down with all hands somewhere to the northeast of Scarborough. She'd been carrying a cargo of zinc and a quantity of cadmium. Her crew wouldn't have stood a chance when her hold had breached. The ship would have sunk faster than a stone.

It was early on Wednesday morning before we managed to get to sea. Boats were heading in all easterly directions on the flowing tide, hoping to earn something before the weekend. There was still a deep swell running from the recent gale, but the wind had fallen away and the rollers would also die as the day went on. In company with Colin in *Our Pride* we were bound for the Ground Edge, which would take about four hours steaming time. This long length of very hard rock, shoaling to thirty-three fathoms stretched for many miles, running east northeast, west southwest. Averaging about a mile wide, this solid ridge was edged by a fifty-fathom trench at the southern side and forty fathoms of soft ground to the north.

Towing the edge of the hard bank, attempting to hold thirty-seven or eight fathoms on the sounder, we had taken a few reasonable hauls by Thursday afternoon. I was now confident we'd have a landing for the morning's market. *Our Pride* was working further to the northwest and Col was on a similar fishing. Though not required, the sonar was scanning in an arc ahead with the sound on low, the BBC radio taking precedence. Suddenly something more than the echo of hard ground came from the machine, out beyond the thousand-metre range, to starboard. This had to be the recently lost merchant ship. There were no other wrecks in this area and though I'd only heard the few short crisp returning signals I was sure this was a wreck. I jumped from the chair to operate the beam manually. The scanner had moved past the target and was now showing soft ground at the bottom of the hole to port. Turning up the volume and pushing the little tiller on the grey console across to starboard again, the strong echo was immediately back. The direction indicator read twenty degrees.

Altering the autopilot to correspond with the presumed lost ship's direction I readjusted the sonar beam to ahead. We were now towing our trawl directly towards the wreck. Stemming the tide, there should be little danger of catching the obstacle and I hoped to mark the sunken vessel on the sounder to get an exact Decca reading. Summoning the lads from below, I quickly put them in the picture before returning to the wheelhouse.

The four appeared from the cabin, grabbed pots of coffee and took the steaming mugs on deck with them. At only two and a half knots we seemed to be taking forever to reach the wreck and I reached for the handset, calling, "*Our Pride*, are yer on Col? Ah think ah've jus' found that missin' ship."

"Oh aye, whereabouts are yer? Over," came the reply.

I reeled off the approximate location so he'd know to run his sonar if he was in the area. I'd give him the precise reading back in the harbour when I'd ascertained the dead fix. We crept slowly towards the object, noticing for the first time a film of oil on the surface. There was no sign of debris but anything that had washed from the ship as she sank would be long gone by now, borne by wind and tide. It was more than ten minutes later when the huge red mark appeared on the sounder screen. This was indeed a big wreck and had to be the newly sunken ship. I took note of the green and purple clock readings, writing them down quickly then pulled the engine to neutral. With the winch engaged, the boat was hauled away from the wreck down tide, back towards the gear. Minutes later the net was safely on the surface and leaving the small amount of fish trapped inside, I turned *Emulator* through one hundred and eighty degrees and shot the trawl back before the tide, away from the wreck.

With the gear down and back on pay I contacted the Coastguard, informing the duty officer that I'd found the missing wreck and that she was lying in thirty-three fathoms of water and was not a hazard to shipping.

"Can you give me the position Sir?" came back an official request. "I'll record the location for future reference."

I didn't know if the position was of any value to anyone intending to salvage the cargo or if this was possible, but if there was a chance the zinc was recoverable, the reading had to be worth something to someone and I declined his request. The location wasn't a problem to mariners so I'd no intention of announcing the position to the world over the radio. Fishermen would find out soon enough.

My intuition didn't take long to bear fruit. A phone call from a very plummy voiced person, who must have been in communication with the Coastguard, said he represented the Salvage Association. Mr Plum quite forcibly informed me that it was my duty to divulge the position of the wreck, as it was a danger to shipping.

I wasn't having that. In the depth she was lying, the vessel was only a problem for fishermen. The man was talking rubbish and I told him so.

When he realised I wasn't going to be railroaded into surrendering my information freely he changed tack, asking how certain I was of my knowledge.

"Look," I said with conviction, "if yer want t' send a team o' divers up 'ere, ah'll tek 'em t' wreck for nowt' if it's not t' one yer lookin' fo'."

This seemed to reassure him that I was sure of my information and Mr Plum made an appointment to visit Scarborough the following weekend.

My opinion of the man on the end of the phone didn't improve when the tall, thirty-something, dressed in trendy clothes stepped from his light blue Porche 911. Oozing what I'm sure he took for charm, Mr Plum introduced himself, holding out a hand, which I shook. The paw was soft and limp.

I gave a heavy squeeze in return. From my point of view there wasn't a lot to talk about. If he was from the 'Salvage Association' whoever they were, then this body had a commercial interest in the wreck and as such the information had to be worth something.

He was keen to identify the wreck positively and liked the idea that this would cost him nothing if I were wrong. Not expecting much for my knowledge anyway, I was pleased to be able to add the cost of a day excursion to my figure, knowing with certainty this was the missing ship. Pete had put the case of identification succinctly during discussions in the pub the previous weekend saying, "It's like tripping over a brick that someone had left in your backyard."

Agreement was reached. At the first possible opportunity, when weather and tides allowed, we'd take divers and a member of the consortium to the wreck site to ascertain the accuracy of my information. The three hundred quid quoted for the location had been agreed immediately by a surprised Mr Plum and I realised I'd got it wrong. He must have anticipated paying more, and I mentally kicked myself. I was disappointed that he wasn't going to accompany us out to the location, but not surprised. It would have been good to show him how others lived. The man drove off in his hotrod motor with a throaty burst of acceleration, leaving only fumes from the exhaust in his wake, returning to his own world.

It would be many weeks before conditions were good enough to take divers on the wreck but eventually, after several postponements we sailed for the site. The days were growing longer and winter had lost its bite. I'd been looking forward to the expedition, knowing I was right about the ship. Every fisherman now had the correct position and not surprisingly, no one had previous knowledge of an obstruction in this location. I was curious to know what had happened to this merchant vessel after she'd foundered. Was she upside down? Had she rolled and spilled her cargo across the seabed or had she just nosedived to the bottom? The latter was my prediction with her accommodation aft and the huge weight carried in her forward holds.

Pete and Jim were waiting on the pier when I arrived at 0530 hours on Saturday morning. These lads, being keen on diving and salvage were interested in the day's proceedings and would be good hands at sea, negating the need to take crew. We wouldn't be doing any fishing. Jimmy, who'd made a full recovery from his decompression sickness, put a light under the kettle and was now collecting ingredients for breakfast.

The charter party arrived on the quayside at 0600 hours. The bags of gear and cylinders were lowered on board then the car parked at the back of the pier for the day. Introductions were quickly made on the driver's return. These two were quite different in dress and attitude from their boss and we struck up a friendly, working relationship immediately. I was surprised there were only two men sailing and even more so on discovering that only one of the pair was to make the descent. This wasn't safe practice.

The non diver, a tall, thin-faced man with bright eyes and an easy manner was dressed in jeans, sweater and yachting jacket in readiness for a sea trip.

Emulator had barely rounded the piers before the smell of frying bacon wafted into the wheelhouse, where the professionals were discussing the forthcoming dive. The lone diver, Mick, was a solid, six-footer with a craggy face and a wide, lined forehead. Here was someone I wouldn't want to fall out with. It was this macho man who was asking direct, relevant questions. What time was slack water at the dive site? What was the depth of water to the seabed?

What was the depth to the top of the wreck? What would be used for a shot rope? Could I be sure of hitting the wreck? How were we to retrieve him from the water following his dive?

I was amazed to discover that Mick O'Kieff was going to dive solo to thirty-three fathoms using compressed air and not mixed gas in his cylinders. Compressed air becomes toxic beyond twenty-six fathoms and nitrogen narcosis is a real danger. On leaving the bottom he would have a huge amount of decompression time to endure before regaining the surface safely. Here was a man living on the edge; a master diver and only by asking the right questions had he lived so long. Mick was pleased to hear I knew a little about diving and was able to respond to his queries with reasonably informed answers. A big fry up breakfast was waiting for us below in the mess-deck so with the theoretical details resolved we went to dine.

The sun was already high above a glassy sea with a lazy, undulating swell that held no threat on the surface for the diver. With the absence of wind and the forecast promising little change, the conditions were perfect. Mick, following a mountainous breakfast spent the next hour unpacking and laying out his equipment, then double-checking gauges, valves and regulators. His triple steel cylinder rig would have made my legs buckle at the knees but he moved the set about the deck with ease.

My two crewmen unlashed a buoy, secured on the top of the wheelhouse then began coiling rope into a basket for the shot line. They were attaching a few fathoms of old chain between the grapnel and the rope when the diver intervened saying he was unhappy with the weight of our grapnel and that he might pull this four-pronged anchor out of the wreck as he hauled himself down the line.

I joined the debate on the deck and while expressing doubt at his reservations, it wasn't me that was going down the rope, so racked my brains, wondering where we could find some heavy weights on board the boat. There was plenty of old chain available, which would do at a push, but this wasn't ideal.

"Have you any iron ballast on board?" Pete asked.

"Of course we 'ave!" I declared, remembering there were some old railway fishplates in the bilges under the engine. These extremely heavy sets were part of *Emulator's* ballast and as such wouldn't normally be touched, but she was such a stiff vessel, rolling quickly, that I was sure the absence of a few of these irons wouldn't affect her stability. With difficulty and using a short iron hook, six of the heavy plates were hauled from their location in the bilge. By the time the pieces were on deck and ready to be lashed back to back in a series of pairs, we were all covered in black oil.

It took four of us to lift this mass over the side and when in position the weight was suspended above the waterline by a length of stout cord. A sharp knife was positioned close by in readiness. The attached chain and line were free to run and the surface marker lay unhampered, ready for throwing overboard. Now all we had to do was locate the wreck again.

"You didn't say how you were going to get me out of the water and back on board," the diver prompted, already thinking beyond the dive. "I thought you'd have had an inflatable boat on board."

"We'll use fender tyres fo' yer to climb up," I suggested unconvincingly then, giving more thought said, "no, t' fish-room ladder will be better."

We'd secure the top rungs of the wooden construction above the boat's bulwark, trailing the lower end in the water for ease of access. Stay lines fore and aft, attached near the bottom rungs would keep the unit in position.

Another mug of coffee was delivered to all hands then we were drawing close to our objective. With about a mile to go I confidently switched on the sonar, though didn't really need the machine now I had a precise, 'Decca' fix to work from. Ping, ping, ping, came the sound as the machine began scanning. The hard ground on the deep edge was soon showing ahead at seven hundred and fifty metres and closing. Shortly after, the crisp, audible echo of our goal came through the speakers. Throttling back we again approached the target at slow speed, the two passengers watching the sonar and sounder screens intently.

"There she be," I said as the big red blob appeared on the sounder, its size giving assurance to the passengers. We were moving across the remains of the flood tide so this wasn't the time to let the shot go. Explaining this to the lads on deck I turned *Emulator* down tide for half a mile before reversing the track and slowly approaching the ship again. Fifteen minutes had passed before we were over the wreck again. Now we were sitting directly above the lost ship and I yelled to the hovering pair at the boat's side to let go the shot. Pete slashed the cord with barely a touch of the knife and the line ran out freely. This wasn't fast enough for the lads and coils of rope were propelled overboard by hand, ensuring no friction impeded the sinking weight. Jimmy threw the buoy clear of the boat's side before the few fathoms of remaining line could flow from the basket and the slack bight of rope was dragged unhindered over the side.

Confident we'd hit the target I moved *Emulator* away from the floating buoy to await slack water. It had been two hours before high water when we'd sailed and slack was four hours after Scarborough in this position so we wouldn't have too long to wait. The diver changed into his dry suit and began assembling his apparatus. Half an hour later with a drain of tide still running, torch in hand, Mick O'Kieff dropped backwards over the side, hitting the water with a big splash just a few yards from the buoy. I checked the time.

The diver wasted no time on the surface. Raising an arm to dump residual air in his suit from the valve in his sleeve, Mick O'Kieff disappeared down the line. Now we could only wait. I made more coffee. The two temporary hands were sitting on the galley step peeling vegetables and had already placed a joint of meat in the oven in readiness for a homeward bound meal, providing all went to plan.

The waiting was interminable and I nervously checked my watch. The minute hand seemed to have stopped moving. Initially, during slack water we could see the diver's air bubbles as they broke the surface but when the ebb began to run, the effervescence was lost to view. An hour had now passed. Thoughts of incidents, accidents and disaster were running through my head incessantly. Had I instigated a fatality? Had the wreck claimed a further life? It was with great relief that bubbles were observed again, drawing closer to the line as the frogman neared the surface. He would still have to spend some considerable time hanging on the line during decompression but at least macho-man wasn't lost on the bottom, only de-fizzing below the buoy. Mick must have been sipping his air like wine to have made it last so long.

The tide was running strongly now and the diver must have been struggling to stay on the line because all of a sudden the buoy lost its wake and began drifting on the ebb.

"'E must 'ave cut the line," I exclaimed. "Ah can still see 'is bubbles but t' buoy's not ridin' t' tide any more."

I disengaged the engine and let *Emulator* drift at a safe distance from the surface marker, leaving the wreck and its secrets behind. We closed to only a few yards from the buoy to assure the diver of our proximity until action man eventually surfaced. Mick gave an assuring wave in our direction then released the marker line. He was probably even more relieved to see us. I moved *Emulator* close alongside the diver, saving him the exertion of swimming.

It took all three men on deck to haul the discarded bottles from the water. His black, rubber fins were hung on a hovering boathook then the big man grabbed the ladder, water dripping from his suit as he ascended. I stood close by with the other passenger as Mick O'Kieff stepped onto the deck. There was no sign of relief or fatigue on his face, only a serious expression.

"How was it?" I asked excitedly. "Was she t' right way up? Is 'er cargo still there?"

The professional said nothing apart from, "this is confidential business mate. He's my boss," and the pair moved forward to the port bow where the diver could impart confidential information to his paymaster.

My initial response was one of disappointment, that I'd found the wreck and been instrumental in putting the diver on the site and was now discarded, but logic said this was a business matter and was strictly on a need-to-know basis.

I manoeuvred *Emulator* close alongside the buoy, enabling Jim to catch the marker with the boathook. He drew the cane shaft into reach, enabling Pete to pluck the light marker and short length of rope, dripping from the sea. *Emulator's* head was turned in the direction of home.

I was dying to know what the tough, tight-lipped diver had discovered but nothing further was said about the dive as we ate the splendid dinner in silence. It was quite surreal that this man had plumbed the depths of the North Sea, pushing beyond the boundary of acceptable safe practice but had now clammed up. Had this been me I'd have been telling the world what I'd discovered.

The company representative was on to his office by mobile telephone as soon as a signal was obtained and he spoke for several minutes, positioned out on the open deck away from any would-be eavesdroppers.

It was almost 1800 hours when we re-entered the harbour. The tide had ebbed and flowed back again since we'd left. It wasn't until we were tied up alongside the quay and the car was being loaded with gear that further information was divulged. As I stood by awaiting payment the leader said, "Someone from a leading salvage company will be getting in touch with you shortly. The man will require the position of the wreck from you and he may possibly want you to mark the site again. You'll receive your payment from this company." With that the pair left the pier, though not as fast or in such style as Mr Plum.

I was left no richer but a little wiser. The ship must be upright and the cargo intact if these people intended to conduct a salvage operation. If she'd rolled, the zinc would have spilled out and had *Renate S* been upside down the load would have been inaccessible.

There was horrendous news when I arrived home and opened the day's post. 'Steelship', the company building our new vessel had gone bust and work on the project had ceased. We were now left with the upside down skeleton in a closed shipyard in the far off county of Cornwall. I rang Bluey with the bad news. It was only last week that we'd paid £5000 for a license for the boat. Licenses were unheard of when I'd had *Emulator* built only a few years ago.

It would be a pleasure to escape to the pub and enjoy a relaxing evening having spent the additional day at sea and then received the bad news about the new boat.

Dotty and I walked into the Leeds Arms to find Michael Winner, the famous film director in the premises with members of his production team. The renowned local playwright Alan Ayckbourn, who'd regularly been insulted by Les the landlord, had produced a classic play, 'Chorus of Disapproval' with the central character, that of a stroppy barman. Not only had the work found great acclaim, the work was now to be made into a film. Mr Winner was in town looking for locations to shoot the movie and ideally, he wanted the Leeds Arms.

The team must have arrived immediately before us and were looking round the premises to assess the pub's suitability for their project. Seeing Les wander to the back room to collect glasses, the film boss stepped behind the empty bar to look for shooting angles. Holding fingers from both hands in front of his face to form a rectangle, the producer swept his makeshift viewer in an arc around the bar from left to right. At the extreme end of the scan the viewfinder was filled with the mug shot of the returning landlord, his face like thunder.

"What d' you think you're doing?" the publican asked.

"My good man, I'm Michael Winner," gushed the producer.

"I don't care if you're the fucking Derby winner, get out from behind my bar," replied the indignant host.

Deflated, the film tycoon was a little contrite. "I'm most sorry my good fellow. I do apologise. Allow me to buy you a drink? "

With the ultimate put down, Les smiled sweetly and said, "no thank you. I've just refused one from a friend. "

The film was shot in the adjacent, 'Leeds Hotel' the following week.

CHAPTER 9

PIPELINES

Having recently fitted a side-scan transducer to *Emulator's* array of electronic gear and with a fine forecast promised, this week seemed a good opportunity to try fishing along one of the many gas and oil pipelines now fixed in the North Sea. A couple of boats had been using this technology for some time, with exceptional results. The fish seemed to be attracted to the pipelines, either for shelter or seeking food.

If we were to pursue this fishing it would mean a change in the distances we'd have to steam to the grounds. The 'Fulmar' pipeline, lying proud on the seabed and running into St Fergus in northeast Scotland, hadn't been in place long and promised to yield good catches. Some pipes were trenched then buried, especially those in the southern North Sea where the tidal effects tended to be far stronger.

A sixteen-hour passage consisting of four, four-hour steaming watches found us near the 'Fulmar' production platform. Everyone was 'slept up' and ready for work when, after pinpointing our position on the chart, I stopped the vessel in forty-six fathoms, slightly to the west of the thirty-inch diameter pipeline and a mile north of the platform. There was almost ninety miles of pipe running north northwest before the line turned due west for another eighty miles. Col in *Our Pride*, who'd also had side-scan equipment installed, was to shoot further down the line so we didn't conflict. There was plenty of pipeline for both our vessels to work on.

With the trawl in the water and a hundred and forty fathoms of warp out, the transducer was clipped onto the after warp and the brake on the new cable winch was released, allowing the bomb-shaped instrument to slide down the wire. A changeover switch had transferred the pulse from the sounder under the boat, to the end of the cable. The bomb would stop at a shackle, five fathoms from the trawl board, transmitting across the seabed to mark the board at the other side of the gear, which showed as a red line along the blue sounder screen. The pipeline should also show on the screen in red when located and needed to be kept between the two boards to get the net in the correct position. With practise and concentration it would be possible to keep the trawl on the pipe.

I was pleased to see the mark of the fore door on the sounder even before the cable had reached its full extent. When stopped, the reading on the screen showed we had thirty fathoms of spread between the trawl doors. Now it was a matter of finding and straddling the pipe. The red object came on to the sounder at the extreme edge of the picture at the fifty-fathom mark and was closing fast. At this rate we would hit the pipe and quickly cross the line with both doors. *Emulator* was directed hard to port, then gradually eased back as the angle of approach to the pipe narrowed. Now I felt able to arrest the boat when the first door had jumped the line and settle the doors astride the pipe. A slight bump indicated the door had jumped over at the same instant the converging red lines met on the screen. I gave her more port rudder but then over reacting had to go to starboard again. Gradually the course alterations became smaller and *Emulator* settled on the required course. Now concentration was required to keep the doors and following trawl astride the line. This was more like a kids game of skill in a seafront arcade than fishing.

After five hours of focusing on the task and fixing the position of the pipeline periodically on a plotter roll for future reference it was hauling time. I was glad of the coffee delivered by Sean, as I hadn't felt confident enough to leave the wheelhouse, something I did several times each watch when fishing normally. We began to haul and the cable winch retrieved its wire and bomb prior to the doors appearing at the boat's side. Laying *Emulator* across the wind all eyes looked to windward with expectation, not knowing if we'd got the technique right.

The water boiled and the bag rose quickly to the surface. "There's nowt wrong wi' that," I called down from the window. "Should be a good lift an' it looks like big cod."

The lads on deck agreed and set to with a will to pull the headline of the trawl on board. If this was pipeline fishing, we'd be doing more of the same.

Col had also taken a good haul but soon after shooting for the second time had snagged a valve on the pipe and badly damaged his trawl. Giving me the position of the obstruction over the radio, he and his crew spent the next hour or so mending and replacing broken wires. That was a serious fastener to be avoided in the future.

Now confident of my ability to keep the vessel on the pipe, others in the crew took towing watches and soon we were all adept at holding the line. We spent two days on the Fulmar and fishing got better as we moved north and west. Even going back over areas previously covered, there were still good catches to be had. Some bumper hauls were taken either side of the bend where the pipe turned to the west and where another valve was located. Fortunately this snag was marked on the chart and easily avoided.

Emulator was now slightly down by the head, sagging with the weight of fish in her hold and the hands on deck had had little respite during the past twenty four hours. Several times during this period I'd made quick visits to the galley to make coffee and sandwiches, rushing these to the deck, then hurrying back to adjust the course. Now as a southerly wind freshened to force five or six I went on deck again with welcome refreshments and announced, "when we 'aul this time we'll call it a day an' mek for 'ome."

The news was received with some relief and as soon as the fish on deck was cleared and put below we hauled once more. There were groans of dismay when a huge haul burst out of the water. This wasn't the usual response to big catches but the work had been gruelling and relentless and was now going to continue. After two hours of bailing bags of fish onboard, filling the few remaining empty boxes with mostly medium sized codlings we were finally able to set a course for home. Now at least I could spend some time helping with the gutting. Without thinking, I set the engine speed to our normal steaming revolutions, switched the autopilot on and was about to leave the wheelhouse. Before I could get through the door, *Emulator* dipped her heavy head in the growing swell and a great dollop of water shot over the whaleback, filling the open deck and deluging the men gutting. I heard shouts of "ease the bugger down," and several other loud, angry expletives from the foredeck.

I dashed back to the controls and eased the throttle to half speed before donning oilskins and heading out to face the music and the weather. The heavy water from each sea had been reduced to flying spray and even then an occasional drenching came our way. Our speed was greatly reduced and this couldn't be increased until the decks were clear of fish. Despite oilskin protection, our clothing was soon saturated. Periodically we'd take it in turns to visit the cabin for a change of clothes, hanging the sodden garments in the engine room where jeans, shirts and jumpers would quickly dry but became salt encrusted. The words of *Emulator's* builder, Derry Forbes were ringing in my ears.

"Ah'm linin' up yerr whaleback tae meet jus' below yerr wheelhoose windows. At some point in the future yerr goin' tae want a shelter-deck."

Well he wasn't wrong and that time was now. The constant stream of cold water down my neck was a forceful reminder. Meanwhile *Our Pride,* fully sheltered from new and with a similar catch on board was ploughing through the seas at full speed, green lumps washing over her while her crew were dry beneath their 'aluminium oilskin'. They'd be home in time for the morning market. We hadn't a chance of making that auction now and the Friday's prices were never as good. *Emulator* was going to get a shelter-deck, and soon.

Many wet hours later I was pleased to put the throttle down and watch huge lumps of sea wash over the even heavier vessel, only to quickly dissipate through her open scuppers. Heavy spray obliterated the wheelhouse windows constantly. She could come to no harm as long as the fish-room hatch was secured and I could see the lid was firmly fastened down with every wash of the windows.

"There's somebody tryin' t' get a message t' yer. Stonehaven Radio's callin' wi' traffic," Col said over a crackling VHF, underlining the distance he'd put between us.

Surprised that there could be a link call for me and thinking he was probably mistaken, I thanked him and tuned the MF set to the coastal station's frequency.

"Stonehaven Radio, this is *Emulator*, Two, Oscar, Bravo, Romeo," I called, giving my vessel's radio call-sign. "Do you have traffic for me?"

"Good afternoon Sir," came the polite reply. "That's affirmative. You have a call from Aberdeen." He gave a frequency to listen on and another to transmit and requested me to stand by while he recalled the number. This was an intriguing mystery. I'd never received a shore to ship call before and only infrequently had occasion to call ship to shore when problems had arisen.

A voice came clearly over the airwaves, "Hello Skipper. It's Mr Andrews from the salvage company. We have a vessel available at short notice and are going to mobilise her to recover the lost cargo as soon as possible. Are you in a position to mark the wreck for us?"

So that was it. The work was about to start recovering the zinc. I assured Mr Andrews that as we had time on our hands at present, we'd divert to the location and buoy the wreck for him on our way home. I was given a phone number to ring to confirm this had been done. Ever efficient Mr Andrews had not mentioned the ship by name or the cargo or position and now with nothing left to say he cut the call.

The operator, who was monitoring numerous radio links on different frequencies was amazed to find my call was ended. He thought we'd been cut off. "Just the minimum charge then Sir. Good afternoon," and he too was gone.

The buoy was dropped at 0800 hours next morning using only a couple of the fishplates from the source we'd used for the diver. There was no chance of these being recovered. The weights, rope and buoy were sacrificial. Hopefully we'd get paid for them.

It was midday when we arrived in port. There was no point in landing our catch now. The ice would melt before auction time and the fish, which had already spent too long on deck before being processed and washed, would look like jam. We'd have to turn out in the early hours to ensure the catch was in the best condition possible for the sale. It was going to be a short period at home, and following next week's fishing trip I was going to Amsterdam with my footballing friends. This excursion would be totally removed from anything my usual day-to-day life brought along.

CHAPTER 10

A DUTCH DASH

We met in the Alma pub near the town centre at 1400 hours on the following Thursday for the annual 'football trip'. An hour later a twelve-seater minibus would take the group to the ferry terminal in Hull to embark on the *Norland* for the 1800 hours passage to Rotterdam. Though friends, we were an eclectic gathering from many professions and though serious at work, were the equivalent of naughty boys out of school when free. We'd previously travelled to London on a couple of occasions and had some great fun but also played five a side football, arranged by one of our group from a national building society. This would be the first time we'd been abroad and the trip was timed to coincide with the 'Queen of the Netherlands' birthday, a time of great festivity and celebration in Holland. I'd packed some sports gear and told Dotty it was a 'football trip' but for the first time there was no organised game. We intended to buy a ball and have an impromptu kick about.

A couple of drinks later our driver, an elderly, grey haired bespectacled man entered the building and his disapproval of the passengers was clear by the expression on his face and the almost inaudible, "tut tut" of tongue and teeth clicking. "You'll be the lads going to Hull. I'm ready when you are," he stated emphatically.

Some of the party had empty glasses while others still had quantities to imbibe. Much to the driver's chagrin, those with a shortage of beer ordered half pints while waiting for friends to sup up, but this quickly became self-perpetuating. There was never a point when all the glasses were empty at the same time. Eventually reason prevailed and the luggage was stacked in the rear of the vehicle and the passengers climbed onboard. Seated behind the driver I was with Brian, a tall, thin-faced lad, a few years older than me. Originally from Barnsley, he had a fantastic sense of humour and we frequently foiled off each other and laughed at the same things. We were also both fiercely competitive in the sports hall.

The bus eventually loaded, we set off and were on our way. Less than five minutes into the journey Terry, who'd drawn the short straw and was riding 'shotgun' with the driver, spied an off-licence. "Pull in there," he called out excitedly, pointing to the shop. "We'll grab a case of beer for the journey."

Approval was voiced from all behind but this enthusiasm quickly turned to dismay as our driver, peering myopically through the windscreen, nose almost touching the glass, ignored the request.

"We wanted t' stop there," I said from behind the pair. "We were gonna get some beer."

"You'll get plenty before the day's out where you're going," the driver replied and continued on his way unfazed.

There were mutterings from the party. This statement, though probably right was an act of treachery as far as the passengers were concerned and shortly after, as we approached an ale house on the road out of town someone from the back called, "there's a pub there mister. Can we stop for a beer?" Knowing full well the request would go unheard.

On the outskirts of town the speed limit increased from thirty miles an hour to fifty. Our man increased speed from twenty to almost forty. Whether due to failing eyesight, fuel efficiency or erring on the side of extreme caution, our driver was not going to be hurried or encouraged to get anywhere near the legal limit. This only gave more ammunition and elicited further suggestions from his passengers.

"There's a tractor behind wanting to get past mister."

"The ship sails at six."

"Try second gear."

We steadily approached a level crossing where the road crossed the Hull train line. Though the barriers were elevated and in passive mode the bus slowed almost to a stop as we approached the rails. I couldn't resist, and looking to the right, down my side of the track called out, "it's all clear this way."

We passed several village pubs on the way to the docks but the driver refused suggestions to stop, though half way to our destination Mr Grumpy was forced to pull into a lay-by following requests to answer the call of nature. "If anyone pees on the side of my bus I'll leave you behind," was the stern warning from the driver and we believed him.

At around five o'clock we arrived at the ferry to be dropped off by a relieved driver. "See you on Monday morning," one of the lads called to the old man as he climbed behind his wheel, having released our luggage from the rear of the bus.

"Don't bank on it," he muttered, then slammed his door.

"He'll be there. He hasn't been paid yet," observed Chris, a prankster who'd been known to go to great lengths with his practical jokes. This of course made him a target for retaliation.

We didn't have long to wait before foot passengers were summoned to board and we grabbed our bags, following other travellers heading for the high gantry. "Would you mind stepping this way sir?" a man in a navy blue uniform said, his beckoning finger selecting me from the group.

Confused, I thought this was an officer from the ship but then seeing the golden portcullis badge on his cap, quickly realised he was a Customs Inspector. I couldn't believe he wanted to search my bag outward bound for Holland. Considering the liberal attitude of that country to drugs and pornography I couldn't imagine what he thought I could be taking there. I'd often been frisked when I was in the Merchant Navy coming home from abroad, but never outward bound. Of course this situation raised plenty of comments from my travelling companions.

"He's a wrong 'un mister. Lock him up."

"Strip search him."

"Get the rubber gloves out," were only some of the comments.

The man wasn't unpleasant or aggressive, explaining he was only making a spot check and I'd been selected at random. After a light rummaging and asking where I was bound and the purpose of the visit, I was allowed to continue on my way. Of course this incident would be flagged up by my pals until someone else stepped into the spotlight.

On board we made our way to the bar but were disappointed to find there'd be no service until the ship sailed in half an hour. A little exploring proved worthwhile when we discovered the Dutch catering staff laying out a huge, buffet of cold and hot food plus some wonderful fish dishes. This was a real banquet and the food was apparently included in the cost of the voyage so was available to all passengers.

As soon as the ship entered the lock linking the huge King George Dock to the fast-flowing Humber all the food became available and we joined the queue for the spread. The meal, accompanied by wine purchased from the trolley service was every bit as good as it had looked and we feasted royally.

Holding his stomach to indicate its fullness, Rod said, "I think a glass of port would go well after that. Does anyone want to join me?" No one was interested in joining him in a glass of anything stronger so the diminutive, bespectacled insurance broker purchased his own port from the bar.

No sooner had Rod put his glass on the table than a mischievous friend sitting adjacent, surreptitiously switched his purchase for a glass of red wine. Taking a sip, Rod's face grimaced. "This port's crap" he stated.

"Take it back if it's that bad Rod," Terry encouraged. Others, keeping straight faces added words of support.

"I bloody well will," the indignant chap said. "It's rubbish." Standing, he headed back towards the bar.

All eyes watched his progress with interest.

Two minutes later a disgruntled Rod was back in his chair, the same glass in hand.

"What did he say?" Terry asked, expressing interest.

"He said he was sorry but it's 'Sandemans' and it's the only one they do."

"Try this one," Terry said, handing him his original glass, to a huge peel of laughter.

"You bastards! You all watched me do that," he said, though laughing at his gullibility.

On its own, this incident was extremely funny but twice previously when we'd all been out together, Rod's tipple had been switched for red wine. On one occasion swapped several times between red wine and port, confusing him totally. I was off the hook now, the customs incident forgotten. Rod was in the spotlight.

Following the feast, a male and female singing duo were performing in the bar at the stern of the ship and we remained there all evening till the entertainers had finished their lively performance after eleven. Jokes were told and previous high jinx recalled in the intervals. Late in the evening the casino proved to be entertaining, though it did seem foolish to wait until late at night when drink influenced judgement before deciding to gamble. Chris was the bold speculator of the party and seemed to scatter chips prolifically across the roulette baize, claiming he had a system. Strangely, he had success, ending the session considerably richer than when he'd started. Others were happy to break even or lose small stakes. It was the early hours before most retired to their beds.

There were some bleary eyes when we were woken by the ship's loudspeaker announcing, in various languages that we were approaching Rotterdam and breakfast was being served in the restaurant. "God! You look rough," Terry, my cabin mate said as we dressed before heading in the direction of the food.

"Yer should see it from this side," I croaked, trying to untangle my vocal chords. "D' yer think you look any better?" I challenged, rallying.

He didn't. With bloodshot eyes and unkempt hair, the tall, blond haired man was decidedly dishevelled. So were the rest of the gang when we met in the restaurant. No one was hungry. The ravenous appetites of the previous evening had disappeared and orange juice seemed to be the only course on our menu.

Disembarking, a short coach ride found us at Rotterdam railway station. Though everyone had woken feeling rough, most had recovered and some humour had returned to the group. Jokes and quick wit were the norm again. There was a forty-minute wait for the train to Amsterdam. "Anyone fancy a beer?" I asked, spying a vending trailer. This was only bravado. It was ten o'clock Dutch time and the last thing I wanted was beer.

"Why not?" said a voice, then others affirmed that they'd also partake, rather than lose face. We shuffled towards the counter. Cans of 'Heineken' were on display and we were about to order a round of this green tinned beer when Chris pointed and called out, "hey, they've got 'Trappist' beer."

Perplexed expressions on the faces around him compelled the speaker to explain. "It's Belgian beer, made by monks in monasteries. They've made it for hundreds of years and its really good stuff."

"Do they make port?" Rod asked.

The upshot was we ordered Belgian beer all round. Sipping from the brown bottle I found the drink a little gassy but quite sweet and very tasty. Another round was ordered before the train arrived. Feeling slightly light-headed I looked at the brown and yellow label. Apart from the logo of an abbey and monks I noticed the strength, eight percent. "This isn't beer. It's bloody rocket fuel," I exclaimed. "Yer could do moonshots on this."

Others examined their bottles but no one complained about the potency or refused to finish their drinks.

Dutch trains are renowned for their punctuality and we were soon clattering north on the short journey to Amsterdam, passing windmills, irrigation canals and bulb fields, vivid with multi-coloured stripes of tulips. We took taxis from the huge, redbricked monolithic station, though one of the many trams trundling from the terminus outside the building would have done, had we known the correct number to take. The carnival atmosphere on the streets was obvious and infectious as we were driven through the main thoroughfares in convoy. The streets were full of stalls, vendors, musicians, various amusing sideshows and scores of people selling what appeared to be old, unwanted junk from their homes. All this material was laid out on the pavements for sale.

Eventually, following a circuitous route, we arrived at our accommodation. "Taxi drivers must be the same the world over," said a disgruntled voice, looking at what he perceived to be the same canal for the third time.

The 'Museum Hotel' a nondescript two star building was uninspiring and dropped further in everyone's estimation when we realised we were to be four to a room.

Intending to deposit our bags then hit town, we made our way upstairs. Terry, one of the quartet sharing my billet, inspected the bathroom then called, "hey, come and look at this."

The bath was stepped, with a seat at one end and a footwell at the other. There was no possibility of lying down in this tub. We were looking at a sit down bath.

"That's nothing," chipped in Wally. "Look at the loo."

Eyes turned to the toilet. This too was stepped. The cupped pan was dry and any deposits would sit in this bowl until the flush washed the waste into the small well at the back.

"Right you lot, take notice. We're going to make a pact," a serious roommate said. "There's to be no crapping in here. It's bad enough having four to a room but dry dumping is right out! If anyone needs to go, then do it in the toilet downstairs in the reception, before you come up here."

This serious declaration was unanimously accepted.

It was late morning when we gathered in the lobby and were about to leave, looking for excitement. A suggestion of, "shall we have a drink in the bar before we head off?" found favour, and following the signs we found ourselves below ground level in an empty bar with a small window, high on the wall at street level.

"What sort of a place 'ave yer brought us to Wally?" I asked. We've got a sit up bath, a dry toilet an' now were suppin' in a dungeon."

The organiser, having just ordered beers all round, was immediately defensive. "My instructions were not to get anywhere expensive. You only wanted somewhere to sleep, so I went for the cheapest option."

Now it was open season on Wally. "We didn't expect a hostel," someone said.

"We wanted one with a toilet," said another.

"Can I have a dump in your room?"

The comments came in quickly then someone noticed the drinks on the bar. "Hey come on, fill 'em up," Brian said. "They're short measures." Being the licensing clerk to the local court, and also enjoying beer, he had a double interest.

The glasses were straight with tulip shaped tops but the beer was only in the lower part of the glass and apart from a froth, which the skinny, pockmarked barman was scraping off with a spatula, beer was absent from the main part of the containers.

"You'd get jail for that in my court," the incensed legal eagle, said.

He was supported by everyone and the reluctant barman put a little more beer in each glass, though the contents never came close to the top.

"This is how we serve beer in Holland," the young man said in surprisingly good English. "We do not fill the glasses to the top."

"I thought we were all t' same now we're in t' Common Market," I muttered, knowing full well that there was very little common in this ludicrous organisation, especially in the fishing sector, as I knew to my cost.

Our disgruntled party downed the overpriced, underfilled glasses and headed for the stairs and daylight to the relief of the bar manager, who was quickly gathering the empties. The sun was shining and the temperature high as we gathered on the pavement with no clear plan, except to head for the busy section of the city that we'd passed earlier. Soon we found ourselves at the entrance to a public park and could hear the sound of live music. "We want to be in here," Chris called out, pointing to the greenery. We followed like sheep to discover various attractions and sideshows taking place within the public area.

A seven-piece band, with saxophones, trumpet, guitars and drums performing on a stage that was normally hitched to the back of a lorry, were terrific. Surrounded by a waving and dancing crowd they played sixties classics as well as up to the minute stuff, while the singer, a tall, thin, totally bald black man, dressed in a silver outfit gyrated for the girls near the front.

"All we need now is a beer," Terry bawled in my ear, counteracting the noise and as if by magic, Brian, standing at his other side pulled his sleeve and pointed to a stall only a few feet away.

I made no objection when, "Trappists all round," were ordered. Whether it was the atmosphere or drinking outdoors but the contents of the bottles vanished quickly. "It might be evaporation with it being so warm," Wally suggested when I held up my empty bottle and scratched my head. Another round was ordered.

However good the music, after a few numbers we began to move off, wandering the paths of the park. We stopped briefly to watch a 'splat the rat' stall, where participants attempted to smash a potato with a wooden mallet. The spud was dropped down a two-foot section of plastic drainpipe, curving at the bottom and directing the tattie across a wooden block. This was entertaining and harder than it looked. Most of the contestants we observed either missed the target or made glancing contact. None of our group was prepared to attempt this and look daft by missing.

A little further along the path was a machine I'd only ever seen at Hull Fair when I was a little boy. A large wooden sledgehammer was offered to passers-by from a cheery man, suggesting they might want to test their strength and ring the bell on top of the tall, striped barbers pole tower. The cost was a guilder for five attempts. Again no one was willing to have a go. We watched several young men attempting then one big strapping Dutchman powered the sliding clanger to its summit several times, contacting with the bell to make a pleasing 'dong'.

"Go on then Freddy, you're a strong lad. I'll fund you to have a go," Terry offered, inviting a response.

Having watched the previous contestant I thought for a moment then said, "Aye OK then, get yer money out. Ah'll give it a bash," taking up the challenge and immediately drawing the attention of the group.

"Don't break it, Nommy," quipped one of the observers as they gathered round and I took the hammer from the smiling attendant.

Rolling up my sleeves I held the long-shafted mallet in both hands, one at the base and the other supporting the head, feeling its weight, then looked at the two-inch metal stud in the centre of the box at the base of the tower. Getting the feel of the instrument I swung the hammer through two hundred and seventy degrees, sliding the hand supporting the weight, down the shaft to join the one gripped firmly at the end of the handle. When the hammer was vertical and both arms fully extended, I swung downwards with all my might. The technique was perfect, but unfortunately the direction was slightly off and the hammer missed the button by a couple of inches, hitting the corner of the box and knocking a few splinters from the head, also removing the smile from the proprietor's face. With howls of laughter ringing in my ears I quickly addressed the button again and using the same method swung the mallet hard.

This time the strike made perfect contact and the slider shot up the rack reaching the top of its trajectory. The bell rang. "Bingo" I called excitedly. The laughter stopped and I turned to the group. "Anyone else want a go? There's three shots left." There were no takers. Twice more I rang the bell, feeling very pleased with myself, though on the final stroke the slider didn't quite make the top, but it didn't matter. No one else was going to try. The vendor, smile back in place gave me a beanie hat with the badge of Amsterdam on the front, as a consolation prize. This headgear was of no value and looked silly but it was a trophy and I intended to wear it for the duration of the trip.

Out of the gardens and heading towards the centre we passed several food stalls selling a variety of snacks. In view were hot dogs, burgers, pastries, deep fried apple dumplings, fish and some exotic oriental dishes. "What about a herring with some onions in bread?" I asked, knowing they'd all baulk at the prospect. Noses turned at the suggestion, but now I felt compelled to taste one of these unique Dutch delicacies. The fillet of fish was not smoked or pickled as roll-mops are, both of which I enjoy. This was just raw flesh with onion and I gypped as I took the first bite when the fishy smell hit my nasal passages but the taste, though strong was not unpleasant. Several pairs of eyes were watching so I devoured the snack unfazed.

"What's that you've got," someone asked Chris, as he picked up a paper plate with three skewers, each holding three pieces of chicken, coated in a coconut sauce.

"Don't know what it is," he replied, "but it looks like 'shit on a stick'."

Others, having assessed the snack also opted for the 'chicken satay'.

Walking along a road, canal to our right, we came to an open market with stalls selling second hand junk. There were old records, shoes, crockery and heaps of other household stuff of little interest or value. Noting our English voices as we drew level with his table, one enterprising trader said, "Do you gentlemen want to buy something?"

Though not in the least interested we paused and 'Robbo', spying a box of assorted cutlery stepped forward. Intrigued, we watched, wondering what his intentions were. He certainly wasn't going to make a purchase, but this could be amusing. The short, stocky, grey-haired builder selected a couple of tablespoons from a box. Nestling the pair back to back with handles balanced in his right hand, the little man cleverly began to produce a pleasant, rhythmic tune. First he clattered the spoons in the palm of his left hand then, gaining confidence he skilfully ran the instrument up and down his left arm then along each of his thighs in turn. We formed a semicircle and began clapping as he continued his performance. Passers-by stopped to watch and the stallholder, sensing a sale, beamed a smile of approval. Then suddenly, mid-tune, the percussionist stopped playing and threw the spoons back into the container.

The trader looked at him askance.

"They're out of tune" the musician said with feigned disgust and walked off.

We quickly followed.

A few minutes later Chris, our navigator, having been to the city previously said, "down here," indicating a narrow passage off a main street.

Again we followed. At the end of the alley stood a dingy bar, one of the traditional Brown Houses, the Dutch equivalent of old British pubs. The wooden floors and décor, darkened with smoke had remained untouched for years. Beers were ordered and we sat at a large, plain wooden table scarred from many burned out cigarettes. Terry and Brian, lighting up, added to the stains.

After a while someone started tapping on the table then began singing, 'Sloop John B' a popular number by the sixties group, 'The Beach Boys.' Within a couple of bars everyone had joined in lustily. Next we burst into 'Running Bear' but the barman came over to our table waving his arms. "Please, please no more singing. Not today. Any other day yes, but today is special." The man, unhappy at spoiling our fun and worried about losing potential trade, explained that today was a memorial day and at the present moment a ceremony was taking place not far away in the city, commemorating the loss of many lives from wartime conflict.

We couldn't argue with this enforced silence and were quiet for a few minutes. "What about a game of spoof?" Brian suggested, "the loser puts a tenner in the kitty."

This source of entertainment found immediate favour and everyone dived into their pockets for coins or borrowed from friends. The game of bluff called for participants to hold a number of coins between zero and three in a clenched hand in view. The challenge is to predict, in clockwise rotation the collective number of coins held. No two people can have the same prediction. The winner of each round withdraws from the competition until only two contestants remain, with a choice between zero and six coins. The win or lose final is quite tense, and can be costly.

Three games of spoof later when Paul had belligerently paid his third £10 into the kitty he stood, put the coins in his pocket and said, "what are we doing here? So far we've been in a hotel cellar and a back alley pub. We really know how to live don't we? I thought we'd come to see Amsterdam."

He was sulking having lost his money, but in a way he was right. We headed off back to the fresh air and sunlight.

Following our leader and probably not by accident we found ourselves in the red light district, not far from the railway station. Viewing the girls in the many windows was extremely entertaining and unlike anything I'd ever seen.

"What time do the next virgins arrive?" a voice in the group asked, laughing.

"Ah think they get a fresh batch in every Thursday," I said.

"That's verging on the ridiculous" came the reply.

African, Asian and Caucasian, some of the women were quite large and totally unappealing but an occasional window held a beautiful, scantily clad girl with beckoning finger, and though no one succumbed, there was a certain attraction and suggestions and innuendos flew thick and fast.

Another canal path in the same area led us to the infamous 'Old Sailor' bar and the sound of more live music through the large, open windows. The place was extremely busy but we managed to shove our way through to the middle of the single room to find a four-piece pop group crammed together on a small platform against the back wall. The lads were belting out familiar sounds at high decibels and were clearly relying on quantity rather than quality to entertain their audience.

Looking round in the crowded room, I took in the surroundings. The ceiling and walls were adorned with nautical memorabilia and a tall, wooden ship's binnacle stood close to our location. A large bell with 'Tina Onassis' etched boldly on the front, hung over the bar. Wally, holding the kitty and complaining, was despatched to order beers. He elbowed and wriggled through the mass of people, attempting to signal the barman, a huge, burly, tattooed Dutchman with short cropped greying hair. Though no longer young, the man looked a no-nonsense character who'd have no problem ejecting any troublemakers out through the door or windows.

Finally gaining the barman's attention, Wally acquired a batch of half-filled glasses on the bar. Terry pushed closer to the counter to pass the drinks over to the group. Holding a glass aloft he looked at the contents then at Wally. "Tell him you want 'em filling up," he said as the kitty man took a swig of beer.

Choking on the froth, Wally, in a squeaky voice spluttered, "have you seen the size of him? You tell him."

We stood huddled together until Chris, returning from the toilet said, "Do not go in there unless you're desperate." He went on to describe a stinking hole in the ground with a couple of hollowed footprints in the concrete floor.

I took note of his observation and opted for the little-used ladies facility instead.

During a break in the noise Chris whispered, "I know somewhere better than this. A pal of mine told me about a nightspot called the 'Honolulu Club'. He said it's really good. Shall me and you give it a try?"

It wasn't much fun in the cramped, 'Old Sailor' but no one looked interested in relocating so I agreed to accompany him and we moved outside to find a taxi. The driver gave us a strange look when Chris told him the destination but said nothing. The journey across the city seemed to take forever in the narrow, crowded streets but we eventually arrived at the destination, paid the driver and entered the darkened premises. The air within the spacious club was perfumed and the music soft. The place seemed quite busy with several couples and a few groups scattered around the room. Two men were standing at the bar nearby and I noticed they were holding hands. Then I saw the server behind the bar heading in our direction and realised something was drastically wrong.

Of uncertain gender, the person with powdered face and red lips wore a sarong, turban and from his/her ears hung a pair of huge, golden looped earrings. My face fell and I quickly looked round again at the clientele, realising instantly they were all men.

I looked at my companion who seemed equally surprised and said, "you twat. Yer've brought me 'alf way across Amsterdam to a bloody gay bar."

The bar person smiled, flashing a set of gleaming teeth and in effeminate Dutch, presumably asked what we'd like to drink.

Reacting to the situation much quicker than I, Chris said, "two beers please," raising two fingers to accentuate the request.

"Ah you are English boys, welcome to the Homolulu Club. What brings you to Amsterdam? Are you here for the Queen's birthday?" the strange man asked of Chris. I stood embarrassed and silent. The pair engaged in conversation while I looked around the room, disengaging from the company. As he moved off I heard the barman say, "Your partner is very shy."

"Where 'ave yer brought me, you prat? 'E thinks ahm yer bloody boyfriend. This place is t' 'Omolulu Club, not 'Onolulu. It's full o' bloody poofs."

Chris, a much-travelled man of the world laughed and admitted that we'd been victims of his pal's sense of humour in recommending this place. He said it was a practical joke and no harm was likely to come to us.

I relaxed a little seeing the funny side of the prank, though still kept looking round uncertainly and didn't want another drink when my glass was empty. "Ah've 'ad enough excitement fo' one day," I said, and as Chris's glass was also empty I took the lead and headed for the door.

Next morning over a late coffee and cheese and ham breakfast I was full of bravado again, explaining to all in earshot how my so called pal Chris had, by trickery, taken me to a gay bar and that I'd had to stand with my back to the wall. I said I'd dropped my wallet and had to kick it to the door before I dare pick it up.

Everyone seemed remarkably fresh considering the excesses of the previous day and all were keen to see some of the sights. At my request we made an all too short visit to the fantastic Maritime Museum during the morning. I could have stayed in this wonderful building all day and vowed to return at some point in the future.

An excursion and tram ride to the fishing port and resort of Scheveningen was next. The extensive sandy beach, surprisingly adorned with topless ladies enjoying the early summer heat, was very pleasing on the eye.

An amazing seafood restaurant close to the fish market was a great discovery and everyone ate their fill from vats of steamed mussels, prawns, smoked salmon and other delicacies, washed down with quality white wine. Our day out extended long into the night, visiting various bars and it was a weary, worse for wear bunch that finally made the late night trip back to the hotel.

It was time to go home. The Amsterdam street parties were over for another year and as if to emphasise this, the men from the city's 'Emergency Services' were washing down the roads and pavements with high pressure hoses. The ferry wasn't due to leave until 1800 hours but there was the serious matter of buying presents for loved ones and we scattered round the shops, agreeing to meet later.

Shopping complete we regrouped at the railway station with a little time to kill before the train departed for Rotterdam though succumbed to a quenching beer. I made the mistake of saying to Terry, "Keep an eye on me bag while ah pop t' loo."

I returned soon after to find my entire bag emptied and the contents lying neatly on the pavement with Robbo sitting alongside the gear, asking passers by if anyone wanted to buy anything.

Back at the ferry terminal the same, usually streetwise Robbo asked Terry to look after his ticket and passport while he visited the toilet. On returning he was most disgruntled to find some wit had drawn a moustache on his passport photograph in blue pen. He was mildly amused when the same artist drew a similar design on his face to that on the document and he approached the immigration desk with a grin.

Unfortunately the officer didn't have the same sense of humour. The man looked at Robbo's face with a perplexed frown but when he saw the defaced passport he erupted and threatened to stop the offender from sailing. Luckily for our pal, the culprit was able to persuade the officer behind the desk that this was a prank that had gone wrong. The ink was quickly removed from the photograph and the man relented, allowing him to board the ship but not without a finger wagging reprimand.

"No sense o' humour, some people," the culprit quipped.

It wasn't a late night in the bar on the return passage and the casino was given a miss by most as our jaded group took to their beds early. The tannoy calling all hands for breakfast was better received than on our previous docking, with the exception of Chris, who looked rough. He announced that his system had let him down in the casino and he'd lost the gains he'd won outward bound. The good-natured accountant wasn't perturbed. He had a very laid-back attitude to life.

I couldn't believe it when, as we passed through the HM Customs section, another navy blue uniformed officer said, "would you mind stepping this way please sir. It's only a random check." I'd been searched on my passage out and had now been selected for another 'frisk' on the return into Hull. I was back in the spotlight again as the crowd, hovering in the arrivals lounge began their banter.

Mr Grumpy, noting our appearance as we left the terminal heading in his direction gave several more 'tuts' then led us, uncomplaining to the bus. Most passengers slept en route and those who didn't had little to say. "You won't be wanting to drop off at the Alma for a drink then?" our driver asked, finally finding a grin as groans came from behind him.

My comment of, "I'll be glad to get back to sea for a rest," summed up the expedition.

"You've had a good time then," was Dotty's first comment on seeing my dishevelled appearance.

"It's been a very cultural trip," I replied with a grin. We went round the Rembrandt Museum, the Reikes Museum and the Van Gogh."

My wife gave me a questioning look.

"We didn't go in any of 'em. We went 'round' 'em all."

"So as long as you haven't brought any culture home with you," she stated matter-of-factly.

It was good to be home.

A mysterious, 'recorded delivery' parcel had arrived in my absence, posted in Aberdeen. I was expecting a small cheque for our services to the salvers of the zinc but nothing of this proportion, so I tore open the lightly wrapped container with interest. A spring-loaded cardboard box file was revealed, which when opened contained nothing but a small brown envelope. "The cheque must be in here," I thought opening the sealed packet. To my surprise there were three red, Scottish £100 notes contained within. This was quite a surprise, as I wasn't expecting cash, and I didn't know such things as £100 pound notes existed.

I thought it would be great fun to offer one of these notes when we went into the Leeds Arms that evening. On arrival I asked Les for a half of beer and a glass of wine. On producing the drinks I gave him the £100 note, expecting him to hit the ceiling and go off on a rant. Ever unpredictable, the bespectacled host raised his glasses, looked at the proffered note then looked again. Without a word he went up the little flight of stairs to his private living quarters, quickly returning with sufficient £20 notes to make up my change. Then, with a smug smile and still not uttering a comment, handed me the correct change, leaving me open-mouthed and completely lost for words.

CHAPTER 11

A PASSAGE TO GRIMSBY

Following a few weeks of consistent fishing with a particularly good trip caught north of Flamborough, *Emulator* was due for a paint-up and I'd arranged to take her to Grimsby. Not wanting to bother my crew, who were planning to maximise their shore time, I asked Dad to make the passage with me. He was delighted to volunteer, though it was some time since he'd been at sea. The old boy loved the novelty of sitting in a comfy chair with the autopilot steering while he studied the other equipment. Dad had fished all year round in an open coble with no aids other than a compass when he was younger. Even when trawling with me in later years in my old boat, *Courage,* he'd sat on a plank spanning the wheelhouse and we'd used short rope strops to hold the wheel in place.

Today would be different though, for as we met outside his house on Sunday evening just before midnight to walk down the hill together, the orange streetlamps highlighted a dense fog, which covered the east coast. "It's a bit thick," Dad muttered as we crossed the road to the pier. As if to echo his words, a deep, mournful boom resonated from the foghorn on the lighthouse, hidden in the gloom across the harbour.

"We'll be alright," I assured him. "We 'ave a radar and t' 'Decca' an' even a Lat'-Long' readout now. We're not gonna get lost."

The forecast gave no prospect of the fog lifting and the lack of breeze gave credence to this prediction. *Emulator* had a quayside berth and unusually, there were no vessels fastened alongside her, so we'd have little trouble leaving the pier. I caught a turn on the iron ladders with a short end of line while Dad let the head and stern ropes go. He'd secure these fore and aft while I fired up the engine and set life into the wheelhouse electronics.

He was standing aft as we passed the lighthouse, where a familiar face appeared at the little square window, looking to log names and times of vessels leaving harbour. Eddie Temple was on watch and, identifying Dad in the glare of the stern deck lights, which were always lit despite regulations to the contrary, immediately picked up the handset of his radio. "*Emulator*, who's that stood aft?" he asked, laughing. "Yer must be desperate fo' crew aboard o' there."

Dad and Eddie were the same age and had been at school together. Both had worked on fishing boats all their lives, apart from war service and the pair, now nearing retirement, were watch-keepers on the lighthouse and also helped to land our catches. Eddie was also our net maker and mender, one of the best in the business. He'd probably forgotten more about net construction than I'd ever know.

Setting the pilot to southeast, I left Dad, now chatting to his pal over the radio and made my way to the mess-deck. Putting a light under the kettle, I sat dreamily at the table till the whistle on the steaming utensil brought me from my reverie. Brewing two mugs of tea I headed for the wheelhouse steps.

The airwave conversation had finished and I sat on the chart table sipping my drink, eyes automatically taking in the radar picture. The screen was reassuringly empty of traffic and the land glowed brightly to the right of the circle. The sounder was marking and discriminating the hard and soft seabed below the vessel, though this wasn't really necessary while on passage. We'd have plenty of water under the boat all the way to our destination. The 'Deccas' were flashing steadily, the clocks corresponding to the master readouts, though we wouldn't need the information from either of these machines until we reached Flamborough Head.

Passing the huge promontory at about a mile and with no sight of the flashing lighthouse due to the density of the fog, we altered course to south by east. I was feeling surplus to requirements. Dad looked comfortable and wasn't about to relinquish the chair so I said, "ah'm gonna turn in. Call me if yer've any problems. Keep 'eading south on t' 'Decca's' red, nineteen lane an' gi' me a shout an hour afore we get t' river." I didn't really have to tell him any of this but felt the need to say something before departing to light the kettle again.

Standing aft on the deck, I peered to the west into the grey void and could see nothing, but then the deep, double 'booom' of the Flamborough Head foghorn, underlined our proximity to the land. Minutes later I handed Dad another mug of tea and a corned beef sandwich.

Back in the mess-deck again my mind flew to a similar passage I'd made to Grimsby years earlier onboard *Independence* when I'd taken Dotty and a couple of friends for the experience. The wind had been fresh offshore on that occasion and the boat, with no ice or fishing gear and little fuel on board, was rolling quite heavily. Pete was a good sailor but Dave had succumbed to the movement almost as soon as we'd left port and had spent the duration of the voyage sitting on the galley step, when not feeding the fishes over the side. Dotty, in the wheelhouse with me, though not ill had kept close to the open window. "D' yer fancy a cup o' coffee an' a sandwich?" I'd asked, wanting to take her mind off the boat's motion and the weather. On her acceptance I'd made the drink and opened a tin of mackerel in tomato sauce, decanting the full contents between two slices of bread. This had clearly been the wrong selection of sandwich filling, as I quickly discovered when my wife took a small bite of the offering and had immediately been sick out of the window. Dotty never sailed on a fishing boat again.

Kicking off shoes and discarding my gansey onto the seat locker, I rolled into the bunk. Reaching for the paperback book tucked down the side of the mattress, I read a few pages then, realising I'd read the same piece twice and wasn't retaining the information, returned the volume to its place and switched off the bunk light. It didn't seem long before I heard Dad shouting down from the alleyway, "aye aye, were three miles from t' 'Checker Buoy', an' it's still thick as a bag."

Rolling from the bunk and slotting my feet into an old pair of slippers, strategically placed by the ladder, adjacent to my pit, I climbed up to the galley, where a steaming mug awaited me. Dad was back in the wheelhouse, not wanting to leave the boat without a watch-keeper for longer than necessary. I climbed the steps, mug in hand. It should have been daylight but the fog was delaying the sun's effect.

The radar was now displaying lots of activity. The long, curved sweep of Spurn Point, the old man's beard on the head-shaped Yorkshire Coast, was distinct. Beyond this low-lying land, many ships could be seen in the river, though most of these would be at anchor, awaiting berths in a Humber port.

I now had the seat and with feet perched on the bottom of the wheel, surveyed the electronic picture ahead. A clever device on the radar indicated the direction of travel of all the traffic in relation to our vessel by leaving a black streak in their track. As long as we continued on our existing course it was simple to identify the ships that would conflict with our inward passage. As yet we were not in the river, only approaching from the north and outside the shipping lane. Several vessels were crossing ahead of us in both directions on opposite sides of the buoyed channel, but none of the ships would bother us. They would be well on their way before we reached the river, but others would follow in their wake.

The airwaves on the VHF were alive with concerned voices as pilots and mariners frequently gave names of vessels, their position, speed and direction to the River Control. In reply the controller gave advice and instruction to the many ships. These were dangerous waters and fog added to the problems. In the days before radar the river traffic was sometimes stopped for days on end when the fog refused to lift. Collisions in the Humber fog were not unusual and brave or foolhardy trawler skippers from the two deepwater fishing ports, under pressure from demanding owners, were reluctant to miss their markets.

Dad refilled our mugs and wordlessly looked out from the port window into the gloom, knowing there was nothing to see. Twenty minutes after being called, I turned *Emulator* to starboard till her nose was pointing west towards the tip of Spurn Point. We were in the shipping lanes now and vigilance was essential. I wiped the black tracks from the radar, allowing new, true lines to form then reported to the River Control that we'd entered the buoyed channel and were heading for Grimsby.

"*Emulator*, thank you for the information skipper," came the reply. "I have you on screen. I was wondering which fishing vessel that was. Continue on your course and present speed."

The Controller had been able to compare the size of the targets on his console and was in no doubt we were a fishing vessel. He'd probably seen thousands of similar echoes over the years.

Another official voice came over the airwaves. "*Emulator, Emulator*, this is the North Sea Ferry, *Norstar*. We are inward bound approaching you from astern. Please keep your course and speed and we will pass you close on your port side." This was the same vessel I'd sailed on with my pals on our Amsterdam trip.

"*Norstar, Norstar*, that's copied sir," I replied, looking at the big blip on the screen, heading in our direction from astern, then turned to Dad. "If that big bugger's comin' right up our chuff, ah'm bloody sure ah'm not keepin' this course." I altered forty-five degrees to starboard away from the approaching giant. Thirty seconds later I resumed our original course.

"I can 'ear 'im," Dad said, as the powerful throb of the ferry's engines echoed from the void astern. He continued peering into the grey then called out, "there 'e is. Ah can just see 'im."

I looked over Dad's shoulder and could just make out the wall-sided hull of the big vessel. She was a quarter of a mile from us according to the radar, revealing the density of the fog.

"'E'd 'ave been bloody close if we 'adn't altered course," I muttered, listening to the throbbing power of the passing ship. Waiting till the ferry had moved on ahead and with no other traffic close, I directed *Emulator* south, across the fairway until we were on the south side of the buoyed channel, then altered back towards our destination. We'd be safer on the wrong side of the buoys and the sounder was recording a good depth of water. There was no complaint from the River Control. At my radio enquiry, the officer on the island entrance to the huge fish dock confirmed the lock was open to the sea.

With half a mile to run to the dock and at slow speed, Dad went for'ard onto the whaleback to look out for the wooden jetty near the dock entrance. "It's there, fine on t' port bow," he bawled from his vantage point. "There's a bloke fishin' off t' end of it," he added. Dad then called to the angler, "are yer catchin' out?"

I could see the wooden structure for myself now and eased the vessel gently towards the open lock as Dad continued his conversation with the man on the pier, the distance between them growing.

It was impossible to see across the huge dock but with the radar on the quarter mile range I was able to direct *Emulator* to port and towards the slipways. As she drew near, we approached a row of 'snibbies', the ubiquitous, light blue painted seine-netters tied with their stems to the pier near the concrete ramp. At the end of the row of boats a quayside berth was available and with a bit of manoeuvring *Emulator* was soon alongside. As there was no rise and fall of tide within the enclosed dock, she was secured with short lines fore and aft.

With the engine stopped Dad and I stepped ashore, heading for the nearby Jubilee Café, ready to tackle a bacon sandwich. We'd only gone a few yards when out of the gloom appeared Brian Leggett, the shipwright. Brian, a stocky, bespectacled man was a cheery soul who enjoyed a chat. He frequently visited Scarborough in his little cabin cruiser and knew Dad from his role as lighthouse watch-keeper.

It seemed quite strange that when I'd first visited Grimsby it was Brian's father, Ernie who ran the family business. Now his grandson Ian was working for the company. The years were rolling by. I'd leave a set of boat's keys with Brian while *Emulator* was on the slip and his men were working on her. When the underwater work and bottom painting had been completed and she was re-floated, a watchman would ensure the boat was secure. It was essential to have a caretaker, as there was much petty-thieving around the dock. A few years ago we'd had our brass port and starboard navigation lights stolen while absent from *Pioneer* for a few hours. Leaving Brian, we headed for our breakfast and to meet our watchman.

The Jubilee Café, one of several snack bars around the massive port, hadn't changed since I was last in the building. In fact the black-painted, wooden clinker built building probably hadn't altered since the days of steam. These premises, always busy, catered for the staff from the scores of fish merchants and the dozens of support services that kept the Grimsby fishing fleet at sea.

We entered through the small entrance porch to the sound of many voices talking across the oil-clothed tables. Boiler suited or wearing soiled white overalls, the workers discussed a myriad of topics while taking their morning break. Joining the queue while Dad found a couple of empty chairs, I observed the three ladies behind the counter, each clad in faded nylon overalls. These women were working at full stretch to keep up with the demand from their customers. A fourth female, her back to the counter was in the rear kitchen, hovering over a giant frying pan and delivering a constant supply of greasy bacon, sausages and eggs to the front counter.

"Yes duck, what can I get yer?" asked the cheery blonde lady with crimson lips, her hair in rollers retained under a headscarf.

"Two pots o' tea an' a couple o' bacon sarnies please love," I replied with a smile and equal friendliness.

The lady slopped a large portion of sterilised milk from the distinctive long, narrow-necked bottle into two of the dozen or more mugs close to her elbow, then with both hands and little finesse, splashed strong, dark tea from the huge metal teapot. Two rashers of crispy bacon were selected from a tin tray and dropped onto a pre-cut breadcake on a small plate, then the process was repeated. The speed of the operation was incredible, though certainly lacked delicacy. Offering a five-pound note, the change, taken from the wooden drawer below the counter was thrust into my hand with equal speed. I picked up a spoon from the cluster immersed in a handle-less mug at the side of the counter, helping myself to sugar from a chipped enamelled basin. Stacking both rolls onto one plate and grabbing the mugs with the other hand, I headed across the room. My cheery friend was already serving another customer from a queue that reached the door.

Acknowledging Dad's waving hand with a nod, I crossed the smoke-filled room, passing wooden benches strewn with discarded tabloid newspapers to find he was sitting with our watchman, Tommy Stogdale. 'Stoggy', a Scarborough man who'd moved to Grimsby while I was still at junior school, had until recently, fished from this port on a smaller boat, working daily not far from the river. Tom still came back to his hometown for a week each summer to look up his old mates and enjoy a yarn about the good old days.

"Now then young Nommy," he said, grinning. "'Ow are yer doin'? That's a fine ship yer've got. She's a bit different from t' old *Emulator*."

With a red, weathered face and now silver haired with furrowed brow, 'Stoggy', in his younger days, was one of the most powerful men of his generation. I still have a vivid recollection from my boyhood days of watching him tow the old steam powered trawler *Emulator*, which my current vessel was named after, across the harbour with his eighteen-foot rowing boat, *Marjorie*. The old trawler, built of iron before the turn of the last century, was around a hundred feet in length. Tom was watchman when she was in port and as her boilers were down, she was dead in the water. The old ship was taking up a landing berth at the fish market and had to be moved. Tom towed her across to the North Wharf with his little boat using a pair of oars. Now he was looking after my *Emulator*, just as he took care of most of the Scarborough boats that came to Grimsby for painting or repairs.

The three of us returned to the slipway to see my work-worn, scruffy vessel emerging from the water atop an iron-framed cradle, hauled into position on the carriage by Leggett's men with ropes fastened to her bows and quarters. Two vertical steel rods standing proud of the water on either side of the trolley had aligned her onto the wooden bilge blocks. The cable drawing *Emulator* up the ramp was thicker than my wrist but this same wire also hauled the few remaining Arctic trawlers from the water when required.

Rust caked on her starboard side from the constant banging of trawl boards fore and aft on the steel cladding, *Emulator* looked unloved and ready for some TLC. Her red bottom, now green with weed and slime was being washed off with powerful hoses as the vessel crept slowly up the slope. The sacrificial zinc anodes on her hull and around her propeller nozzle were almost eaten away. They were doing their job and would be replaced with new for old.

As we stood chatting and recalling old times I was aware of someone standing at my side. "Ahm 'ere," said the young voice. Sean, a person of few words had arrived in his car to collect us and take us home.

Dad and I shook Stoggy's hand and though I didn't need to, said, "look after 'er," then turned to follow our driver.

"Don't you worry, she's in good 'ands," Stoggy answered. "See yer next week."

The drive home was horrendous. The fog hadn't thinned at all and though Sean was driving steadily, I'd much rather have been at sea with the radar going.

The following morning while Dotty was out of the house there was a knock on the door and on answering I discovered the Sea Fisheries Committee's inspector on the doorstep, briefcase in hand. What was this about?

"Mr Normandale?" said the sallow-faced man unnecessarily. He knew full well who I was. We'd crossed swords often enough. "May I come in?"

"Of course," I replied stepping aside to allow him access while racking my brains to think what crime I'd committed to warrant this visit. I hadn't done anything wrong recently as far as I could recall. "Is this a social call?" I asked. I'd asked the same question last time I'd been interviewed and I received exactly the same answer.

"I'm afraid not. It's business," he replied in his funereal voice, missing my irony by a mile.

"A'll put t' kettle on then," I said, "tea or coffee?" I left the tall, thin chap sitting at the table preparing his book and pen ready for the interview. I chuckled to myself at the thought of this dour man calling round for a coffee while passing. On his previous visit

I'd recorded my interview on a cassette tape, much to his dismay but didn't think this was necessary at present.

Taking cups from the kitchen cupboard I made the two drinks and with a plate of biscuits, returned to hear the case for the prosecution.

"I don't think there's anything in this," the officer said, "but I'm investigating a report from a Filey cobleman that your vessel, *Emulator* was seen fishing in the prohibited area in Filey Bay last week." He gave details of the time and date and looked at me for a response.

"Ah, of course," I recalled. We'd been in the prohibited area briefly while shortening the distance to home on Wednesday night around darkening. It hadn't been a serious or extended breech and I was sure this couldn't be proved. The inspector was letting me know I'd been seen. Lifting my cup I sipped my coffee while thinking of a response. "Euk" I said, as a strong smell of bleach hit my nasal passage. "Is your drink alright?" I asked, concerned. "Mine tastes of bleach."

He raised his cup, sipped then assured me his beverage was fine.

That was a relief. I returned to the kitchen, dumped my drink and, rinsing the cup made myself a fresh brew, now distracted from the interview. Returning, I said, "It's jus' occurred to me what must 'ave 'appened. We'd 'auled our trawl on t' edge o' t' area on our way 'ome. We were steamin' slow an' guttin' our last 'aul while we were in t' area. We were 'omeward bound, not fishin'."

"I thought that would be the case," the inspector replied quite affably, "but I had to investigate." He stayed for a while, finishing his drink and talking about the current quota problems facing the industry, none of which were of his department's making.

The officer made his farewells. I could still taste bleach.

On her return I said to Dotty, "did you leave some bleach in a cup in t' cupboard?"

My lovely wife coloured a little and said, "yes, there was a stain in the cup. I left it to soak. Why?"

140

"I almost poisoned the fisheries inspector," I said. This wasn't true but I could imagine the newspaper headlines, 'Fisherman attempts to poison investigating officer.' Why Dotty had put the cup in the cupboard and not left it in the sink I never discovered.

The fog had gone when Sean drove one of the crew and myself back to Grimsby to bring the boat home. On his return to the harbour he would help the other two to prepare the gear for taking on board, ready for sea. *Emulator* was looking pristine when we got to her berth. I was delighted to see my boat looking so good. Stoggy couldn't have been more proud of her if he'd done the painting himself. "By 'ell, she's a fine ship," he said again with great approval. Tom threw off the ropes and called out, "see yer when ah'm up in Scarborough this summer," then with a wave and a grin turned and headed for home. Tommy Stogdale had spent most of the past week on board *Emulator* taking care of my vessel.

Looking across the dock as we departed, it was sad to see the North Wall with not a single trawler tied up. Not too many years ago this quay had been full from end to end with North Sea and Arctic trawlers, so many ships that they were occasionally double-banked. Amazingly, crews joining these vessels would climb aboard up a single ladder onto the whaleback with their kitbags, despite the usual influence of drink.

The smaller class of these ships had become obsolete, requiring too many crew but the bigger vessels had been forced from their main fishing grounds in Icelandic waters due to international pressure to keep the NATO base at Keflavik. The exclusion of foreign boats from these waters was part of the agreement to retain the strategic base focusing on the Soviet Union.

Thousands of men had lost their jobs in Grimsby, Hull and to a lesser extent, Fleetwood and Aberdeen. Fine ocean-going ships had been taken to the breakers yard long before their time. I couldn't help thinking how close to home these international agreements were getting. Our politicians had already surrendered our fish and grounds to the European Union behind closed doors.

* * * * * *

Dickie Elliott has died. Dick, one of the loveliest men who'd ever walked the piers had passed away at sea. He and his shipmate Ernie had been hauling pots a few miles to the southeast of the harbour in their coble, *Who Cares* when Dick had collapsed. Poor Ernie, with no idea what to do, could only cut the rope connecting the pots and bring his friend home at full speed, knowing he was probably dead. Dick will be sorely missed, not only by his family, but by everyone who knew him.

I'd known Dickie Elliott all my life and as a boy was one of many youngsters who'd sailed with him in his little motorboat, *Kathleen and David,* named after his children, in the years before he'd teamed up with Ernie. More recently the pair had taken Danny and the lads of his generation to sea with them. Dick's funeral was to take place at St Mary's Church later in the week and the occasion would be extremely sorrowful.

Danny and I, in our best clothes, made our way up the hill to the imposing church overlooking the town to join the scores of mourners milling around outside the beautiful old building. Most were reluctant to leave the daylight until the cortege arrived.

The vehicles in view, we joined the shuffling crowd making their way through the iron-studded wooden doors at the rear to find the huge church already packed and it was difficult to find seats but people shuffled along the pews allowing as many as possible to fit in.

The sight of the pallbearers carrying the casket followed by Dick's widow, Mary supported by David and Kathleen and their spouses, then other equally distraught relatives, brought a lump to my throat and moisture to my eyes.

The service was intensely moving and I found it impossible to sing any of the hymns. When the eulogy to this special person was read out I could feel tears running down my face and pulled a handkerchief from my pocket, passing another to an equally distraught Danny. The mariners hymn, 'Eternal Father' concluded the emotional send off for the gentle man and soon we were back outside. Few were willing to leave the church grounds and I stood with many fishermen and friends from the diving club where

Dick had been a social member. "He got a good send off," was the expression heard over and again from solemn faces.

I took a red-eyed Danny home then met up with the divers in the Leeds Arms. The remainder of the day was a haze as we raised glass after glass to our absent friend and I had no recollection of going home. There were no complaints from Dotty. Dick was one of the first people I'd introduced her to when we met and her affection for him was such that she couldn't bear to attend the church.

* * * * * *

The phone rang and I answered with my usual, "ullo."

A quiet, confident voice said, "I've got it Fred. The bank has paid up. One year to the day you signed for the boat. It went without a hitch."

Recognising the voice, my manner changed immediately. 'That's fantastic, Stephen. Well done, thank you. Ah'll ring Bluey immediately an' tell 'im the good news."

Stephen Drury, a young, bespectacled Scarborough solicitor, slightly Dickensian in appearance had travelled on our behalf to Truro in Cornwall to the branch of the bank used by 'Steelship' and had requested the manager to honour his guarantee. Stephen had now successfully recovered the instalments we'd paid to the bankrupt shipyard. For the first time in ages we could look to the future.

A few weeks later there was more good news on our stalled building project. Ken Marshall, the Managing Director of 'Cochranes', the famous trawler building shipyard in Selby and Goole, following a phone call, had sent a quotation. For an additional £50,000 above the original contract quotation, workers from his company would travel to Truro, cut the existing structure into three sections and transport these pieces to Goole. There they would weld the sections together again and complete the vessel to our satisfaction. Our project was back on track.

Back at sea, we were at 'Bruce's Gardens', seven hours steaming time from home. This was an area of long, narrow strips of hard ground and stones and we were fishing well, catching mainly haddocks in the dark, but not having much success during daylight hours. Neil, a swarthy, black haired, ruddy-faced character was with us for the week while one of the regulars was on holiday.

Neil had been with us in the past and was a useful hand to have aboard. I'd left him in the wheelhouse on a four-hour watch to trawl across various pieces of light, shady ground that we'd not fished much recently. The weather was fine and there were no other vessels anywhere near.

I'd been 'turned in' a couple of hours when Neil called me urgently. "I've marked summat on t' sounder. Will yer come and look at it? It's a queer lookin' thing."

Quickly out of bed, I was up the ladder in seconds. It's only a short period of time between marking objects below the boat on the echo sounder and reaching the same object with the trawl. If this was a wreck, seconds could be the difference between snagging and prevention.

The red mark on the screen, about the size of my little finger end looked distinctly like a wreck. Neil had been on the ball watching the sounder, and there was still time to stop the boat before the trawl reached the position. "There shouldn't be a wreck here," I said, as much to myself as to the watch-keeper and reached for the throttle. I paused, my hand on the stainless steel lever and I looked again at the mark. It looked very much like a wreck but this could be a huge ball of cod.

My mind began to whirl. I couldn't be a hundred percent sure there were no wrecks here, though I had been in this area several times before. We had a pair of combination rope/wire cables between the doors and the net. These were not as strong as the wire and chain bridles and would part easily if this was a wreck and I'd lose my gear. With mixed feelings I drew back the throttle, easing the engine, quickly writing down the position of the target. Even as I did so I knew I'd made the wrong decision.

The crew dashed from their beds as they always did when the engine eased without warning and we began to haul the trawl. In less than ten minutes the net was alongside and much to my

144

chagrin I noted a few large cod thrashing in the upper part of the netting. "Bugger!" I shouted loudly from the window. "We've just missed a bloody big bag o' cod."

Taking the wing-ends on board, we dodged slowly back and forth over the readings looking for the mark, but the 'bird had flown'. For the remainder of the day I trawled back and forth covering the region comprehensively, but to no avail.

I was really mad at myself for not standing on and backing my data, so it didn't help when Neil, grinning said, "fortune favours the brave, skipper. Yer'll 'ave t' put that down as the one that got away."

Matters got worse with the dark when we hauled and the quarter-rope on the after end of the trawl somehow became caught in the propeller, stopping the engine. There wasn't much rope in the screw and it would cut out easily, but I had no diving torch to illuminate the problem. There'd be no light from the boat's deck reaching inside the prop's nozzle. We'd have to wait till daylight, but then an idea hit me. We had a very good torch in the engine room that I regularly used for examining the bilges and other inaccessible parts below. If I wrapped this light in a plastic bag it might do the trick.

Leaving Mick to find a bag and some tape, I kitted up into the diving gear and with the Heath-Robinson lamp switched on, jumped over the side. The torch stayed lit. It was only a few minutes work to chop out the offending rope and I even managed to hold on to the stainless steel clip spliced into the end of the quarter-rope. The flashlight failed as I surfaced but it didn't matter. The cost of a new torch was insignificant compared with the time saved. Putting the clip and soggy plastic bag into the dangling bucket, I climbed the dangling ladder back on board, bringing an end to the run of bad luck.

CHAPTER 12

DENMARK

We were heading east-northeast and the 'Navstar' navigator with its latitude and longitude readout computed a forty-hour steam at our current speed. My pals, Syd and Pete were onboard and we were bound for Thyboron in northern Denmark. I'd never forgotten the passage back to Scarborough last year when we'd been continually drenched while punching into a strong southerly wind while clearing a deck load of fish. We'd been forced to ease our speed due to the mass of heavy spray and had missed the market. Now *Emulator's* builder, Derry Forbes' words were about to come true. He'd predicted that I'd fit a shelter-deck on the vessel before too long.

Having seen numerous quality aluminium improvements on Grimsby vessels modernised in Denmark, I'd consulted friends from the port and all had recommended 3Js, a company named after the trio of owners of the business whose surnames began with the letter J. This company had an excellent reputation for fabrication. I'd subsequently met the three men at their stand at the Fishing Exhibition in Scotland and having seen albums full of their work, had no hesitation in asking the company for a quotation. I wanted to continue working over the starboard side on the vessel but intended to fit a three-quarter shelter-deck enclosing most of the foredeck and all the port side.

The three Js had arrived in Scarborough in a hire car from the ferry terminal in North Shields, armed with note pads, long, reeled tape measures and a stack of cardboard sheets. Refusing a late breakfast the men had set to in a workman-like manner taking dozens of measurements and joining the cardboard together to make templates. Every dimension was checked twice and agreed before being committed to paper. The men's English was reasonable and we had no trouble communicating but the readings they were taking were in metric, a totally alien medium to me. After more than an hour of precision tape work the men were satisfied with their results and agreed to an early lunch and a beer before heading for the evening ferry back to Denmark.

The men had wasted no time on their return and a thick envelope with a 'Danmark' stamp awaited me at home the following Thursday. I opened the wad with enthusiasm but my face dropped when I looked at the bottom line. The price was astronomical and far beyond anything I'd envisaged. I couldn't run to this sort of figure. Then the penny dropped. The quotation was in Danish crowns. An enquiry to the bank gave me an exchange rate of approximately eleven crowns to the pound and made sense.

This was a similar price to quotations I'd received from Scotland and was acceptable, but the main attraction of 3Js was the two week time scale to complete the work. Four to six weeks was the estimate from north of the border.

"Is it my watch yet?" Syd asked, entering the wheelhouse with two pots of coffee. "A person could get bedsores aboard 'ere," he said, grinning.

We were supposed to be doing four-hour watches but with nothing to do but sleep or read below, no one was prepared to relinquish the helmsman's chair. In the wheelhouse, apart from keeping a lookout and plotting our course on the chart, the radio helped to pass the time. We'd long since lost the signal for the little television set perched on a shelf in the mess-deck.

The weather remained fine and we slowly and uneventfully crept across the North Sea. At dawn on the second day we could see strange structures on shore that were not readily identifiable, though as yet the low-lying sandy coast of Jutland was still invisible. As we grew closer, it became apparent that what we could see were windmills. Not the conventional, four-bladed buildings of old, that can still be seen in Holland; these were slim towers with three-fingered, aeroplane-type propeller blades. It was Pete, a knowledgeable engineer who identified the edifices as wind turbines, generating a proportion of Denmark's electricity needs. These futuristic, alien structures seemed ugly blots on the simple, and now visible sandy shoreline. There would be little power generated today. The blades were still.

Thyboron was now in sight and the chimney of what we later discovered to be the fishmeal factory was emitting a thin, grey vapour vertically into the clear sky, underlining the lack of wind. Though we could see the town, the harbour was behind a long, north-facing strand that formed the southern end of the access to Limfjord, where a system of navigable canals and natural lakes crossed the northern part of the country. Turning slowly to starboard we followed the green buoys to the port's entrance, marked with red and green towers, into what was revealed to be a huge harbour, lined with scores of various types of fishing craft. The smaller, pale blue gillnet vessels were berthed together and were easily identified by the dozens of flag-topped, cane buoys with white polystyrene floats, stowed on board each craft. Dozens of anchor seiners, also pale blue were very similar to the vessels in Grimsby, each boat fitted with a pair of large rope reels on their foredecks. A row of vessels lined the fish market, discharging the fruits of their labour in readiness for the morning auction.

In another section of the harbour the air was cloying with a strong, powdery smell emitting from the fishmeal factory. Seven or eight red-hulled industrial fishers, sunk to their gunwales with sandeels were berthed alongside. A couple of vessels were having their catches pumped out while others waited to be discharged. I'd seen some of these ships to the southwest of the Dogger Bank, where a huge fleet of industrial ships gathered in the spring each year, coinciding with the emergence of the giant shoals of sandeels.

These 'shit-catchers', using extremely fine mesh, each took hundreds of tons of mostly sandeels but they also fished for sprats, herring and pout, with the unfortunate by-catch of many edible species, mature and undersized. Once onboard, this cargo soon turned to a mushy soup and it wasn't easy to identify the different fish. The annual quota for this fleet was set at one million tons, which was always taken. This huge extraction must be causing massive damage to the food chain, as most fish feed on sandeels. In May and June almost all the fish we caught had bellies bursting with these little eels.

The processed meal is used for animal foods and for feeding the burgeoning salmon farming industry while the quality oil extracted is an ingredient in many food products. The sad statistic is that it takes about eight tons of wild fish to rear one ton of farmed stock.

I spied the 3Js logo, a three-bladed ship's propeller within a circle, with the letter J between each blade, simple but very effective. Two blue boiler suited men took our ropes as we tied alongside and in no time we were stepping ashore. I shook hands with Ole, one of the Js, introducing him to my friends. "Where do we find t' Customs Office Ole," I asked, holding up my passport.

"You don't," he said. "You are visiting fishermen. It is not a problem. Come and have some coffee." The big, round-faced man led us across the harbour road and into the company's canteen where we were offered strong black coffee, bread, paté, cheese and savoury titbits. This was a very friendly welcome that bode well for our relationship.

"Is it possible t' get a crane t' lift our fishin' gear from t' boat?" I asked. "We'll need t' get it back when we tek t' boat 'ome again."

A telephone call fixed this. "The lorry will be here in half an hour," he said.

Breakfast finished, Ole showed us the new landing winch, hinged fish-room hatch and the bag hatch, which would be hydraulically raised to let the codend swing inboard to the middle of the boat. These pieces were ready to be fitted as required. The shipbuilder then took us into an adjacent shed where to my amazement the prefabricated shelter-deck was constructed and waiting to be offered into place. The top section was of embossed plate, ensuring good footing. Both my companions were engineers and were extremely impressed, not only with the preconstruction but also with the quality of the work.

Back on board men were removing the convex iron strips from the port side top rail while others were scraping the surface ready for the coach-bolting of thick, aluminium plate to the bulwark top, this shaped to match the curve of the boat. The new shelter would be welded to this material.

A flat-backed truck with a power block attachment arrived at the quayside and the driver alighted, drawing stabilisers from the four corners of the vehicle. With little communication apart from thumbs up each time the lift was attached, the cheerful trucker transferred trawl boards, three nets and the heavy rock-hopper ground gear from the boat to his wagon. The back of the truck was piled high with gear. "Ring me when you require this returning," the driver said, smiling. Then he was gone.

We appeared surplus to requirements now so began packing our personal effects, ready to leave *Emulator* for shore accommodation, intending to stay overnight and make a mini-tour of the area before taking the ferry from Esbjerg the following day. There was so much to see round the region that was different and progressive compared with back home.

Syd, having cleaned the galley, came ashore with a bagful of rubbish and in vain looked around the immediate area for a bin or skip. "Leave it on the quayside," one of the workers said. "It will be collected."

The black plastic bag was placed on shore by my sceptical friend and within five minutes was picked up without comment by a van-driving port worker. The whole port and infrastructure seemed clean and in good condition. There was no rubbish floating anywhere in the harbour, unlike most ports. "We have no tide here or in the Baltic," Ole said when I mentioned how clean everything was. "We have to make sure nothing gets dumped into the water."

Of course! That's what was different. We'd been in harbour for about three hours now and it was still possible to step on and off the boat at quay level. How strange was that? I'd forgotten how little rise and fall occurred in this area. We were all part of the same North Sea but the tide didn't affect this part of it to any degree. We had a fair amount of tidal range at home, and in the

English Channel a massive rise and fall took place, yet we were all connected. I pondered on this strange phenomenon for ages without reaching any logical explanation.

We were taken by Ole to the Fishermen's Mission, a short drive into town, on the way passing the biggest admiralty patterned anchor I'd ever seen. This huge, black painted street ornament with reproduction wooden stock was in the centre of a road junction and part of the traffic system. We stopped outside a brightly coloured building with the word, Somandshjem over the door.

The 'Seamen's Home' was basic but spotlessly clean. A canteen restaurant with wooden tables offered a good selection of food and strangely for a mission, bottles of beer. The little single rooms were rudimentary, with no radio or television but were perfectly adequate for our needs.

Following a bite to eat we made our way back to the shipyard where another surprise awaited us. The new shelter-deck was being offered into position, held in place by a mobile hydraulic crane. This was incredible. Another of the workforce wearing the ubiquitous blue boiler suit with a 3Js badge emblazoned, was cutting the edges of the aluminium fabrication with a big ripsaw, shaping the after end of the structure to fit around the wheelhouse.

"It's like trimming the crust from the edge of a pie," Pete observed. He, far better than I, was aware of the skill involved in doing this work.

"At this rate they'll have the job finished by the weekend," Syd said. "We might as well stay over here."

He was joking but the major structural work would indeed be completed by Friday but, like building a house, the second stage of fitting the intricate parts would take longer to complete.

Considering the size of the harbour the town was quite small with a compact main street. The social life focussed around three small bars, one with an old fishing boat's wheelhouse forming its entrance and it was here we started our evening. The bar was quite spacious and busy, though the room was very smoky with most of the customers indulging. Like most fishermen's bars the walls were decorated with photos of fishing vessels but in addition

Ebbing Tide

there were numerous name plaques from boats that had either been lost or scrapped.

The choice of beer was limited to draught lager or bottles of Tuborg and Carlsberg but these were quite acceptable and not expensive. Next we crossed the road, studded with beer bottle tops to another of the bars, a smaller place with the same choice of beer but with a quiet, pleasant atmosphere. A very small, rotund man wearing a white boiler suit, on hearing our English voices, introduced himself as Eric, an electrical contractor at the harbour. In appearance this was not a man I could easily envisage climbing over fishing boats and up and down engine room ladders, but several men, clearly fishermen, spoke to Eric while we were in his company and each said he was the best electrician in the business.

It seemed essential to visit the third hostelry, so bidding goodnight to our rotund friend, we headed for 'The Kanalan Bar' to complete our tour, though it was now late in the evening. Loud sixties music greeted us as we entered the small bar. The customers here were younger and some were dancing. The atmosphere was buzzing though it wasn't easy to talk. The locals were friendly asking, above the din and between tracks, what we were doing in their little town. It was revealing that all these people could speak English yet none of us had a second language. "It's the pop music," a young girl said. "We learn the words of the songs then want to do more English at school."

It was a late breakfast of coffee, cheese, hotdog sausage and pieces of herring, accompanied by bread rolls, which seemed a strange combination, but was enjoyed nevertheless. Work was coming along apace on *Emulator* when we finally arrived at the yard. There were still several hours to kill before we were due to set off on the two-hour drive to board the 'Esbjerg to Tyne' ferry so more time would be killed strolling the harbours.

"You should set off early and visit the museum at Roskilde," Villy, one of the Js suggested. "It is worth a visit. They have excavated some old Viking longships. The driver will wait for you."

What an opportunity this was. We were all maritime history enthusiasts and it was unlikely we'd get a chance like this again.

HRH Prince Charles with the author at the Teesside restaurant.
Photo JWP Reeveley

An unusual catch, a 10 stone halibut.
L-R Russell Cryer, Danny Normandale, Gordon (Gogga) Mann,
Mick Bayes, Sean Crowe, Sid Withers.
Photo FG Normadale

Emulator back in Scarborough harbour, still iced up.
Photos FG Normandale

Bluey, Skipper of Independence had found the cod. Timmy Tyson celebrates.
Photo George Brockwell

Pete and Jim with a special find.
Photo FG Normandale

Team photo on an earlier dive trip.
Photo FG Normandale

Jim Butler leaving Emulator
on the rescue helicopter.
Photo Alan England

Gutting fish on board Emulator pre shelter-deck.
Photo FG Normandale

New aluminum shelter-deck being fitted to Emulator in Thyboron,
Denmark. Photo FG Normandale

Allegiance ready for naming and launching.
Photo FG Normandale

Allegiance, arriving in Scarborough on her maiden voyage.
Photo FW Normandale

The Mermaid.
From a video by Chris Coole

Undaunted's launching.
Photo FW Normandale

Undaunted on trials.
Photo FW Normandale

Emulator leaving the River Hull towing the new vessel.
Photo FG Normandale

Quickly packing our few belongings, we piled into our car. The driver had little English but had been given instructions and headed down the flat, straight roads towards Esbjerg via Roskilde.

Our chauffeur was content to remain with the car and visit the café, while we wandered around the stylish, modern building with great interest. There were five ships varying from ten to more than twenty metres in length in the temperature-controlled hall. Knowing a metre was about three feet enabled me to get some perspective. These ancient craft, carbon dated to the 11th century, had lain in silt and mud undisturbed until their discovery in the early 1960's. The vessels had apparently been used as block ships in the entrance to the Roskilde Fjord to deter raiding Norwegians. "Vikings raiding Vikings, that's novel," Syd suggested, raising a laugh.

The ship construction was incredible and cleverly documented in several languages. If there was a negative aspect of the wonderful display it was that these vessels had been deliberately sunk, so would probably have been old craft before they were scuttled. They would have been stripped of any artefacts or remnants of cargo before being despatched.

The driver was waiting patiently near the exit and an hour later we were in Esbjerg. The ferry, operating on a summer only schedule, was an old vessel that had been a cruise liner in former life and our beds, deep in the bowels of the ship in a sixteen-berth cabin, were directly above the propeller shafts. This had probably been crew accommodation in her earlier days. Sick bags were conspicuous on every bed, along with a towel and soap. Hopefully the bags wouldn't be required in our case.

Though we'd had a heavy night previously there was only the bar to visit following dinner and another extended stay. I awoke feeling slightly dopey with a dry, unpleasant beery taste in my mouth, to see Pete was almost dressed. The loudspeaker was announcing breakfast prior to the ship's approach to the Tyne. There was no sign of Syd. Scrambling into trousers and following Pete, I headed for the gent's washroom, toilet bag in hand. Here we found Syd, washed, beard trimmed and shaved around the edges, his hair neatly groomed.

"Bloody 'ell Syd, we're not breakfasting wi' t' Captain," I said in a croaky voice.

"Years of Navy training boys," he said with a grin. "You can get away with almost anything if you look the part."

"Well you certainly look the part now," Pete said, minutes later when Syd was attired in deck shoes, slacks, casual shirt and cravat. "You look like 'our man in Havana'."

This was Dotty's sentiment when she met us as we disembarked in North Shields. "Two scruffs and a gentleman," she said, earning a beaming smile from the tailor's dummy and shrugs from the tramps.

I now had a week and a half ashore and no boat to inspect or work on, though there were always new plotter rolls to make and old ones to replace. Even these mechanical plotters would be obsolete soon. There were new, colour screen CVP plotters on display at last year's fishing exhibition. These worked on the latitude and longitude system rather than the Decca lattice of our current machines. This was the future, but there'll be a mass of work involved converting the Decca information to the new format. Both systems will have to run concurrently for an extended period to cover the vast amount of data accumulated on my plotter rolls.

There was bad news at the National Federation of Fishermen's Organisations (NFFO) meeting in York at the weekend. The government, in the form of Trinity House, was intending to extend its 'Light Dues' charges for the upkeep of lighthouses and buoys around the UK coast to include fishing vessels. This compulsory levy had traditionally been paid only by merchant ships in home waters, but with the reduction of the merchant fleet we were expected to make up the shortfall. The feeling of the meeting was one of outrage. "We won't pay it."

"We don't use 'em."

"They'll have to take us all to court."

A policy of non-cooperation was adopted. We seemed to be falling out with the Government on several fronts.*

---

* High profile prosecutions ensured everyone paid their 'Light Dues', though no other nations in the EU demanded their fishermen pay this tax.

Further new legislation had given the Department of Trade and Industry (DTI) mandatory powers to inspect fishing vessels every four years to ensure safety equipment, which included pyrotechnics, life-buoys, liferafts and fire-fighting gear was kept up to date, though liferafts were serviced annually. I didn't know anyone who didn't conform to these requirements already but it was reasonable to expect some would flout the rules. The problem was the proposed charge of £46 per hour including travel and office time, which was outrageous. This cost would quickly escalate. To add insult to injury nails had to be drawn from all wooden vessels to ensure their fastenings had not decayed. My lovely *Emulator* would have to have the wood around these nails burned away by blowlamp to expose the heads, allowing some of her large, galvanised square pins to be drawn, then replaced. The holes in the plank would then be plugged with putty. This regulation made my blood boil.

As if things weren't bad enough, fish prices were now at rock bottom due to foreign imports and the new quotas were restrictive and creating further problems. The fun and freedom had gone out of the industry and honest men, who'd done nothing illegal in their entire lives were being forced to break the law to make a living.

My time ashore passed quickly seeing more of Dotty and our family, who were quickly growing up. Paula was now at sixth-form college and Danny would soon be leaving school. There was no doubt what he was going to do then. He'd been waiting all his life to go fishing.

It was a more sober crossing of the North Sea for my crew and me on the return ferry passage to collect *Emulator* from the shipyard. There would be plenty of work to do from the onset, cleaning the vessel, rigging the gear and taking ice and stores onboard.

My vessel looked terrific and was ready for us when we arrived and it didn't take long to organise the return of the fishing gear. The driver, who must have loaded the truck himself, was back with our gear within an hour of my requesting it. There was a charge for this service of course, but the efficiency was second to none.

I asked Sean to go to the ships' provisioner for a week's supply of stores. Despite language difficulties he returned having placed the order but with a perplexed look on his face, and with a scratch of his head said, "they didn't 'ave any bacon."

"Course they've got bacon," I replied, "this is Denmark. They bloody grow it 'ere."

"That's what ah thought, but they on'y 'ave small chunks o' smoked 'am," he insisted. "T' man in t' shop said t' Danes don't eat bacon, they send it all to England."

It was strange having the big lump of aluminium in front of *Emulator's* wheelhouse from a viewing perspective, especially when manoeuvring her in a confined space, so it was a little unnerving leaving this strange port for the first time, but I'd quickly get used to the structure.

It took a thirty-hour steam to the west to reach familiar grounds where I could be sure of the terrain and would have no problem finding fish. Three days of steady fishing found us with sufficient catch on board for a wage and to pay the fuel expenses of the two long passages. It was evening when we arrived home, to discover two local fisheries inspectors present on the quayside watching the boats land, and checking catches. Why was this? Things were changing, and not for the better.

Chapter 13

Allegiance

Our new vessel was finally ready after all the troubles and delays and we'd decided to call her *Allegiance*. Her registration number was to be SH 90 and Bluey's mother, Irene was to name and christen the vessel, but I was in big trouble with Dotty. I'd brought some fish home in the car the previous weekend but the bag of fillets, collected from Alliance's processing factory, had tipped over, leaking juice into the vehicle's carpet. Of course I'd forgotten about the spill so hadn't clean it up and had omitted to mention this. Now the smell in the car was really strong. We were supposed to load family and overnight bags into the vehicle in readiness for driving to the launching, but when Dotty opened the car door, the pong had hit her.

"We can't go to Goole in that!" my wife exclaimed. "It's horrendous."

"We'll 'ave t' go," I countered. "It's t' new boat's launchin'."

Leaving us standing by the car with the doors open, my wife went back into the house for some spray, returning with the strongest air freshener, which was liberally directed at the offending location, making it impossible to breathe. All the doors were left open for a further five minutes then we loaded up and set off for the venue, but not before winding all the windows down. It was a very draughty drive to Goole.

Two hours later we'd booked into the hotel, changed into our finery and strangely, were heading for the Capricorn Club for the reception, not the launching. Due to the late high water, we'd planned to have the celebration meal first then launch our, as yet unfinished craft, into the River Ouse. Following the ceremony we would return to the venue for the formal speeches and toasts.

The club was already full when we entered the building. Many of our two families and lots of friends had travelled to Goole to help us celebrate the event. Everyone present was enjoying a glass of something prior to the meal and were in no hurry to leave the bar, so it took the staff longer than expected to get the guests seated.

The Capricorn staff had pulled out all the stops and everyone was enjoying a splendid feast, but the meal was taking longer than planned; the clock was moving against us. By the time the first two courses had been served and cleared it was time to head for the shipyard. The desserts would have to wait.

It was already high water and the crowd was gathering around the podium, which was decked out with red, white and blue bunting. On the staging, the official party of Bluey, his wife Julie plus parents Tom and Irene and the yard's managing director Ken Marshall were joined by a tall, well built clergyman in white robe and vestments. We were delighted when Charlie Bubbins, this old friend from years past, had agreed to come along and bless our new craft. Reverend Bubbins had been the Curate at St Mary's Church in Scarborough. He had sailed on the lifeboat several times and had christened our daughter, Sarah. He and his wife Dorothy had later moved to Teesside, then Manchester and had been assigned to some of the roughest parts of these cities. Charlie had always kept in touch and when asked, had been delighted to come along and play a part in this ceremony, refusing any offer of travel expenses.

The proceedings began and for a few quiet, serious minutes Charlie said a prayer for, and blessed the new vessel, still clad in her dull, grey undercoat then Mrs Sheader, in true style played her role. The small, plump lady in a clear, slight Norfolk accent named the vessel, and echoing the vicar's words, asked God to bless her and all who sailed in her. The bottle of champagne broke with a pleasing crump, which triggered a huge round of applause. Following her excellent performance a bouquet of flowers and a memento of the occasion were presented to the beaming lady.

Looking down the slipway I was surprised to see the water had left its mark on the concrete and there was now at least ten feet of wet ramp in front of the onlookers. The boat hadn't moved yet. Were we going to miss the tide? I was standing next to Norman, the yard manager, a small well-dressed, elderly man with wavy silver hair and a neat clipped moustache. "It's ebbing fast," I said, trying to keep the concern from my voice. I should have known better. Here was a man who'd supervised dozens of launches and of much bigger vessels than this one. He was in complete control.

Though it was now almost dark, Norman pointed to a small branch, moving very slowly upstream, visible in the loom of the lights from the shipyard and he said, "it might be ebbing here onshore, but there's still a trickle of flood going in midstream."

This was a real revelation. I was well aware that the tide flowed later offshore than on the coast but hadn't realised the phenomena extended to the very reaches of tributaries and in places only yards from shore. Everyone was waiting, wondering if there was a problem. A few minutes later, when the water had receded even further from the ways, another piece of driftwood was sighted, lying static in the middle of the little river. "OK lads, let her go," Norman called to his men by the ramp. Wooden chocks were knocked out, retainers released and *Allegiance* began her first and most important journey. Our lovely new ship slipped effortlessly into the river stern first, parting the murky water and creating a small wake, accompanied by three rousing, ringing cheers. With little available light the grey vessel quickly merged with the river's gloom. A harbour tug was on hand and quickly took control of the loose craft, towing her the short distance to Goole Docks, where her fit out would be completed and she'd receive her topcoat. The crowd, now feeling the effects of the cool evening air quickly disappeared in the opposite direction.

Back in the Capricorn Club it was time for the much delayed desserts and coffee then Ken Marshall, now in the role of 'Master of Ceremonies' stood to say a few words of his own. He kindly said we'd been good people to work with and that Cochranes had been pleased to pick up the pieces, literally, of our Cornish disaster. He made everyone laugh when he said this was the smallest vessel the yard had built but it was the biggest launching party. Ken then thanked Mrs Irene Sheader for her perfect performance, raised a toast to the lovely lady then introduced her son, Tom 'Bluey' Sheader, Junior.

This was the moment my partner had been dreading. Bluey was a very good skipper but like most fishermen hated limelight and publicity. He was holding several pages of the speech he'd written and had been practising for the past few days. After only a few lines and several stumbles Bluey, in frustration said, "oh bugger it" and threw the sheaf of paper into the air. The pages fell and scattered. Speaking from the heart he gave a short but sincere speech, again thanking his family and the shipyard for a wonderful vessel and me also for my part in the venture. He ended his brief performance with a toast to the management and workers of Cochranes shipyard.

Now it was my turn and I thanked the shipbuilders for saving our project from disaster, transporting the parts from Cornwall and bringing our vessel to completion. I then thanked Ken and Norman in particular for their professionalism and the management of the Capricorn for the great reception. Now it was time for a final toast to our *Allegiance*.

A rock band, struck up and the floor filled with dancers. It was party time. Bluey and I had agreed to fund a free bar for the night and I'd reminded him to bring £500 for his share.

The revelling went on long into the night for those staying the course and it was well past two in the morning when I found Bluey and took him to the bar. "One fo' t' road," I suggested, then chinking glasses, said to Bluey, "'ere's to a successful venture." I took his share of our bar funds, adding a similar amount of my own then asked the manager to tot up the cost of the evening. We received less than £10 each in change, plus a drink on the house.

There were lots of thick heads at breakfast next morning, including Danny, who though officially too young, had managed to obtain a supply of drink by asking sympathetic friends, making for the bar. I wasn't feeling too good either. I looked up from the bacon and eggs that I'd been pushing round the plate, to see Bluey heading in my direction, a worried look on his face.

"Freddie, I 'ave a problem. Ah've searched me pockets inside out an' been all over t' 'otel room but ah can't find me money. I 'ad five 'undred quid in me pocket last night at t' party, but ah can't find it anywhere now."

"Oh no!" I said in horror. "Where did you 'ave it last? Ah'll 'ave t' lend yer it," but I couldn't keep my face straight any longer and his relief was palpable when I told him he'd already paid.

Dotty and I and our family left Goole around mid-morning. The car was still smelling and horrible. We passed the grey-painted *Allegiance* on our way to the main road and could see workmen climbing all over the boat like ants, intent on her completion. Next time we'd see *Allegiance* she'd be wearing her dark blue livery and be ready for service.

* * * * * *

There was much concern around the harbour when I walked on the pier after returning early from sea. The Bridlington stern trawler *Anmara* H 91 was missing with three hands aboard. The vessel was on her first trip since having a new engine installed and had been seen earlier in the week by the fishery patrol boat *North Eastern Guardian*, fishing north of Flamborough Head. The blue painted craft was last seen on the previous day by the lighthouse watch-keeper heading towards Scarborough. She never arrived. The watch-keeper had gone off watch at 0800 hours thinking she'd turned around and headed for her home port.

Thinking back, I recalled that I'd looked out from my bedroom window at the sea the previous morning before breakfast and most strangely had thought, "I wouldn't want to be out there today." The wind had been strong from the northeast with a steep swell running. *Anmara* would have been broadside to the waves. This must have been about the time she was last seen.

There was still no news of the missing vessel when we sailed on Saturday night, though there was now no doubt that she had foundered. Confirmation eventually came when the body of her skipper, Dave Barratt was found on shore a couple of days later, this following a report to the coastguard by a member of the public.

There was still no sign of the wreck or of the two missing crewmen. The boat's liferaft was found under Bempton cliffs a few miles to the south later in the day. The flimsy craft was empty.

With dreadful timing considering the tragedy back home, I was onboard *Allegiance* towards the end of the week with Bluey and his crew. She was now fuelled and her freshwater tank was full, giving her a draft of about twelve feet. This vessel would certainly tow her fishing gear well. Following successful trials on the upper reaches of the Humber, commanded by a yard appointed skipper, we returned to Goole, where we signed to accept our lovely new vessel. She was finally ours. *Allegiance* steamed briskly down river on her passage home with a following tide, passing under the Humber Bridge and heading towards the open sea with skipper Bluey in the wheelhouse. She began to lift to the swell as we rounded Spurn Point and had a comfortable, easy movement, giving us confidence for her future role as a good sea boat.

With a few miles to go *Allegiance* was now decked out with bunting for her arrival and a large blue flag with the prominent white letters, N & S, was at her foremast. This house flag had been specially made by friends for the occasion and flew proudly as *Allegiance* rounded the piers to welcoming cheers from our families and friends. Sadly there was still no sign of *Anmara* or her missing men.

On Saturday morning, with the tide flowing, I sailed on *Emulator* to conduct a sonar search close along the shore. Pete had volunteered to assist and we scanned up and down the coast in the most probable area, between the high land of 'Redcliffe' and the point at 'Whitenab,' but found nothing. I hadn't been able to discriminate between rock and wreck with the sonar.

I sailed that night on another fishing trip, disappointed at the failure to locate the wreck, intending to look again the following weekend. *Allegiance* also sailed on her maiden fishing trip. Pete continued the search on Sunday in his small dive boat, *St Hope* intent on finding *Anmara,* despite having no sonar. He'd searched for some considerable time and had almost given up hope when he spotted a length of green twine on the surface that seemed to be riding the tide. Curious, he picked up the line and followed the lead upstream. As the line tightened and began to point downwards, his sounder began to mark the wreck of the *Anmara*. He'd found the missing vessel. Despite the poor underwater visibility of late spring, he organized a diving trip to examine the sunken vessel, knowing beyond doubt that he'd found the missing boat.

Returning from my fishing trip on the following Thursday, Pete informed me of his discovery. He said as he began to mark *Anmara* on the boat's sounder, and realising this was the position where three men had lost their lives, a feeling of great sadness overwhelmed him in an instant. On diving the wreck to confirm its identity later in the week, he discovered the boat's trawl net to be festooned around the sunken vessel's stern gantry. There was no sign of the missing men. He'd reported this to the police and then, when requested, had taken the police diving team to search the sunken vessel, though these professionals were not as competent in the sea as the diving club members. These men were more used to searching lakes, canals and rivers in shallow water. They were unable to search the wreck.

Allegiance landed her first catch the following morning and true to tradition her first box of fish was auctioned for charity. Bluey requested that the cash went to the '*Anmara* Fund'.

"The Royal Navy are coming tomorrow," Pete said when I met him later. "The entrance to the accommodation is blocked with a huge ball of netting. Can you pull the stuff clear with *Emulator*? We can't move it with our boat. We've left a line attached on a buoy, ready." He was spending a great deal of time attempting to find the lost men.

We sailed that evening and within an hour had taken the attached line, made this fast on the boat's for'ard gallow and gently engaged stern gear, easing the obstructive net free and dragging the big sheet of green braided twine to the surface, well away from *Emulator's* vulnerable propeller. There was no possibility of diving the wreck now with tide running and visibility down to zero due to the silt cloud we'd created. The navy divers would get inside *Anmara* the following day when conditions would be more suitable.

Next morning a fishing boat reported a body floating on the surface near the wreck. The inshore lifeboat was launched and her crew recovered the missing man, which wasn't a pleasant task. We must have freed the remains from the wreck when dragging the net clear. It was the body of Paul Briggs.

"Someone should tell the bloody politicians this is the real price of fish," a voice in the lifeboat station said as the sealed bag was brought ashore. There was no sign of the third man, despite the navy's best men searching the black interior of the wreck.

* * * * * *

Two months later the salvage vessel *Eurosalve II* arrived to recover the wreck of *Anmara*. The professionals wasted no time in raising the sunken vessel but were refused entry into the harbour with the recovered craft by the Harbour Master. The boat was placed on the beach to be searched and surveyed when the tide ebbed. Despite the prayers of his family there was no sign of the remains of Peter Ward within. He would never be found.

The wreck was taken to Hull and later scrapped. At the inquiry into her loss it was recorded that she had been overwhelmed by a huge wave.

* * * * * *

For the past few months Bluey had been fishing well in his new vessel but he and Julie had gone to America on holiday, a break they'd had booked for some time. Ian Wallis, his right-hand man was left in command. It was only August but we had virtually run out of cod quota to catch, yet the fish was so plentiful it was impossible to avoid catching the stuff. The Producer Organisation managing the monthly allowances for the Scarborough and Bridlington fleets had eked the quota out as sparingly as possible, but there simply wasn't enough to last to the year-end. The pot was almost dry.

I attended a meeting in London along with other fishermen from the area, pleading for more fish quota from either the government or from other PO's that still had fish to catch, but to no avail. We received only sympathy and it was explained that for us to get more cod, others had to be prepared to transfer some of their supply and there was no slack in the system. This was what we'd expected before we set off, but we had to try. Whenever we'd met Mr Gummer, the Fisheries Minister, he'd always said, "If any of your representatives want to meet me at any time, for any reason, my door is always open."

As we left on this occasion, having heard the same rhetoric, someone muttered, "It's a pity your bloody ears aren't."

Some vessels were landing fish undeclared in their logbooks, running the risk of £50,000 maximum fines for a first offence. Subsequent offences would attract unlimited fines and up to two years in prison. Most fishermen were now lawbreakers through no fault of their own. It was becoming a nightmare scenario with Fisheries Officers, who had formerly been friends, now cast in the role of policemen and inspectors.

The same expressions were heard daily on the quayside and the radio. "What's the point in dumping the stuff? It's dead."

"We can't cheat t' bloody bank manager but maybe we can cheat t' inspectors an' try t' keep goin'. We're payin' tax on the stuff."

"We've got kids t' feed and mortgages t' pay. Don't they understand?"

Feelings were running high. Our crews were paid a share of the profit their boat made when voyage expenses had been deducted. If we couldn't land fish we'd soon have no men. Skippers began finding innovative ways of getting the fish ashore away from the prying eyes of the fish police. These inspectors now turned up at the harbour around the clock, unannounced, attempting to catch fishermen red-handed. For the first few weeks of the prohibition the illuminated light in the Fisheries Office was a valuable clue to the presence of the inspectorate, but when they realised this beacon was a 'giveaway' the lights were left on constantly, making the policemen's detection more difficult. The officers became more skilled at reading tide tables and turned up as the boats were arriving at the end of their fishing week, attempting to continue their usual pattern of working.

Tactics changed as fish merchants began sending their lorries to rendezvous with boats in other ports where there was little policing, ranging between Hartlepool to Grimsby in an attempt to maintain their supplies. Of course this arrangement suited the merchants very well. They didn't pay as much for the 'black' fish and having gained sufficient stock for their requirements by the 'back door', they didn't need to buy as much produce at the market, thereby depressing the fish prices further.

One enterprising skipper, who'd caught a huge haul of cod early in the week and was hoping the inspectorate wouldn't be expecting any landings, had arranged for a 'sentry' to sit in a vehicle close to the chief inspector's house for several hours during the night in case the man left home. The observer was armed with a mobile phone, ready, if necessary to give notice of a potential visit, while the crew loaded the bumper catch into a waiting lorry.

Another skipper arrived in port, his crew topping the landing gear in the harbour entrance in readiness for a quick landing, only to find two officers waiting on the quay. He informed the inspectors that it was his intention to leave his fish below, tie his boat up across the harbour and move back to the fish market to discharge next morning, prior to the auction. The disgruntled policemen were going to have to wait most of the night before inspecting the catch. They could see the boat in total darkness lying starboard side to the pier, opposite the fish market, in full view of their office window. This vessel had to be berthed port side to the quay to land her catch.

What the inspectorate didn't realise was that at high water, the boat's deck was level with the pier and the shelter-deck shielded any activity from prying eyes across the harbour.

Some thirty or forty boxes of prime cod were pulled to the deck by hand from the illuminated fish-room and stacked on the darkened quayside.

The vessel's lights were then switched on and the boat crossed to a landing berth at the quay, to be greeted by grinning inspectors. The crew began to discharge their catch with no sign of cod, and the waiting men began to show impatience. When the final three boxes of fish arrived on the quayside the policemen were confused and not a little tetchy. Now the fishermen were grinning and one said, "that's the lot. There's nowt else t' come up," but then inadvertently looked across the harbour to where the few remaining boxes of cod were being quickly and unceremoniously thrown into the back of a van. The furious officials headed round the harbour at best speed but arrived breathless as the vehicle pulled away.

This game of cat and mouse couldn't last. Someone was going to get caught. My phone rang at home on Thursday morning at about 0500 hours. I'd not been asleep long, having recently landed our catch. It was a while before my dull brain came to life, but eventually I reached for the handset. It was Ian, Bluey's temporary skipper.

"'Ullo," I said with croaky voice and fuddled brain.

"Fred, it's Ian, we've just been caught by t' bogeyman landing twenty boxes o' cod."

I was immediately awake. "OK, ah'll be down in a few minutes," I replied. "Don't worry, it was bound to 'appen," I added, attempting to reassure him, but knew this was going to be serious.

There was no sign of the inspector when I arrived on the pier ten minutes later but the twenty boxes of fish were stacked and sheeted over with a large synthetic cover.

"E's jus' gone t' ring 'is boss," Ian said, glumly.

Irrationally I said, "Right, quick, lets get rid o' t' evidence."

Willing hands pulled the sheet from the cod and someone slid open the market doors leading to the back of the pier, allowing the boxes to be quickly stacked in a nearby baiting shed. Twenty empty boxes were piled up and the cover dragged back over the stack, which again was not a good idea but seemed so at that moment. Everyone continued their work cleaning the boat and replenishing its store of clean boxes ready for the next voyage. I stood on the deck talking to Ian and awaiting developments.

The tall, balding, bespectacled official arrived back and immediately noticed his sheeting had been tampered with. Lifting the corner of the cover, the man was incandescent with rage on discovering his proof had disappeared and hurriedly scoured the market searching for the lost fish before coming to the boat and asking where the cod had gone.

Of course no one had any idea what he was talking about.

"You've only made it worse for yourselves," he stated as he stormed from the pier to get the District Inspector from his bed once more.

I returned home but couldn't sleep, running the sequence of events through my mind. On arriving at the pier next morning I was quickly informed by Terry, our agent that both Ian and I were 'in the shit' and we could either voluntarily agree to meet the inspector for an interview at an agreed time, or we would be legally obliged to do so in due course. We opted for the former.

At the appointed time on the following Friday morning we arrived at the local fishery office for our separate interviews. This official interrogation was to be conducted by an unknown official from the MAFF head office in London. I opted to be first in the firing line, entering the inner office to see a small, thin faced, snipe nosed man with unblinking, poker player's eyes, sitting behind the desk.

At his side was Mike, one of the local assistant fisheries officers, nicknamed 'Pavarotti' by fishermen, due to his build and beard, though not usually to his face. Mike at least, tried to be sociable with an attempt at small talk.

The pair didn't know at this point that we'd decided to own up to the offence and plead guilty, aware that the Court would always find in favour of authority and we'd be forever persecuted in the unlikely event that we won.

The proceedings commenced with a formal caution by the officer just as I'd seen on police programmes on television. The junior officer laboriously recorded the questions relating to the event and my subsequent answers, word for word. Every page of writing was underlined with pen and a ruler below the transcription to prevent additional material being added at a later date.

The inquisition was intense and unpleasant. At the end of the hour long interview I was asked to read the document and sign each page as a true record of the proceedings. This was serious stuff. We were going to be the example that would deter others from attempting to land unrecorded cod for the remainder of the year.

I insisted that the instruction and responsibility to remove the fish from the pier was entirely mine, but of course this didn't absolve Ian from landing the alleged illegal cod in the first instance. "Where is Mr Sheader?" the diminutive official asked as my grilling came to an end. "He'll have to be interviewed."

"Yer'll 'ave t' get on an aeroplane," I replied, finding some humour for the first time in the day. "'E's in America."

Without a hint of expression the wooden character replied, "As joint owner of the vessel he is also implicated in this alleged offence, whether abroad or not. Even if he's totally ignorant of the situation he must undergo an interview on his return. Please tell him to get in touch with his local inspector."

What a welcome home Bluey was going to get, but at least his holiday would be untroubled.

"What 'appens now?" I asked, as I stood to leave. "Who decides if we get prosecuted?"

"I'll submit my findings to my superior and he will make his decision," the poker faced inspector replied. He may as well have said, "We're going to prosecute you."

Mike surreptitiously winked as I moved to the door. He'd been a fisherman when younger and was a decent bloke and didn't enjoy being a policeman. This officer had got the last laugh on a young Scot's skipper, fishing from Scarborough who persisted in calling him 'Pavarotti'. When the skipper's boat missed the harbour entrance for some unknown reason, running aground undamaged by the Spa Wall, close to some big stones, Mike's subsequent remark to the skipper, "you were 'scotch on the rocks, yesterday," stopped any further 'Pavarotti' remarks from the young skipper.

I waited in the adjacent room while Ian faced a similar grilling. He reappeared forty-five minutes later looking pale. We were free to go and though we weren't informed that the Court House was looming, there was no doubt in my mind.

The summons came a couple of weeks later and gave the option of appearing in the Magistrates Court or Crown Court, the latter being for more serious offences. We took advice from our friendly Dickensian lawyer Stephen and opted for the local court, hoping for a lower profile case.

"You'll get fined ten percent of the prescribed maximum fine for a first offence," my friend from the Magistrates Court said in the pub after our five a side football on Saturday night.

"Ah thought there was a maximum fine that Magistrates could levy?" I countered, hoping for some insight into the proceedings.

"The law states that there's a maximum fine, but with a rider that says, 'or whatever sum is prescribed'," he replied grimly.

"That's not fair," I said, a little too loudly.

"When you get to the building, look what it says over the door. It doesn't say, 'Fair Court' it says, 'Law Court' and before you ask, I won't be going near that particular Court Room on the day you're there. It'll be one of my associates who'll be taking the case."

So that was what we'd get. Ten percent of the £50,000 maximum fine was £5,000. If only it had turned out that way.

Weeks later the three of us, dressed in our best gear sat in the lobby of the Court House among several of the town's habitual criminals and hard cases, waiting to be called. Our boats were tied up and the crews not earning while our case was being heard. Half an hour later we stood side by side in the dock like criminals, facing the three magistrates. A posse of MAFF men, including the local inspector who'd made the original report, were also present to enjoy their 'day in court'. The Chairwoman, slight, with short straight, grey hair and clad in a brown square patterned tweed suit had a thin, severe, frosted face and looked at us with total disdain. On either side of the lady were elderly males, both bespectacled and wearing suits with similar ties, though one's glasses were perched precariously on the end of his nose like a wise owl. These pillars of society were to decide our fate. I wasn't confident, but at least I had a good idea of the outcome.

The charges were read out clearly by the unfamiliar, black-robed clerk and he asked each of us how we pleaded.

"Guilty." We replied in turn.

Our case wasn't helped when the Bench heard from the prosecution that the fish evidence had gone 'missing'. The Chairperson raised her nose as if there was a bad crab present, showing her disapproval.

Stephen, our representative, mitigating on our behalf said the fish that had been caught were already dead and to throw them back was not only senseless but also immoral. He pleaded that the vessel was almost new, costing a huge amount and that her monthly repayments were astronomic. Our brief went on to say that we couldn't land cod now until January and that our revenue would be greatly reduced, through no fault of our own.

Having heard the prosecution's case and our guilty plea and mitigation, the Court rose and the Bench retired to consider their judgement. "We'll get a five thousand quid fine and probably some costs," I said to my accomplices confidently. "It'll be tough for a while, but we should get some time t' pay."

Forty long minutes passed before a bell sounded and the clerk called, "All rise."

Our peers returned to the courtroom looking stern to pronounce our sentence. When the trio had settled on their perches and silence reigned, Mrs Bad Crab cleared her throat. "We have taken into consideration your early, guilty plea. We have also considered your circumstances and that for each of you this is a first offence. This said, we have decided that each of you will be fined £5000.

"Each of us?" I spluttered quietly to my fellow criminals.

The battleaxe hadn't finished yet. "Furthermore, each of you will pay £500 towards the prosecution's costs."

I was totting up the amounts in my head as the proceedings went on and had reached £16,500. "That's outrageous," I whispered through gritted teeth.

There was still more to come. "We take a dim view of the boxes of fish going missing and fine you jointly a further £1000 for the value of the aforesaid fish. We expect this total fine to be paid within one year," was the final insult.

As we left our positions and headed for the door I glared at the Fisheries Officers. "Seventeen an' a 'alf thousand quid. I 'ope you're bloody 'appy now. Is that what yer call justice? We've been well an' truly shafted." I barked my anger at the silent policemen, who seemed as stunned as we were at the severity of the penalty.

As soon as we were out of the Court Room I said to my companions, "If we'd 'ave nicked the bloody fish we'd 'ave been fined a couple of 'undred quid." I felt totally betrayed by the judicial system. We'd certainly been made an example of. The gloves were well and truly off. We'd be landing no more cod for the remainder of the year. Those who did would be extra cautious.

CHAPTER 14

POTTING

I'd been thinking about the large number of lobsters we'd caught while diving off the Humber, so the following spring, after more quota reductions had been introduced, and still smarting from the injustice of the court case, I decided to try working pots in the area where we'd spent our summer expedition. This was a radical change for *Emulator,* as we'd have to acquire a large number of pots, fit a pot hauler and davit and locate some portable deck tanks to keep the live lobsters in. I hadn't been potting since I was with Dad in his coble *Alison* when I was eighteen. The sonar would be a boon as there were many uncharted wrecks off the Humber, as well as those marked on the computer readout we'd sourced from the Hydrographic Department. These were all identified on the admiralty charts. There would be others yet to be discovered. The computer readout gave the names of the wrecks when known and the details and date of the sinking, plus the orientation and depth. This area from North Norfolk to the Humber is a vast expanse of water, littered with debris and was hardly ever fished.

I ordered two hundred large, plastic-coated, metal parlour pot frames from a company in West Yorkshire and some black 70-millimetre sheet netting to cover the tops and ends of the pots. Unlike conventional pots with two tapered entrances, or 'spouts' the parlour type had a third, internal spout leading into a separate compartment within the pot, where it was almost impossible for the creatures to escape from, once caught.

Dad spent several weeks of his spare time cutting up old trawl netting into the correct width of meshes, then constructing sets of spouts, two small entrance openings and the larger, parlour spout. Ever studious, Eddie, our net mender devised a simple, labour-saving method of hitching the spouts in place at the same time as the cover netting was secured.

For the remaining weeks prior to changing over from trawling we took a number of bare frames to sea each trip, returning with completed pots, assembled by the watch-keeper in the wheelhouse or the crew during any extended down time, working around the cabin table. This enforced labour didn't find universal favour, but it was the only way to ensure we obtained the required number of pots quickly. I assembled many at home on the rug-covered coffee table, though didn't expect anyone else to take frames home. As a lad I'd made lots of smaller pots for my Dad, braiding all the netting and taking at least three hours for each. Now, with the prefabricated spouts and sheet netting, I could complete a pot in about an hour and fifty minutes.

Nearer the time, a delivery of twenty coils of 16-millimetre rope arrived. These were cut into ten-fathom lengths and would join the individual pots into fleets of eight. Heavy four-pronged anchors for the ends of each fleet were acquired and polystyrene marker buoys assembled on stout canes with red or black flags attached, indicating north or south on each fleet. We were soon to discover that when fishing in busy shipping lanes we'd lose many of these buoys, some ships actually steering at the markers. A plastic five-gallon oil drum was initially substituted when we had no replacement buoys aboard, then realised that oil drums were free, more buoyant and readily available and these soon became the norm.

We sailed on Saturday evening heading for the Dowsing, catching the flowing tide, which would make a huge difference to the sixty-five mile overnight passage. Stowed below in the fish-room were several frozen blocks of horse mackerel, which we were to use for bait.

The sun was making its appearance when we slowed to half speed and switched on the sonar. The lads on deck had assembled and baited four fleets of pots, all fastened to the new rope ready for deploying and were now awaiting instructions. The pots would have to be shot with the tide to keep the rope taut through the wreckage, as slack line would wash about on the bottom and become tangled in the debris. It was to be trial and error gauging the strength of the tide to hit the wreck with the middle pots of the fleet. The first sunken ship we were to shoot our gear on was the *Dromore Castle*. This ship, 412 feet in length and 5,242 tons was sunk, like the *Fireglow* and several other ships in the area by mines in December 1941, but not dispersed until 1949. When I'd dived on this wreck the previous year there was only scrap iron plate strewn around the seabed and it was impossible to appreciate that this had ever been a ship.

We now had a new Decca Mark 53 navigator which, as well as giving a Decca readout also converted this data into latitude and longitude, though the machine only updated this reading every eight seconds. It was quite frustrating initially, holding the required longitude, shooting north with the now ebbing tide. I watched the latitude readout increasing to where I thought we should let go the buoy and anchor, only to see the wreck on the sounder and realise I'd missed the moment. Three attempts later I gauged the distance correctly and shouted, "leggo."

By late afternoon we had gear shot on a dozen wrecks including the dispersed *Antiope* 4545 tons, and several others that we'd dived the previously. A pack of plain postcards in a plastic box was my record of fleet locations and I numbered, and when possible, named the wrecks we were shot on. I couldn't wait to haul the pots back to see if the investment and effort had been worthwhile. Hopefully, we were on pay.

The next few hours were spent scouting for other sunken vessels from the hydrographic data. Some were found easily, the sonar reflecting loudly, while others were not located at all. These undiscovered ships must have been smashed to smithereens, lost under the shifting sands, or were not in the positions given. The lads were already lifting more pots from the fish-room. When time allowed, these would be assembled into fleets to hit the new targets.

We'd completed a good day's work and dinner was ready. *Emulator* was now heading back to the first fleet we'd shot. While Sean took over in the wheelhouse in the busy shipping lanes I sat and enjoyed the filling meal. "After dinner we'll go back t' first fleet we shot an' see if there's owt in it," I announced to the three men sitting around the table.

This decision found favour, as the lads were as curious as I was to see some results. Dodging into the tide there was no difficulty in getting hold of the downstream buoy with a small grapnel, spliced in the end of a light line. The anchor on the end tow was quickly pulled to the surface by the grooved wheel of the hauler. It was important to keep *Emulator* dodging into the tide with the rope leading slightly off the boat's side and almost up and down so the pots were plucked cleanly from the wreck and not dragged into the wreckage to become snagged.

The first pot came up and contained two good-sized lobsters, both located in the parlour, each would weigh about 2 pounds. The next pot contained two more of the creatures but these were slightly bigger. I was now marking the wreck on the sounder and excitedly watching for number three in the fleet to appear. This was like Christmas, not knowing what was in the next parcel. Kevin, standing at the boat's side lifting the pots inboard excitedly yelled, "Bloody 'ell, look at this bugger, it's full!"

The inside of the third creel was just a mass of crawling black creatures and they were huge. I couldn't assess the number of lobsters contained from my vantage point, even when craning my neck out of the wheelhouse window but there must have been four or five big specimens and some of these must have weighed 5 or 6 pounds each. The next pot contained another good quantity then the results began to taper off again as we moved further from the wreck. It seemed the giant lobsters were kings of the wreck and the lower order lived on the fringes. The net result was twenty lobsters from this one fleet but these creatures more than filled a fish box. Their combined weight must have been more than 60 pounds. *Emulator* was quickly turned and lined up for the wreck and the pots shot back accurately. I was getting the hang of hitting the wrecks now and this was an encouraging start.

We prepared a couple more fleets then spent the night outside the buoyed channel in sufficient water for safe navigation, taking spells to man the wheelhouse till first light when, following a big fried breakfast we began hauling our gear again. The results were equally as good on every wreck as we'd experienced on the previous evening. The biggest lobsters were living in the heart of the wreck and the smaller sized specimens on the periphery. By evening we'd hauled all the gear, shot pots in four additional wrecks and were on our way to Scarborough. Our deck tanks were almost full of lobsters plus we had several boxes of crabs, covered by wet bags and stacked where the overflow from the tanks would keep them moist as the boat rolled. The downside of fishing in this area was that it would be morning before we reached home and there'd be no point in turning straight round after landing the catch, as it would be dark when we arrived back on location. At least the pots were fishing in our absence.

Edwin Jenkinson, universally known as 'Sailor' a portly, pale-faced, lugubrious, balding Filey man was standing on the quay waiting for us as we tied up alongside. There were so many families of Jenkinsons fishing in cobles from Filey that they all had nicknames to prevent confusion. Even the schoolteachers in their classrooms used these nicknames and this was accepted without any fuss. Trab, Snosh, Tint and Dilt were all Jenkinsons in the Filey fishing industry and there were many others. The family name was so widespread a local resident had published a book entitled, 'The Jenkinsons of Filey'.

A former coble fisherman who launched from the beach at Filey, Edwin was now a fish merchant and shellfish dealer and was buying our catch. He was pleased to handle our lobsters and paid a fair price, though was less enthusiastic about our boxes of crabs. "They're all full o' watta at this time o' year," he said mournfully, pulling at the few strands of hair combed across his head. "There's nowt in 'em. Ah on'y get a bit o' meat out o' claws. Ah don't really want yer crabs."

Pleased with our results we sailed again overnight on Tuesday, once more arriving at sunrise, keen to see what the pots had caught in our absence, knowing the gear had now been left for two nights.

The results from the wrecks we'd worked before were still very good, though the average size of the lobsters had reduced slightly. The wrecks would have to be rested and visited infrequently if we were to continue this mode of fishing. There was no shortage of sites to exploit. "These next few fleets should be good," I called out to the lads on deck. "These are t' new wrecks that we found last trip. Ah reckon these pots should be full o' lobsters."

Indeed, the first couple of pots gave excellent results and we were optimistic of a record yield from this fleet but then disaster struck. It was carnage. Inside the third, fourth and fifth pots there remained only one large, living lobster and the remains of many others. These creatures were not just dead; they had been broken and torn to pieces. With the bait gone, the territorial creatures had turned on each other with calamitous results. The fighting must have been spectacular but grisly. There was a major lesson to be learned here for us. We must never again leave pots on any new wrecks for more than one night or we'd only get the winner in each cage.

We had a good day of fishing despite these losses and again had time to find new locations, though I was both surprised and disappointed when looking for the two biggest shipwrecks in the region. *Ahamo* was an 8,600-ton tanker, sunk by a mine in April 1941 in a relatively shallow section of the shipping lane. Two months later *Fleet Tender C,* a converted carrier of almost 4000 tons was torpedoed by a German E boat and somehow became stranded on the wreck of the *Ahamo.* Both ships were total losses and as hazards to shipping were initially dispersed by bombing in September of that year. This job was completed more effectively in 1949.

Now I could find virtually no trace of either ship. The scrap, which should have been ideal territory for lobsters had completely vanished apart from a few isolated bits of shady ground on the sounder on top of the sandbank. Of the combined deadweight of over twelve thousand tons, nothing at all remained above the seabed. The dispersed ships had been completely swallowed up. It seemed that the deeper the water, the more likely the wreck would be intact.

186

We now had gear on twenty wrecks, including some that had been huge ships when afloat. These vessels were now mostly smashed and unrecognisable, the remains strewn wide and standing only a couple of fathoms above the seabed. Over the past few days we had lost a few pots that had snagged in the wreckage. We could only haul until eventually the pot rope parted. This was inevitable though I quickly learned not to haul from the other end of the fleet until the tide turned. The remaining pots were better left, as hauling with the tide only created more losses. It was very sad that any crabs and lobsters in the lost pots would be captive forever.

"We're losin' a lot o' time steamin' 'ome an' back," I said to Edwin when we next landed back in Scarborough. "It teks thirty-six hours each time."

"Why don't yer land in Grimsby? Me an' Richard 'll drive there an' pick yer stuff up," he offered.

"That's a great idea," I said, though we'd still be faced with a four hour steam each way from our nearest fleet of pots to the Lincolnshire port, and the dock was only open for two hours either side of high water. We wouldn't be able to stay in the port for long, but we'd take that opportunity in future when the tides were favourable.

Entering harbour on Friday morning after the usual overnight passage I couldn't fail to notice a sleek, gleaming white, forty-five foot GRP* cruiser with a for'ard wheelhouse, berthed on the North Wharf. This had to be *Perception*. Her owner, Simon Barningham had commissioned this new build to replace his former vessel *Sagacity*, which had proved inadequate for his needs.

Simon, a stocky, tousle haired, red-faced, pleasant character was not cast in the mould of the average fisherman. His accent was more from the countryside than the 'Bottom End'. Originally he'd been a bookmaker with a love of angling and had owned a small, wooden craft in the outer harbour. With the development of more accurate navigation equipment he'd been able to target local wrecks consistently and had made some amazing catches. Realising there was a living to be made doing something he enjoyed, Simon had

---

*   GRP glass reinforced plastic, commonly known as fibreglass.

built *Sagacity*, a faster, lighter, thirty three foot GRP vessel to enable him to work further offshore. Carrying only one other deckhand, and frequently this was his attractive, raven-haired wife Janet, their results, using only rods and lines were excellent. Sometimes they were bringing in upwards of 100 stone of good cod, though working many miles offshore, the little vessel occasionally got a pasting on her homeward passages.

This pioneering venture had quickly led to his latest vessel. Several wannabees had tried to emulate Simon's success but all had fallen by the wayside. These challengers either lacked the ability to find the wrecks consistently and plot the tidal flow across the lost ships, or hadn't the strength and resilience to pull string after string of big fish to the surface from deep water. I was well aware of what stamina this took from our short periods of wreck fishing during diving trips. I wouldn't want to earn a living this way. Simon relished the challenge.

In this new vessel he was to work even further offshore, sometimes more than a hundred miles from home and would stay overnight. On the open deck he began carrying insulated plastic tubs holding ice to keep his catch at peak freshness, commanding premium prices for the pristine, hand caught fish. Simon would work far offshore and make friends with several Danes, also fishing on the wrecks with gillnets. These men were also amazed by the tenacity of the angler.

As Simon continued pushing the boundaries, the intrepid angler lost his stocky figure, becoming leaner and wirier, the long, rough, fast passages and uncomfortable nights taking their toll. Then one day, suddenly and inexplicably, Simon Barningham died. His funeral was attended by scores of people that had respected his pioneering spirit, including some of his Danish friends. No one took up his mantle, and as cod quotas reduced, the opportunity of hand lining for this species was no longer available to anyone with sufficient will.

* * * * * *

There was something wrong when we arrived back to our gear after the weekend. The pots that were supposed to be on the *Fireglow* were not on the wreck and the buoys were too close together. "Some bugger's 'auled these," I declared as we approached to pick up the down tide buoy. This prediction proved correct when the first pot came to the surface. Not only was this creel empty, the door had been left open and the other pots were in a tangled heap, just below the surface. This bunch of creels was pulled up and held alongside as I dodged *Emulator* into the tide, easing the load on the rope against the retaining anchor. With much effort, the lads on deck selected and cut each pot lose from the hauling line as it came into reach. When the gear was successfully recovered, the line was untangled then new strops were hitched on to each pot. The whole string was then reassembled and redeployed. This exercise was extremely time consuming and so unjust. I was seething with anger.

"The bastards, the thievin' bastards," were the only words I could find. The pleasure of knowing what was in the pots had been taken away; replaced with the knowledge that someone had stolen part of our livelihood in our absence. Had this been an isolated incident it would have been bad enough, but the day went progressively downhill. Of our twenty fleets, two had been interfered with and emptied but worse, two more strings were missing altogether. I was now incandescent. Not only at the loss of income, we'd lost twenty percent of our day's pay, but that these totally inconsiderate scum were also stealing our means of making a living. Each pot was a cost and took some considerable time to construct. Though we could replace the lost gear from our remaining supply of spare gear below, this was fast diminishing and meant we couldn't shoot on any additional wrecks.

There were no problems the following day and no sign of any bandits, so the gear was intact and the catch improved. Though still angry, there was nothing to be done and with all the gear back in position we headed for Grimsby and a rendezvous with Edwin.

It was still daylight as we passed Spurn Point and a familiar voice came over on the VHF radio. "*Emulator, Emulator,* is that you just passin' Spurn, Nommy?"

Recognising the voice of Brian Bevan, the much-decorated Coxswain of the Humber Lifeboat, I reached for the handset.

"Hiya Bri. Yeh, that's us, inbound fo' Grimsby. 'Ow's things wi' you? Ah see yer still livin' in solitude."

Spurn Point is the southernmost tip of the Yorkshire Coast and these shallow, treacherous waters are far from the nearest habitation, requiring a permanent lifeboat crew to be located on the isolated peninsular. These men and their families were the only inhabitants on this long strip of sand, apart from migrating birds that stopped in huge numbers at this landmark sanctuary.

"Yer must 'ave a good trip o' fish aboard if yer goin' in t' Grimsby. Where 'ave yer been workin'?" Brian had a good knowledge of the fishing grounds, having worked on boats in Bridlington and Scarborough for several years before joining the lifeboat service.

He was quite surprised when I said we were not trawling but potting out to the east and southeast of the river. We were going into the Humber port to land our catch directly into Edwin's van on the quayside, intending to come back out again immediately. Bri' expressed his disgust when I told him about our losses but then on a more positive note said, "If yer could get Edwin t' pick yer stuff up at Spurn, some of our lads would bring yer boxes ashore for yer. We 'ave a little coble that we use for pottin' close to t' coast when it's fine weather. It would be quicker an' cheaper for yer than goin' t' Grimsby."

This was an even better idea. We could save an hour steaming each way from Spurn to Grimsby, plus we'd have no dock dues to pay and we could land in the Spurn bight at any state of the tide. It would depend on Edwin. If he was willing, we could do this in future, but the drive to Spurn Point wasn't an easy run. The road was narrow and meandering, even reducing to single track in places. I arranged to ring Brian when I'd spoken to Edwin about this possibility.

Tied up alongside the North Wall in the vast Grimsby Dock, we began passing the boxes of lobsters onto the quayside, where a reasonably happy Edwin and his quiet but willing assistant Richard took the plastic containers, stacking them gently in the van. "These lobsters seem dopey," Edwin mumbled, his impassive face beginning to frown. "There's summat wrong with 'em."

He was quite right. The lobsters were lethargic and not flapping their tails or moving their claws. Edwin nipped one of the creatures at the end of its tail with thumb and forefinger and the lobster flapped its tail, though not vigorously. "They might liven up when we get 'em in t' tanks back at 'ome, but yer can 'ave t' dead 'uns back."

When we passed some boxes of crabs his face fell further. "Ah'll tek 'em, but ah don't really want 'em," he mumbled.

Their van loaded, the pair wasted no time in pleasantries. The doors slammed, a three-point turn was executed and the vehicle headed towards the dock exit and the road north. There'd been no time to mention possibly landing at Spurn. We were in no rush to leave so decided to have our evening meal before departure. The dock gates wouldn't be closing for sometime yet.

The obvious reason for the lobsters lethargic state struck me. "It'll be t' river water," I exclaimed to anyone in earshot. "We've steamed up river against t' ebbing tide and we've 'ad t' 'osepipe pouring int' t' lobster tanks. It'll be mostly fresh water, not seawater. They'll live longer out o' t' water. Lets 'ope they perk up again."

To our great relief, on our return home we discovered that Edwin had managed to save virtually all the lobsters and our loss was insignificant.

"What are you lot up to?" asked a stout, bearded man as he approached out of the setting sun; a huge grin spread across his weathered face.

Recognising Olaf Christiansen, the gentle giant, I returned the smile. This was a pal of many years and I was delighted to see him. The big fella had noticed our vessel in the dock and driven round to see us. We stood for a while reliving old tales and discussing mutual friends. When he asked about our current mode of fishing I told him of the success but also of our loss of gear and missing catch of the previous day.

"That makes some sense now," he said, nodding thoughtfully. "The *C------* landed some lobsters yesterday. The skipper, D---- and his crew dragged the baskets out of view fairly sharpish, but I saw 'em. He hasn't any pots in the sea as far as I know, and I wouldn't trust him as far as I could throw him."

Looking at Olaf, I thought he could probably throw this crook a considerable distance, preferably into the dock but I took this information on board and now knew who had stolen our gear and affected our livelihood. My old pal departed with a wave, saying he'd let me know if the suspected thief landed any more lobsters and we went on board to eat.

With our filling meal over and the dishes washed up and stowed in their racks, the ropes were thrown off and *Emulator* was manoeuvred through the narrow concrete dock entrance into the dark river to follow the buoyed channel to the sea. With the engine at less than half speed we were swept along at a good speed on the ebbing tide back towards our pots. There would still be a few hours to kill before the dawn.

Daylight came and work commenced. Having hauled and replaced three fleets into the same locations, we had about four miles to steam to the next wreck. A small target was showing clearly on the radar at about this distance. As we drew nearer it became apparent that this blip was a small, decked boat in the vicinity of our gear. The weather was flat calm and as we drew nearer I picked up the binoculars, highlighting a black and red-hulled craft lying stopped in the water. On reading this boat's port letters and numbers and checking these in the 'Fishermen's Almanac' I realised this was the vessel, *C-----*.

The rage I'd felt on finding our gear hauled and missing flooded back and I shouted to the lads on the deck, "that's the bastard that's been 'auling our pots." I couldn't wait to get to this boat and fervently hoped the crooks wouldn't steam away.

Strangely, the boat didn't move off as we drew closer and I eased the engine down on approach, giving her a huge surge of power astern, throwing a cloud of black smoke skywards from the exhaust. *Emulator* came to a standstill about ten yards from the smaller craft. The three unsavoury characters aboard the vessel were looking in our direction. My four crewmen, three of them big strapping men, were leaning outboard from *Emulator's* side, their anger as great as mine.

"Put us alongside the bastards, Ah'll pull their fuckin' 'eads off," one of them bawled loudly. The others concurred.

I leaned out of the window as far as possible and bawled, "you've been 'aulin' our gear yer thievin' bastards. If yer so much as look at any more of our pots, ah'll fuckin' sink yer, an' that's a promise. Keep yer thievin' 'ands off 'em."

Looking guilty as sin but no longer making eye contact and without a word, one of the trio made his way to the little wheelhouse and engaged the engine, directing his vessel away from our position and towards land. He'd got the message in no uncertain terms. There was no way the thief would admit to his crime and I'd no proof of his theft so our lost pots wouldn't be recovered, but our gear would never be pirated again for the remaining time we were potting.

This period of grace was cut short, for a few weeks later, having landed several times at Spurn Point, anchoring in the lee of the headland, our lobster catches reduced dramatically, despite our finding new wrecks. This was the time of year when the creatures in this region holed up to cast off their shells. As we caught fewer lobsters we seemed to catch more and more crabs and our merchant became disgruntled. "Ah keep tellin' yer, ah don't want yer crabs. Ah's on'y tekin 'em t' get yer lobsters an' there aren't many o' them these days."

It was the end of our potting experience for the time being. The boats to nor'ard were making a bare living trawling, catching mostly whiting and haddock while trying to avoid cod and working within the restricted quotas. Reluctantly we hauled our remaining gear, stowing the pots below and returned home to convert *Emulator* back to trawling, though I was now aware of a potential alternative fishery. To pursue the job properly off the Humber, a faster, more manoeuvrable vessel was needed. Would this be something for the future?

We fished on, doing our best to avoid cod, of which we were only allocated a few boxes each week and scratched a living catching mostly haddock, whiting and other species, though the quota on haddock was tight. There was a desperate need of more fish quota. The slow starvation was affecting everyone. The fleet's earnings were well down on the previous year in the port. Seven boats had been sold recently, some given up by men who wanted out of the unprofitable industry while others were selling their large vessels and quotas to downsize, buying smaller boats. The government, in its wisdom had deemed that vessels under ten metres in length were not a threat to fish stocks and allowed these craft to fish free against a separate, plentiful government quota.

Ever ingenious, fishermen began to build vessels under ten metres, trawling with large horsepower engines to exploit this loophole. For many, this was a route to freedom from regulations, but some of these overpowered, sometimes unstable 'rule-beaters' would be lost, with fatal consequences.

In the years to come the under ten metre fleet, with their separate government administered quota would increase from hundreds of boats to thousands, as skippers jumped on the 'free fishing' bandwagon, eventually causing slow starvation in this type of vessel also.

The New Year didn't bring any comfort, only further cuts in quotas for those still remaining. The NFFO began lobbying the government for a decommissioning scheme to bring the fleet in line with the fish available, but there was little enthusiasm from Whitehall.

To their credit, the government had taken about a hundred large, foreign-owned vessels based abroad, from the British registry. This at least would help to conserve fish for the UK fleet. These ships had been sold abroad and the new owners had retained their UK registration numbers, so were eligible to fish against British quotas. These were predominantly Spanish owned craft, fishing in the western approaches, though a few belonged to northern European companies and fished the North Sea.

These vessels, known as 'flag of convenience vessels' or 'flagships' were laid up until huge Spanish pressure was brought to bear on

Britain through the European Court. Forced to capitulate, then to pay massive damages for loss of earnings and access to these owners, our government seemed to give up the ghost on its fishing industry.

CHAPTER 15

A SPECIAL BIRTHDAY

The clock had passed midnight and it was now Thursday, but not just any Thursday. Today was my fortieth birthday. We were on our way home with a good trip of fish onboard and I was looking forward to a special weekend. We'd be in harbour soon and there was plenty of time to get the catch on the market, replenish the boxes and for a few hours kip at home before breakfast. The Crescent Hotel was reserved for the following evening for a party with family and friends. It was sure to be a cracking night.

Not long after 0400 hours, showered and with my stinking, discarded clothes dumped in the laundry bin, I was on my way to bed. Not for the first time I thought how strange it was that these clothes didn't smell at all when I was on board the boat and neither did any of the crew's garb. In a pile on the bathroom floor, my dirty clothing stunk.

"Happy birthday," said a very sleepy Dotty as I climbed into bed beside her.

"Thank you," I replied. I was still wide-awake and I'd be ages winding down before nodding off.

Rat tat tat went the knocker on the front door. The heavy, brass dolphin banged loudly. It was daylight, but still early. "Who the bloody 'ell's that at this time o' mornin', an' don't they know we 'ave a doorbell?" I snapped at the rude awakening.

"You stay in bed. I'll see who it is," Dotty said, donning her dressing gown and heading for the stairs.

I heard the door open and words exchanged, then Dotty's raised voice saying, "our cars" and "our wall" then "go away." The door slammed loudly, causing the knocker to bang with the force.

On her return I said, "What was that all about?"

"It's a man with a clip board and a hardhat. There's another one in a big yellow digger. He asked if we could we move our cars. He wants to knock our wall down and had the cheek to say, go and get your husband. Who does he think runs the house while you're at sea all week? I told him to go away."

There must be some mistake, I thought. The land adjacent to our house was officially still on the market, though there was a preferred bidder. He intended to develop not only this land, but also my old school beyond the plot and the workshops opposite. We'd made an offer for the land in the hope of preventing our home being overlooked by a terrace of new houses, but were not optimistic. We were not property developers. Meanwhile this new departure was an unforeseen threat. The Council hadn't accepted any bids or approved any plans as far as we were aware. There must be a mistake. Hopefully the workmen had gone away.

Rat tat tat, rat tat tat, went the knocker again, and if possible sounded even louder.

"Righto, ah'll tell the buggers," I growled. "I was 'oping for a good day t'day, but it 'asn't started very well." I grabbed a pair of clean jeans from the cupboard, pulled them on, then bare-footed and bare-chested, stormed down the stairs, opening the door swiftly, expecting to see the foreman on the threshold. Instead I saw the man's head wearing a white hardhat looking up at me through the railings. He was standing on the lower level of the steps, peering up in my direction. Was he expecting me to open the door with fists flying?

"Ah Mr Normandale," said the tall young man, safe behind the metal frame. "Can you move these cars? We want to drop this wall." He repeated the request he'd made to Dotty, pointing to the ten-foot high retaining wall supporting the land on the hill above our house.

His associate, a big, brawny man clad in overalls and obligatory hardhat had climbed from his excavator leaving the engine running and was now pressing on the front end of the old yellow car, rocking the suspension as if assessing his ability to move the vehicle. The conspicuous, 'Vauxhall Chevette' was Paula's pride and joy and was personalised with a huge, black-painted, red-eyed bat covering the entire bonnet.

As if on cue Paula's bedroom window shot open and leaning from the void, our daughter joined in the row loudly. "That's my car. Keep off it," she shouted at the driver, pointing to her batmobile.

I was angry now and addressing the foreman said, "look mate, that's our wall, they're our cars, now fuck off."

The man went red in the face and looked quite flustered. Hearing another voice from his right near the corner of the house the foreman turned in the direction of the sound. A look of relief spread across his face when he spotted Chris Coole and Terry Pearson grinning from ear to ear, the former brandishing a bottle of rum. Others joined the pair and the group burst into a loud, "Happy birthday to you."

"You bastards!" I yelled. "Yer've set me up. Ah've been well an' truly 'ad'. Ah knew you buggers were gonna do summat today, but ah thought ah was safe in bed."

This was an outrageous birthday spoof from my footballer pals. I was aware they'd do something crazy today, as I'd taken part in several wheezes myself when significant birthdays had arisen within the group, but I'd expected this to occur on board *Emulator* later in the day. I'd been asked by Terry the previous weekend to turn up at midday for a meeting with a TV reporter. Knowing this was my birthday I guessed I'd be letting myself in for a surprise.

The digger driver, who clearly hadn't been included in the prank was now leaning against his vehicle, plastic hat in hand, scratching his head and looking perplexed.

"It's OK mate, we've changed our minds. The job's off," Chris said to the confused workman, who'd been looking forward to some legal vandalism.

Another pair joined the company and I now recognised the foreman who'd banged on the door, starting the incident. In the absence of helmet, donkey jacket and clipboard he was Adam, an actor who was appearing at the Stephen Joseph Theatre for the season, now smiling and relaxed. His companion, Stephen Mallatratt was grinning like the Cheshire Cat. Seeing the pair in company, I put two and two together, immediately calculating that Stephen, who was an actor and playwright as well as a television writer, must have enlisted Adam to play this leading role.

Stephen was a friend who lived close by and who we'd met in the Leeds Arms some time ago. A tall, thin, tousle haired, quiet man, he was a real observer of human nature. This trait showed in his work when writing for the popular television programme Coronation Street, where we occasionally heard local expressions and familiar names spoken by the cast. Stephen had adapted the famous novel, 'Woman in Black' from the book by Susan Hill into a record-breaking stage show in London. At the show's sell out premiere in the small, former school-cum-theatre in Scarborough, he'd arranged for four additional chairs to be placed in the aisle for us, omitting to say these were situated in front of the sound system. When, during the performance one of the players gave an intense, shrill scream, Dotty almost hit the ceiling from a sitting position.

Having calmed down a little now, though still annoyed at my own gullibility, I congratulated the villains on their great spoof. I'd been taken in hook, line and sinker. Why didn't I stop and think? Now another pair of conspirators arrived and I learned they'd been filming the entire event from a house across the road and that I was in due course to be presented with a video recording of the day's events. This was a film Dotty would be unable to watch for years after, without her pulse racing.

The weather turned dull and wet during the morning, an early precursor to a stormy autumn. I went about my routine harbour business, talking to various tradesmen, asking each to address the problems listed on my job-sheet, in preparation for *Emulator's* next trip. Finally I visited the Alliance Office to settle the recent catch and calculate the crew's pay.

Terry couldn't avoid laughing when I put my head round his office doorway and said, "I thought you took it very well this morning, considering you hadn't been in bed long. Your face was a picture."

"I 'adn't much choice," I replied ruefully, "an' it was a great wheeze but remember, it's your turn next year. It'll be your big four '0,' an' ah'll be in on t'e act."

As I made to leave the building he called, "don't forget you've an appointment aboard your boat at twelve o'clock."

"Ah'll be there," I answered with a knowing grin. What else was in store?

The rain was torrential as I hurried along the North Wharf to where *Emulator* was berthed. I'd deliberately avoided visiting the boat during the morning in case I interrupted any preparations that may be taking place. Now as I stepped onto the wet starboard gunwale and looked under the shelter-deck, I realised my fears were groundless. Beneath the aluminium cover protected from the weather, a large crowd of friends, were congregated all holding charged glasses. A pair of trestle tables, laden with food and drink had been placed on the port side.

Another chorus of, 'happy birthday' began as I jumped across the stowed trawl to the deck, to be handed a glass of red wine. All the culprits from the morning prank were present plus others who couldn't make the appointed hour. Everyone on board had by now been informed of the morning's events and most had witty remarks to offer.

From within the group near the front of the wheelhouse, though not visible, a female voice called, "is that Mr Normandale?" Curious, I turned in the direction of the mystery voice and the men parted, revealing a real, live mermaid. On closer examination this apparition was a blond-haired delight, dressed in a green, scaly tailed outfit with matching bra, barely containing a magnificent cargo.

"Wow!" I declared at the eye feast. "There can't be many o' them in a pound."

To my amazement the fair maiden reached to her back and proceeded to unfetter her wonderful bosoms. Her top discarded, the lovely lady began to read a poem commencing, "Today's your birthday Mr Normandale, and I have come to say ..." but no one was listening. Everyone was looking.

Walking the few steps to the mermaid's position, I stooped and with no little effort lifted the damsel up into my arms. The blond fishy-lady put one of her arms around my neck for fear of being dropped, which brought her closer and was very pleasing.

"Be careful" she whispered, "I'm heavy."

"No yer not," I replied manfully, then announced to all present, "Ah don't think we 'ave a quota for these. Ah might 'ave t' throw 'er back."

Amid the laughter, and with dreadful timing, Dotty arrived at the vessel to be helped onboard and didn't appear too keen on my new friend. I felt compelled to gently return my well-endowed messenger to the deck then, sourcing a bottle and a couple of glasses poured my wife and the sporting lady a drink.

"She was nice," I said to Dotty, attempting conversation and feeling guilty of some unspecified crime, as we moved across the deck to the food.

"She was fat," retorted my wife.

Detecting bad vibrations, and feeling the need to change the topic of conversation I swiftly said, "that was a great spoof the lads played this morning."

This was also a sensitive topic. "I didn't find it funny at all. It was very upsetting."

Dotty's mood lightened when the lovely lady departed and with Terry and Chris in close proximity our conversation switched to other pranks that had been perpetrated over the years. We all laughed when recapping Brian, the magistrates' clerk's birthday celebration at the Rugby Club.

Robbo, the builder had spent a full day assembling a mock up wooden court dock, complete with stocks for wrists. At his party,

Brian had been persuaded to stand in the construction. Before he was aware of his peril the victim's hands were fastened securely in the stocks and the prisoner was secure. Lots of trumped up charges were levelled at the accused and he was found to be guilty of each offence. The plan was that the accusers would splash the guilty party with wallpaper paste as punishment. All the participants in the conspiracy had brought along different coloured goo. Instead of paste, I'd made a gallon of 'Strawberry Delight', a tasty, creamy pink dessert. Unfortunately for the victim, I'd missed the rehearsal in midweek and wasn't aware that I was only supposed to fleck a little of the product on the prisoner, and I was the first witness appearing for the prosecution.

Centre stage and entering into the role with enthusiasm, I accused the now worried man of persecuting poor, hardworking, innocent fishermen during the course of his daily business. "What happened to justice?" I asked the audience, remembering Brian's comment prior to our nightmare court case. "Guilty or not guilty?" I asked the baying crowd, all standing a safe distance from the unfolding events.

A resounding, enthusiastic, "guilty," echoed around the room.

With equal zeal I declared, "I sentence you to be gunged," then directed the entire contents of my bucket at the helpless victim. The ooze, reluctant to leave the container hit the poor chap full on the chest, splashing up to his chin and despite its viscosity, flew everywhere.

A huge gasp, then peels of laughter rang out from the observers as the enormity of my action was realised.

Variations of, "you were only supposed to use a little," came at me from several directions.

I could only hold up my hands and plead innocence. No one had told me I wasn't supposed to use the whole bucketful. After all, a precautionary plastic sheet had been placed on the floor.

Of course, my action gave carte blanche for what followed. The prisoner was accused of being a bandit at golf, a bad loser at football and even of having a big nose. On each occasion Brian was found guilty and given the same treatment, though amazingly, for someone fastened securely by the wrists, he managed to dodge the bulk of the slop on a couple of occasions. Even so, at the end of the performance the poor chap looked as if he'd emerged from a swamp.

To rousing cheers Brian was released from his clamp and exited in the direction of the club's shower room leaving a snail trail on the wooden floor. Fortunately a change of clothing had secretly been brought along for the occasion.

The onboard party didn't last too long. Most of those present had to return to work in the afternoon, though what would be achieved in the way of productivity with the amount of wine consumed was debateable. There was an evening event to look forward to yet.

Dotty and I along with our three bairns arrived at the Crescent Hotel in good time for the evening celebration where fifty guests, family and friends were to enjoy a sumptuous meal. To my surprise Chris Coole and Ian Marshall were already on the premises. Ian armed with a movie camera and Chris was dressed as Alan Whicker, the well-known television travel presenter, complete with false moustache and Australian bush hat with dangling corks. The pair approached our group and Chris, addressing Dotty, spoke into the microphone. "When did you first come in contact with Fred Normandale, Dorothy?"

Initially lost for words, Dotty stuttered a little, but then said, "I've never heard of him."

Of course when he asked our family, Danny said, " Ah've always known 'im, 'es me Dad."

Paula, matter of factly said, "I know who you are. You're the one who tried to move my car this morning."

Little Sarah, still holding her Mum's hand smiled sweetly at the camera. She was on television.

As the guests congregated in the bar prior to the meal this mischievous pair approached each in turn asking various questions along the same lines and of course receiving answers of a similar nature, all denying any knowledge of Fred Normandale.

"We always eat here."

"Who?"

"Never heard of him," were repeated over and again until the presenter, with no material to work with, faced the camera and said, "well there we have it. No one has heard of this person. We're clearly at the wrong venue. This is Alan Whicker in Scarborough, handing you back to the studio."

The excellent meal was served by cheerful, efficient staff, who also enjoyed the banter and good humour of the guests. But later, back in the bar, after the feast, I grew worried when the main participants in the mischievous capers of the morning disappeared up the stairs. Clearly there was more high jinx lined up. My anxiety heightened when a sheet of polythene was placed on the small wooden dance floor in the adjacent room.

Soon after, the partygoers were invited in to where half a dozen crusty seafarers, attired in oilskins, sea-boots and sou'westers and wearing false whiskers and beards, stood in a line, armed with song sheets. A chair was placed in the centre of the plastic sheet facing the unlikely choir and I was invited to sit.

"Here, take your shirt off and put this on," Brian said, grinning and handing me an old tee shirt. "It's more than you did for me, mate."

The motley crew began to clear their throats and tune up in various pitches and at different speeds before not so much bursting, as staggering into song. 'What shall we do with a drunken sailor' was the number they were murdering with naughty, amended words frequently interspersed. The chorus of 'Way hey and Nommy's 40, way hey and Nommy's 40,' featured regularly and everyone quickly picked up the lyrics and joined in. Initially I was lightly splashed with whatever drinks the singers were holding, mostly red wine but then audience participation meant I became wetter. Ray Trotter a fisherman friend of my age stepped forward holding a pint of beer while the singers continued their performance. "Ah've always wanted t' do this," he said grinning, then poured his full glass over my head, drenching not only the tee shirt but my suit trousers too. This stunt brought a huge laugh from the audience.

The singers ended their song to rapturous applause, which I was pleased join in. I'd been in enough birthday performances to know the effort and fun that went into pulling these stunts together, and it was pleasing that people had made the effort to give a friend a birthday to remember.

Late in the evening when most of the guests had taken their leave, the proprietor Paul said to Dotty and me, "there's a spare room if you want to stay the night, you're very welcome." This was certainly sporting considering the mess the guests had made of his floor. While accepting his offer, I mentioned the mess, which the plastic sheet had been unable to contain and offered to pay for the clean up.

"It's OK," he replied with a smile. "We're decorating next week. You don't think I'd have let that lot carry on like that any other time."

We awoke next morning following a dreamless sleep in the hotel's best suite and dressed to go for breakfast. My still wet, and now uncomfortable trousers were a stark reminder of a very memorable day.

For years after, whenever I jokingly mentioned to Paul at the Crescent that we were thinking of having a birthday party, he'd reply, "we're full."

* * * * * *

It was almost Christmas again and Dotty and I were in the Leeds Arms. The pub was very busy and there was a great atmosphere. Les and his barman Bill were rushed off their feet keeping glasses filled.

"Where's your Christmas decorations Les?" someone asked.

"I haven't got time to mess about with decorations. I'm far too busy keeping the place clean and the bar stocked, without that sort of stuff. They only collect dust."

"Bah humbug!" I said. "Where's your Christmas spirit?"

"The only spirit you'll get in here is out of those bottles on the top shelf," he replied, pointing upwards.

The more grumpy Les became, the more his customers ribbed him. "We could have a night singing carols," someone suggested.

"Not in my pub you couldn't," came the reply from over the bar. His assistant, a clone of his employer, concurred.

"What a misery Les is," I said to Dotty when we got home. "It would be really funny if there was a carol evening in the pub."

Paula, who'd been sitting up babysitting said, "I could make a poster advertising it."

This really wasn't a good idea but having had several beers it seemed like one at that moment and I agreed.

The result from Paula's art class during the next couple of days was fantastic. The poster, with a light blue background looked very festive with lots of silver glitter, but it was the wording that made me laugh. 'Sing a long a Les', said the banner headline. Below in smaller wording it said, 'with Bill on drums'. The date given for the performance was two days hence.

That evening I was in the pub again and discretely showed Paula's work to those present before surreptitiously pinning the poster to the cellar door near to the back room en route to the ladies and gent's facilities. Not one could miss it.

Strangely, maybe because they were too close to the location when passing, or people were bent on entering or exiting, but no one noticed the display. Les walked passed it on numerous occasions, even going down into the cellar at one point. Everyone was chuckling and sniggering and the landlord knew there was mischief afoot but couldn't see what form this was taking. His frown had returned.

Towards the end of the evening I could contain myself no longer and as he was passing to collect some glasses I pointed to the poster saying, "that's gonna be a great night Les. Ah'm really looking forward to it."

He looked at the artwork, which measured two feet by eighteen inches and took in its contents. Those around stood with bated breath awaiting his reaction, expecting him to explode and rip the poster down. As ever, he did the unexpected.

"That's very good," he commented. "Someone's put a lot of time and effort in on that," then walked off. This was certain praise for Paula's work as Les was a talented artist himself. The poster remained in place up to and past the advertised date, though of course nothing happened on the day.

At lunchtime on Christmas Eve I was standing at the bar, close to where a smart young lady, clearly not a frequent visitor to the pub, was reading the advertisement with interest. "That sounds like it was fun, Les. I'm sorry I missed it."

I looked at the landlord, wondering what he'd say.

With a lovely smile at the disappointed female he said, "Oh! It went really well. You missed a good night."

I almost choked on my drink.

* * * * * *

Bluey and Julie had gone on holiday again, leaving Timmy to take the boat, Ian having previously left to take command of another vessel. Tim had been with Bluey since leaving school, firstly on *Independence* and then *Allegiance*. Now in his early twenties he was a very competent young man. Tall and lean with a ready smile and pleasant manner, Tim was a good all round hand and was pleased at the chance to take the vessel to sea.

Fishing about forty miles northeast of Whitby, things were going well with fish going below with a pleasing frequency until a problem came up, literally.

The doors were up and unclipped and the winch man was hauling on the bridles while the other hands on deck waited to take the quarter-ropes. It became obvious there was some additional weight on the top wire on the fore end. As the floats on the headline surfaced, an object close to the first orange ball became visible. This heavy piece was about four feet long, cylindrical, drainpipe-thick, clean and painted. On closer inspection, the stencilled letters USAF were clearly visible. "It's a bloody rocket," the nearest man said.

Gingerly, two men were able to detach the weapon from its location and lower the piece carefully to the deck. All hands quickly dragged the slack net of the trawl aboard before lifting a good bag of fish up the boat's side.

While the men were hauling the net, Timmy was talking to the coastguard via the MF radio, describing the unwanted catch and expressing his concern.

The coastguards didn't take long to identify the ordnance from Timmy's description over the airwaves. *Allegiance* had trawled up an American heat-seeking missile. "Head for the shallow water to the north of Whitby," the officer instructed then needlessly added, "try to keep the thing cool." The rocket was already on the foredeck, covered with sacks and with the hose playing on it.

It wasn't long before a helicopter was hovering overhead and three servicemen were lowered individually to the after end of the vessel. "This is from the Gulf War," the first of the men said on removing the wet bagging from the rocket. "It was very careless of the yanks to lose it."

Allegiance was heading southwest but it would be three hours yet before the vessel would be at the designated location. The disposal men took no time in making themselves at home. One promptly found a comfortable berth on the spare net and went to sleep while a second discovered the kettle and television on the mess-deck. It was down to the team leader to prepare a detonator and charges.

As the vessel steamed towards the shore the sun disappeared and *Allegiance* entered a fog bank, causing the sunbather to vacate his berth and join his boss. Eventually on site, close inshore along the coast from the ancient port, the final member of the trio joined his teammates and the charge and detonator were attached to the missile. The bundle was carefully lowered over the side and the officer quite casually called out to Timmy, "head out to sea skipper, full speed." Thirty seconds later there was a 'crump' and a fountain of white water shot skywards.

It was low water in Whitby and the fog still thick, so helpfully, the Whitby lifeboat was launched and her crew took the servicemen on board, disembarking the trio and their kit near the fish market. Within minutes *Allegiance* was heading back out to sea to continue her fishing trip.

I was standing on the West Pier in Scarborough when Timmy stepped ashore. He grinned and said, "Fred, can yer tell Bluey not t' go on 'oliday anymore. Summat always goes wrong when 'e's away."

Heading away from the boat along the pier with a couple of fishermen, we reached Sandgate Corner. A lone person, leaning on the railings turned his head in our direction as we approached. Swivel-eyed, sloping shoulders and a head like the cartoon character Popeye, this person was a throwback to the days when this site was the domain of ne'er do wells and critics. This bunch would pick fault with anyone making an effort to be successful, though none had ever achieved much themselves or even tried. "Hiya lads," the loner said to my companions in a whining voice.

One of the pair acknowledged the man but as soon as we were out of earshot said, "what a pillock. 'E's never done a stroke o' work in 'is life. 'Es been kept by t' State since 'e was born an' will probably go to 'is grave t' same way."

"'E 'asn't a good word for anyone who does work either," added the other. "If 'e put as much effort in t' bein' useful and 'elping people as 'e does bein' negative, 'e'd be a bloody saint."

I concurred and said, "Ah try not t' worry about people like 'im. Ahm on'y interested in folk that 'ave constructive things t' say. If yer let the bastards grind yer down t' their level, yer'll achieve nowt. They're on'y jealous," I said with feeling.

Chapter 16

Undaunted

Les at the Leeds Arms has retired. He's bought a bungalow on the edge of town and is hoping his favourite customers will call by to see him. The property is new and Les, being a skilled bricklayer and stone worker is going to put his own stamp on the place. The new tenants of the 'Leeds', Simon and Hilary, were customers previously and they're unlikely to change things in the pub, though there'll only ever be one Les. His deadpan face and unique approach to running a hostelry can't be imitated. It's the end of an era.

* * * * * *

Over the past few months I'd been thinking more about the prospect of potting at the Dudgeon and Dowsing. Though lobsters were the more valuable stock there was a market for crab if these could be transported to a processing factory on the east coast of Scotland. The price was only £5 a stone but there was potentially a huge quantity of crab off the Humber, so if I fished the wrecks for lobsters with short fleets then had longer lengths of gear for crabs, then both stocks could be maximised. First I'd need the right boat for the job. *Emulator* was too slow and not manoeuvrable enough. I'd require a vessel that could get to the grounds and back in a day while being big enough to carry a substantial number of pots. Sean was more than capable of taking *Emulator* and would jump at the chance of skippering her permanently.

My mind was made up and I began looking round for such a vessel. After much searching and following up advertisements, including a wasted trip to Jersey to look at a boat, I decided that the only way I'd get the ideal vessel was if I had one purpose built for the job. If I could find the right shell, the boat could be fitted out at the local Scarborough Marine yard. There were several companies constructing GRP boats on the south coast but having seen drawings of a 'Halmatic' craft from a yard that built RNLI lifeboats I decided this was where I'd get my basic hull. She would be forty-five feet in length with a good beam. Next I had to decide on the size of the forward cabin from three basic designs then select engines, as the engine beds would be moulded into the hull.

I opted for the middle of the range for the boat's accommodation, which would give plenty of deck space and allow for a berth with a couple of bunks, a gas stove and toilet. For engines I chose twin 'Sabres,' each with 385 horsepower. These, at full revolutions would give a top speed of nineteen knots, though this would be for emergency purposes. We'd cruise at seventeen knots to and from the grounds, which was more than double the capability of *Emulator*. At this speed the boat should sit up in the water and plane easily and be more economical.

The order was placed and the dark blue shell would be delivered to Scarborough in three months. Meanwhile I began making pots in any spare time I had and continued trawling, desperately trying to avoid going over quota, though our monthly allowance was low. How stupid life was becoming when we had to go to places hoping not to catch too much cod.

The chrysalis hull arrived and was manoeuvred into the boatyard's workshop. This would metamorphose, emerging again, transformed into a beautiful and totally different creature.

Meanwhile the fisheries minister, John Gummer, no friend of the fishing industry, had recently returned from negotiations in Brussels where further cuts were conceded by the UK delegation. Unsurprisingly he announced, "We got the best deal possible for our fishermen."

In Scotland things were no better for fishermen. Andrew Bremner, a top skipper had been taken to Court, prosecuted and fined for punching a fisheries officer. This clearly was not a sensible thing to do, but every fisherman knew his frustrations.

* * * * * *

Undaunted eventually emerged from the cocoon, towed on a trailer and was hauled to the North Wharf by the builder's Land Rover ready to be craned into the water. It was a bitterly cold day and family and friends were huddled round for the naming ceremony. She was going to be christened, not by Dotty or my Mother but by Christine, a lovely family friend. Christine said she had always wanted to launch a boat but clearly would never get the opportunity. Her husband John, a quiet, unassuming man with a lovely sense of humour said, "if you think I'm building a boat, just so you can launch it, you can think again."

With Dotty and Mum's approval I'd suggested that for an undisclosed sum to the local hospice, we'd be pleased for Christine to christen and name our new vessel. In all her finery, with glamorous suit and matching hat Christine, in a clear, articulate voice called, "I name this ship, *Undaunted*. God bless her and all who sail in her."

The lady swung the bottle of champagne towards the stem of the boat and the glass shattered in an instant, throwing champagne spume over all in proximity. The smash came as no surprise, as the bottle had been doctored and gouged deeply in several places. The vessel being of glass-fibre construction would however still have been damaged by the impact but Alan, the yard's owner/manager had taped a piece of thin, stainless steel to each side of *Undaunted*'s stem which together formed a sharp angle. The bottle had no chance.

Four waiters and waitresses from the nearby Lancaster Inn, dressed in white flimsy tops and black trousers or skirts complete with pink sashes, were on hand with trays of sparkling wine for a toast to the new boat, which had been quickly lowered into the water and the slings unhooked. These poor folk must have been absolutely freezing from the bitter easterly wind blowing in off the sea. Most of the guests were wrapped up in topcoats. Hot teas and coffees would have been more appropriate.

The few guests who wanted to look on board the new craft didn't stay long and soon everyone was ensconced in the Lancaster. This old building had been a pub for centuries but the ancient mariners who'd inhabited the harbour in years past wouldn't have recognised the place. It was now locally known as the 'pink palace'. Its current proprietor 'Stan the man' was a flamboyant, gay character who'd certainly stamped his own style on the place. The curtains were pink and there were pink tablecloths and flowers on the previously bare tables. Stan, beanpole thin with sharp features and watery eyes sported spiky, dyed blond hair. He had engaged the forever-young, 'Danny Wilde' as entertainment for his establishment and the one man rock concert was a big hit, playing to full houses. This afternoon the rock singer was to entertain our party.

Danny Wilde, small in stature, thin with bright eyes and a lined brow, sported looped gypsy-type earrings, a white frilly shirt and black flared trousers. The diminutive artiste stepped onto the little stage to rapturous applause. Unfortunately this sound was from a tape machine, part of the array of gadgets the singer engaged to play the noise. Looking at least sixty, he wore a long black wig to cover his greying crew cut. Danny sang popular sixties and seventies stuff to a musical backing tape, though his guitar added something to the performance occasionally. He'd frequently change some of the lyrics with self-praising words of his own.

The entertainer was churning out his material and the guests were enjoying the performance, some were dancing to the beat. The launching party was going with a real swing despite Danny continuing to play the phoney applause at the end of each number, hoping to encourage his audience to join in. This irritated as many as it enthused.

At the mid point of the afternoon an intermission was announced and a huge buffet spread, prepared by Dotty and her friend Sandra was served in an upstairs room. The pair had received quite a shock when they'd turned up earlier in the day and found Stan wearing only a towel. He'd insisted on laying out the splendid food in a professional manner for best presentation, though never thought to dress first.

During the brief interlude I took to the stage to say thanks to the boatyard for completing and commissioning the lovely craft and to Stan and his staff for their hospitality, then Danny Wilde struck up again. Now dressed in a white 'Elvis' suit, the performer built up the second part of his act to a grand finale then burst into the classic Presley hit, 'American Trilogy'. With strobe lights flashing and a fantastic big band sound from his machine, Danny belted out the song then, with a great fanfare to conclude the performance a waitress stepped onto the stage and passed a white towel to the singer. The dynamic performer mopped the perspiration from his brow and casually hung the cloth around his neck then stepped from the stage, exiting the nearest door. Stan, on cue leapt onto the tiny stage and into the spotlight, microphone in hand. The now gaudily dressed landlord proclaimed, "Danny Wilde has left the building." The lights dimmed dramatically. The show had ended.

The landlord's announcement was slightly misleading. There was no limousine waiting outside for the star. Danny had stepped into the broom cupboard.

It had been a great afternoon and certainly like no other launching party I'd ever been to. Now it was time to get to work.

Next morning I was on the pier early. The easterly wind had died away leaving a lazy swell. I watched *Emulator* sail with mixed feelings; I was pleased for Sean but had I done the right thing? I felt a little uneasy at my change of vessel and direction but it was too late now for any doubts, the dye was cast. I wandered round to the pier to meet up with my two crewmen and began assembling the fleets of pots and attaching anchors and buoys on the quayside.

The two hands I'd shipped up for this new venture were Kevin, Sean's younger brother who'd been on board *Emulator* for a period and Robert, a fisherman from Bridlington. Robert was an unknown quantity. He'd heard I was building a vessel to go potting off the Humber and had more or less invited himself to join the crew. He had plenty of experience of potting, having worked with his brother John out of Bridlington for years on a coble, before graduating to a small keelboat. Initially they had fished on wrecks around Flamborough but had eventually worked as far away as the Norfolk Coast and even occasionally landing catches into Ostend across the channel. I was still a novice at potting so hoped to learn from Robert.

Of average height with a round, red face and short, straight black hair, Robert was a strange man. He had large, unblinking, staring eyes, which were frequently focussed in my direction, though he would rarely speak unless the topic was work related.

However odd Robert seemed, he certainly knew about making pots and must have spent days on end completing the frames I delivered to Bridlington for him, before the boat was ready. He'd even bought and netted a dozen large pots, the size he'd used with his brother, but without consulting me. Reimbursing him for the expenditure, I had to ask him not to make any more. These pots were so big we'd have difficulty handling them on the smaller vessel.

Early next morning we loaded up the boat and headed out with our first cargo of pots. *Undaunted* was stacked high with enough fleets of eight creels to target a dozen wrecks. When we sailed again we'd deploy two fleets of sixty then haul the wreck pots. Within two weeks we would have six hundred pots in the sea.

The boat performed wonderfully and even fully loaded planed at sixteen knots. Dotty had prepared a large pan of beef stew for our dinner, so as soon as we were northbound the catering sized cauldron was placed on the stove top to heat up, after being securely fastened in place with the fiddle.

Whenever possible we'd try to travel with the tide, as this would make at least two knots difference to our speed. The vessel's fuel capacity was a little over four hundred gallons but *Undaunted's* consumption of two hundred gallons for the round trip meant it would be prudent to refill her tanks after each voyage.

After three days of carrying pots to the grounds and hauling those already deployed, it became clear that we wouldn't be able to continue at this pace every day. The work was physically demanding and the days were long. Though the boat had a couple of bunks, it was almost impossible to lay down while on passage unless the sea was flat calm. I'd bounced off the deck-head on a couple of occasions while horizontal, with Kevin on watch. The vessel steered straight and easily on autopilot, so apart from monitoring the radar and ensuring the boat didn't divert from the line on the plotter screen there was little to do while on passage but view the small colour television, handily located on the console. The shock-absorbing helmsman's chair was the most comfortable place on the boat.

We soon steadied into a good routine, sailing every second day, leaving the harbour around 0300 hours and arriving at the grounds a little over four hours later. I'd previously laughed at people who commute to their place of work and here I was spending almost nine hours each day travelling to and from the fishing grounds and the ride wasn't always pleasant. Our catches varied but we were regularly landing between 200 to 300 pounds of lobsters and 200 to 300 stone of crabs each trip. Getting the crabs to the Scottish processing company was still a problem until I bought a transit van. Now on the days we weren't at sea I drove the catch to meet up with link transport at a pre-arranged rendezvous and kept in touch with the driver of the articulated lorry by phone. This venue could be anywhere from the Humber Bridge or Hull Fish Dock in the south or nearer home on the outskirts of York or Guisborough, depending on the trucker's schedule. I was a white van man.

The pair back at home would be making oil drum buoys to replace those lost by shipping or constructing new pots. They would work till midday. There was always work to do when we were not at sea.

We sailed early on Sunday and approached the first wreck. After the first two pots were on board, with good results, the rope became extremely tight and before we could stop the hauler, the rope parted. The line must have chafed on some sharp plating. "Don't worry about it," I called. "We'll come back later when t' tide's eased an' 'aul 'em from t' other end.

Continuing to pull other strings of gear for a few hours more, we eventually hauled a short fleet on a wreck yielding only moderate results. Keeping these pots onboard, we enjoyed a well-earned mug of coffee while heading back towards the wreck with the broken end. Before hauling the remains of this fleet, we shot the pots we'd retained onboard very close to those already stuck in the smashed up wreck.

It was now slack water and we moved towards the remaining end of the partial fleet. Taking the buoy on board then hauling to the anchor, tension began to come on the rope as the first pot came into view. "Be gentle with it," I requested Kevin. "Don't break it or we've lost 'em. It's on'y shallow 'ere. Ah can always dive for 'em while t' rope's attached for me t' go down."

The first pot appeared and was recovered aboard with several lobsters trapped within, but the line tightened and was threatening to part. "Cut t' pot off and slack t' line out," I instructed.

Robert, slashing with the sharp knife from the baiting tray, swiftly achieved the severance. As the rope was paying out and tension eased I said, "now cut t' rope an' fasten a spare buoy t' end. Ah'll kit up wi' me divin' gear an' clear 'em. "

Fifteen minutes later, clad in wetsuit, mask, fins, weight belt and single fifteen-litre tank attached to a buoyancy aid, I flopped over the side as Kevin took the boat close to the marker. I knew from experience I wouldn't need a torch. While I was underwater the pair would deploy the metal diving ladder I'd commissioned for easy access from the water.

The visibility was crystal clear and I could see the coarse sandy bottom and rusty plating of the wreck long before I neared the bottom. The wreck was charted as *Cavehill* (possibly) and was 1556 tons. The ship had sprung a leak while on passage from Newcastle to Amsterdam in 1921 and was now totally fragmented. The wreck made no structural sense at all. The offending pot was stuck under a piece of girder and the rope beyond was free. It was no problem at all to drag the pot sideways clear of the obstruction and it was very pleasing to see some black creatures within. Swimming easily along the ten fathoms of line and breathing gently I came to the next pot, which was clear of obstruction and contained another good catch. I wasn't in the least bit cold within the neoprene membrane and with no tide running and the clarity of water incredible, the diving experience was extremely pleasant. As I approached the next pot, again free of encumbrance I noticed a cupped disc lying on the bottom, partly covered by the golden sand. Holding the object aloft I indentified this as the brass cover from a ship's steering wheel, and realised there was lettering etched on the piece, though not easily decipherable in my current situation. What a discovery!

Following the line again and elated with my find I came to the end pot of the string of four, again full of lobsters and then beyond, the tangled rope that had somehow become fouled around a piece of wreckage. This knot had caused the earlier breakage. Even holding the piece of brass with my spare hand it was quite a simple matter to untangle the mess. The pots were now free to be hauled. Looking away from the wreck while still holding the rope, I could see another pot not too far away and realised this must be one from the recently deployed fleet. Incredibly, lying atop of the pot, attracted by the bait but not yet having worked out how to reach the juicy morsels was a big, bright blue lobster. I couldn't resist the urge and, swimming easily over to the site, grabbed the beast across its back. The huge claws came up attempting to grab me, but in the position I was holding the creature, this was impossible. Now I had a large lobster in one hand and the piece of brass in the other. If only I had a goody bag.

I hadn't far to swim back to the surface line, but was faced with a dilemma. I had to hold onto the rope to control my ascent but both hands were full. I looked at the brass cap then at the lobster and was reluctant to lose either. The artefact was by far the most desirable so I put the lobster between my knees and grabbed the rope with my now-free hand, beginning my ascent back to the surface. There was still hardly any tide running or I'd have been forced to use my legs to fin and the lobster would have flapped off back to the bottom. With difficulty I was able to vent my buoyancy aid as the air within expanded, while still holding on to the piece of brass. As I made my way slowly up the rope I looked down at the creature between my legs and was horrified to see how close its open claws were to a very sensitive part of my anatomy. I quickly moved the orientation of the animal to a less dangerous position with the rim of the cover. A few minutes later I was on the surface. Releasing the rope I put a little air in the buoyancy aid then grabbed the crustacean again, holding both trophies aloft. The men on the boat only a short distance away spied me instantly and headed in my direction.

Passing up both trophies then my fins, I ascended the ladder, grinning from ear to ear. The experience had been both amazing and rewarding. "T' pots are clear," I said, "an' they're full o' lobsters."

Kevin passed me a mug of coffee as I dressed and having examined the 'find' said, "T' wheel boss says, *Hyden* on t' top and London on t' bottom." The wreck was listed as *Cavehill* (possibly). I wondered if *Cavehill* had formerly been called *Hyden* or was this just another mystery of the sea?

We hauled the now freed gear without difficulty and the lads were delighted with the results from the four missing pots. The contents of these creels plus my blue lobster filled a plastic box and must have weighed at least 50 pounds. The day continued uneventfully and the recovered catch added to a particularly good landing.

At the first opportunity of a Wednesday evening at home I presented the now polished artefact to the diving club. The piece was mounted above the bar and as far as I'm aware, remains there to this day.

The following week I was to dive on another unknown wreck when an anchor was stuck and the other end parted. Swimming down the line on this occasion I was amazed to see the heavy four-pronged anchor had dropped neatly down a small hatchway, no more than two feet square on a piece of otherwise indescribable scrap. The shot was a bullseye. No matter how we'd attempted to pull up the grapnel anchor, one of its prongs must have been hooking under the combing. The odds of achieving such a shot must have been millions to one. The dive took less than ten minutes from surface to surface.

Undaunted was an ideal craft for taking diving trips and as I now had the positions of scores of accessible wrecks I decided to place an advertisement in the 'Diver' monthly magazine offering her services to diving clubs in the region. I was able to offer two separate dives on consecutive slack waters on different wrecks, many miles offshore. Though unable to guarantee that the wrecks I'd take the parties to were pristine and un-dived, I had in mind, intact sites at reasonable depths that had certainly not been stripped of souvenirs.

Following an enthusiastic response from the York 'Excalibur' club, the following Sunday at 0400 hours *Undaunted* left the harbour to sail east southeast for fifty miles with ten divers on board. Each one had brought two separate cylinders, as unlike on *Emulator's* trips, I had no compressor available for recharging the sets. I'd also brought along two fifteen-litre bottles. It was great to be able to take divers commercially and to get a dip myself too.

We were heading for a site where two wrecks were positioned side by side in thirty-seven metres. The *Jersey* was a steam powered trawler that had been sunk by a U boat in October 1916. *Sea Pearl* was a small Belgian trawler that had caught its trawl on the wreck in September 1967 and capsized while broadside to the tide. The skipper had been picked up by a passing Grimsby vessel after being spotted sitting on the upturned hull and waving frantically.

On site in a little over three hours, and with another hour to spare before slack water, I prepared the shot line. The divers looked on keenly and would have no trouble deploying the plonker when the wreck was pinpointed. *Undaunted* was so much more manoeuvrable than *Emulator*. Her twin engines and rudders enabled her to turn in her own length. With accurate readings the first wreck, marked on the print out as *Jersey*, was located. The divers had split themselves into two groups and the first wave began to kit up while the other team dropped the shot at my behest.

The first six frogmen were sitting on the boat's side as we drew close to the buoy and looking out of the door just before putting the engine into neutral, I was gobsmacked to see the tools the group were armed with. Hanging from their belts along with the usual goody bags and torches were crowbars, hammers and chisels. Were they going to dismantle the wreck? "Yer won't need weight belts wi' that lot," I called out.

The oil drum was only ten feet from the boat as the divers dropped over her side. The visibility looked excellent as we watched the first group submerge, heading down the rope. It was quite sometime before the bunch disappeared, such was the clarity of the water. Their combined bubbles continued to boil on the surface. These exhaust gases would split into three groups when the divers hit the bottom to begin moving around the dive site.

The others began to kit up ready for their dive and I donned my wetsuit and prepared my kit ready for quick deployment.

"It's only a small wreck," one of the first of the pair of divers commented as they climbed the ladder back onboard, having previously passed bottles, torches, fins, goody bags and toolkits to the willing hands on deck. "The vis' is fantastic and there's no tide. It was a terrific dive. I got a lobster."

"It's a first war trawler," I restated, having informed everyone of the wreck on the passage out. "They weren't very big."

Leaving Dave, who'd dived in the first group and appeared a competent boatman, to look after *Undaunted,* I dropped over the side following the four frogmen who'd been waiting impatiently to get in the water. It was weird dropping through the streams of bubbles and impossible to see anything below me except the nearest diver but this would soon change when we reached the wreck.

Pausing above the sunken vessel to get my bearings as the others moved away, I realised there was something wrong. This wasn't *Jersey,* this was a smaller vessel and was intact. This must be the little Ostend vessel, *Sea Pearl* that had snagged its net on the wreck. Had I taken the wrong position from the information I'd consulted? It wasn't too important. We were going to dive both wrecks anyway. I could see the two pairs, or their torch beams as I leisurely inspected the sad little craft; her foremast lying over the port bulwark in the desert. The trawl winch stood as expected in front of the wheelhouse but this structure looked very strange. Instead of windows the little bridge had a series of portholes. I contrasted this with my own vessel's panoramic views and the limited vision offered from this wheelhouse and I shuddered. It must have been a dismal place to steer from and a nightmare for the lookout, usually the same person.

It didn't take long to circle the little wreck and pleasingly, because the bottom was sandy, there was no disturbance of silt from the other divers to cloud the visibility. I was startled by the sudden sound of banging, resonating through the water, amplified as all subsea noises are. The scrappers must have found something to remove. Finding myself back at the fallen mast I followed the structure to the seabed and was delighted to see the copper masthead light still in place with glass intact. The iron rods the lamp was slotted on to were quite decayed and required little levering back and forth before the light was loose and mine. I could still hear and feel the vibrations of the banging but decided to leave the little craft and head towards the nearby shot rope, trophy under arm, making my way slowly up the line to the surface. I'd only been fifteen minutes but the start of the new tide had already begun to run.

Dave brought the boat gently to a stop and I passed the lamp to one of the divers who'd been first on the wreck and was now dressed only in his woolly under suit. "Where did you find that?" he asked, slightly miffed. "It's a beauty."

Spitting my mouthpiece out and grinning, I said, "Oh! It was still attached t' mast, lying on' t' seabed at t' side o' t' boat."

"Bugger," was his reply.

The others followed up the line soon after, one carrying a porthole that had been removed by brute force from its location on the wheelhouse. Most of the divers had lobsters in their bags and they'd all enjoyed the dive immensely.

We now had more than five hours to kill and nowhere to go. Checking the readouts I was pleased to see the hydrographer had transposed the readings and had the wrong vessels names in their database. The enthusiastic divers recovered the plonker and shot-line then it took only a few minutes at slow speed to locate the real *Jersey* and re-deploy the shot and buoy line ready for the next dive.

The kettle on the little two-ringed stove was continuously boiled till all on board had been provided with hot drinks to wash down their own sandwiches and snacks. There were a few other wrecks in the area so I took *Undaunted*, at half speed to some of these locations to confirm, amend or delete the information as supplied on the readout, for future use. Valuable information was never wasted.

We dived the real *Jersey* on the next slack water and again the conditions were excellent. The wheelhouse and deck structure had long since gone from the old ship at deck level but at the stern I discovered a small rectangle of black and white ceramic tiling. This must have been the galley and I felt a little sadness at the thought of the ship's cook toiling around this small space while juggling his kettle and pans as the ship rolled to the swell.

Nothing significant was recovered from *Jersey* apart from lobsters but again the dive was a great experience and soon we were heading for home. Dotty's catering-sized pan of beef stew and potatoes was the 'icing on the cake' for the York crew who'd had a terrific day out. This was the first of several trips the group would make on *Undaunted* during the season.

We passed Flamborough at half a mile; the lighthouse flashing brightly and we now had less than an hour to run to home. We'd be back in the harbour at 2200 hours. It had been a long day for the divers. "Do any of yer want a beer before yer go 'ome," I asked.

"You haven't got beer as well?" was the universal reply.

"No but t' Leeds Arms 'as. They close at 'alf past ten. Tell me what yer want and ah'll ring t' order in. Yer drinks'll be on t' bar when we get there."

I rang the pub on the boat's phone and relayed the shipping order to Simon. It would be nearly closing time when we'd offloaded the gear and I'd secured the boat and shut down the machinery. At 2220 I walked into the pub with my new friends to receive our drinks. The divers raised their glasses to a great day out but didn't stay too long. Twenty minutes later they were supping off their drinks and heading for the door. It would be almost midnight before they reached home and most had work the following day. I'd be onboard *Undaunted* heading back towards Flamborough Head again with my crew before daylight.

* * * * * *

"Tom, do yer like trout?" Herby, skipper of *Crystal Sea* asked his neighbour when the pair met in the street the following weekend.

"I love all types of fish Herby," replied the Police Superintendant with a smile. Tom was the nephew of Dickie Elliott and though his mother's family was steeped in fishing, Tom's career had taken him in a different direction.

"Ah've been gettin' a few lately. Ah'll leave yer some on yer door," said the rotund, jovial fisherman.

Sure enough, the following morning the policeman found a string of large, silver fish hanging on his door handle.

Two weeks later Tom answered a knock on his door to discover a concerned Herbert on the doorstep. "Can you give me a reference, Tom?" the tubby trawler-man asked.

"Of course I can Herby," the Superintendant replied. Come in. What's the reference for?"

"It's for t' magistrates." The skipper replied with a mischievous grin. "Ah got caught poachin' trout a couple o' days ago on an estate just outside o' town. Ah'm due up in court next week."

* * * * * *

Sincere was missing. She was last seen around midday the previous day, fishing close to shore in the narrow strip of sand somewhere north of Scarborough between Creek Point and Robin Hoods Bay. Terry Hunter, skipper of this little under ten metre vessel always contacted home a couple of times each day but had failed to do so on this afternoon. Kath, his wife had attempted to phone the boat's number but the line was dead.

The Whitby and Scarborough lifeboats had been launched but after much searching the volunteer crew had seen no sign of the missing craft and this could mean only one thing; *Sincere* was no longer afloat. The fresh southeasterly wind and ebbing tide wouldn't have carried a broken down vessel offshore, only northwestwards towards the 'Bay'. Terry was an experienced skipper and if his boat had merely broken down he would have deployed the vessel's anchor then used his radio or phone to call for assistance. The little vessel must have sunk. No liferaft had been found before darkness fell, so the skipper and his crewman Ken must be presumed lost.

I'd sailed with Terry in an earlier and larger *Sincere*, A555 when I was a teenager. We'd fished offshore for thornback skate with long lines, baiting with herring and mackerel then, following this late spring fishery, the boat had been converted and we'd turned to trawling.

It was now daylight and along with several other boats and lifeboats, sounders running, we were looking for the lost vessel. Coastguards combed the shoreline.

"She's 'ere." Brian Cox, skipper of *Challenge* called on the radio an hour later. "She's right at t' north end. 'E must 'ave been turnin' across t' wind an' tide an' she's been pulled o'er." He gave the 'Decca' position and radar distance from the nearest land. Following this first fix Brian reported the distance from the North Cheek of Robin Hoods Bay, giving a cross bearing. Several boats passed slowly over the position, marking the strange mound on the flat sandy bed. Now at least divers would be able to search the wreck for the missing crew.

A few days later, in answer to a request from the police, though doubtful they could do the job, I took a team of their divers to the wreck site where they intended to search the sunken vessel. As soon as they encountered the swell and tide the sergeant in charge had second thoughts and decided this was beyond his team's jurisdiction. I'd heard this previously when *Anmara* was lost. It was a wasted day as far as I was concerned but I had to volunteer.

The following weekend a team from York 'Excaliber', who'd been on *Undaunted* earlier in the summer, volunteered to dive the wreck to search for bodies, but the visibility was very poor. The divers tried, but couldn't say for certain whether the lost fishermen were in the wheelhouse or little cabin. Royal Navy divers later confirmed there were no remains in the vessel. The only hope now was that the bodies of the missing men would be found on the surface or be trawled up by the other boats fishing this sandy bottom.

Terry's son Mark, a teenager, couldn't sleep following the loss of his Dad and spent many hours alone on the outer pier looking out to sea, wanting his father home.

Bill, who'd also sailed previously with Terry and with me in *Courage* years ago, was now working single-handed, trawling in his own under ten metre vessel *Julie Anne*. Bill was determined to find his former skipper's body and spent days towing his net up and down the likely area of drift and it wasn't so much divine intervention as sheer doggedness that he eventually trawled up the remains of the missing skipper. Sadly his crewman Ken was never found.

Poignantly, Ken's car stood on the quayside for several days awaiting an owner that wasn't coming back, before the vehicle was taken away.

Sadly, *Sincere* was another under ten metre vessel lost due to government legislation, allowing this class of vessel to be exempt from quota restrictions.

Mark Hunter, Terry's son, joined the Coastguard service as a volunteer soon after his father's body was recovered and was to spend many years helping others in difficulties along the cliffs and shoreline.

* * * * * *

Mum had bought me an unusually striking jumper for Christmas; different to anything I'd seen before and quite distinctive. The Aztec pattern wasn't something I'd normally wear, but I put the garment on to go to the pub that evening.

There were several favourable comments and I was quite pleased with my new acquisition until, an hour later and dead on time as always, the 'pub bore' entered the door and for once caused a huge roar of laughter. This was indeed strange as people normally closed ranks and looked away, hoping not to attract his attention. The man headed directly towards me and I could hear people chuckling, then I noticed his sweater. Though larger than the one I was sporting, his jumper was identical to mine. No wonder everyone was laughing. I felt the eyes staring in my direction awaiting a reaction.

Totally oblivious to the rumpus he'd caused the man looked at my new present and his eyes lit up. "Eyup Fred," he said, pointing to my top. "We could be brothers."

"We bloody well couldn't," I replied, and playing to the amused audience pulled the jumper over my head. Rolling the garment into a tight ball I dropkicked it through the open door and into the street, thus creating even more laughter.

Having made my point, I did quickly retrieve the sweater before any passing vehicle wheels spoiled the material, though didn't put the thing back on again. In subsequent days I was to see several men sporting the same design around town, apparently from Marks and Spencer's best-selling Christmas range, but never wore mine again.

To escape the attention of my wannabe twin, I caught the eye of someone I desperately needed to talk to across the room and edged away from my unwanted companion. I was extremely surprised when a couple of minutes later, 'Stoff' walked into the pub and stood next to the rotund, dour chap.

A Londoner, Stoff had recently moved to Scarborough with his wife Jenny, who was a local girl. Jenny had travelled extensively from her late teens, had lived in America and enjoyed a successful career as a restaurateur before moving back to her roots in the 'bottom end' with her husband. The pair now lived in a large, former guesthouse that had been rundown beyond belief when they'd bought it. They were now restoring the property to its former glory. The previous occupant on departing had stripped the place to the extent of even removing light-fittings and would probably have taken the wallpaper had he been able to remove it.

Stoff, a tall, well-built man was a witty, affable character with twinkling eyes and a mischievous sense of humour: not prerequisites for his occupation as a prison Governor. He travelled the thirty-plus miles from home to the category C establishment each day astride a powerful motorbike.

Already into the second of his usual four pints and delighted to have someone he could talk at, the bore began with his standard greeting of, "evening."

"How are you?" Stoff asked. "I've seen you in here before." Not waiting for a reply the Governor continued, "Did you see the programme on TV last night about the Terracotta Army."

"They're Chinese," replied the dour man in his slow, monotone voice. He was looking forward to imparting his knowledge and monopolising the conversation and placed his empty glass on the bar. His third pint was on its way.

As the man began to speak Stoff interjected. "Eleven thousand of them have been unearthed so far."

"Yes I know, they're al..." the drone was again cut off mid sentence by another interruption.

"They all have names," Stoff stated with authority.

Frustrated the chap took a long swig of his beer, reducing the contents of the glass by half. Quickly putting his glass down the man drew breath and was about to launch into his knowledge on the subject when the Londoner began speaking again. The pub was now silent as the entire clientele looked on, realising they were witnessing something special.

"There's Ying Dan Dong, Do Jim Gosh, Su Ling Jan, Li Sung Jing." He was concocting these names spontaneously and delivering them with conviction.

The beer disappeared amid the endless names and his fourth pint appeared on the bar as if by magic. The glass was grabbed and a big gulp taken as the list continued. A worried look had appeared on the face of the man trapped in the corner and compelled to listen to non-stop drivel.

"There was Jo Long Tee, Ku Fung Sang," pausing for effect the speaker asked, "How many is that?" He was opening and closing the fingers of both hands as if counting in tens but then, as the listener drew breath to say something; anything, Stoff carried on again with the diatribe of fictional characters. Minutes passed and the fourth pint had disappeared leaving fresh froth on the glass and on the face of the now panicking bore.

Finally managing to find his voice the tiresome chap loudly and with real passion in his voice for the first time ever announced, "I have to go now." He pushed past the narrator, grabbed his coat and shot out of the door.

Stoff, with a perplexed look on his face, turned to the onlookers and asked, "Was it something I said?"

He received a loud cheer and some applause. The Governor had obviously been briefed about the danger of being sent to sleep at the bar and had been proactive.

The miserable chap still called for his four pints each evening, but would look round the pub warily as he entered, making sure he avoided the tall Londoner.

Stoff loved the atmosphere in the Leeds Arms but did occasionally stay longer than was wise. Jenny arrived in the pub one evening to inform her husband it was time he went home and insisted on escorting him back to the big house in nearby Princess Street. Surprisingly, once indoors he'd quickly dressed for bed then said to Jenny, "I'm going to sleep in room eight tonight."

While thinking this was peculiar, but knowing at least Stoff was home and would be in bed, Jenny humoured her husband and said goodnight, then though it wasn't late, also went off to bed. As soon as the house was quiet Stoff left the former guest room, tiptoed downstairs and still wearing his pyjamas and slippers, totally unperturbed, returned to the pub, where he remained till closing time.

The following day, when Jenny heard about this crazy stunt she was horrified and at the first opportunity confronted her husband. "What on earth do you think you were doing going off to the pub in your nightclothes?" The irate lady asked.

Stoff eyeballed his wife with his wonderful confused countenance and said, " Jen it was really strange, just like in that book. I opened the door of room eight then everything went cloudy and I found myself walking through the door into the Leeds Arms."

The key to room eight now hangs permanently in the Leeds Arms.

* * * * * *

Danny had finished in the boat he'd been working on and was between jobs. Not liking the idea of him laying in bed while I was leaving to go to sea in the early hours, I conscripted him to sail on *Undaunted* with me, knowing this would encourage him to find a permanent berth. Our similar temperaments clashed when we fished together. My lad didn't like potting or working with his Dad and less than two weeks later he was back trawling.

Undaunted sailed as usual with three crewmen, though Kevin had stood down and my cousin Dave had filled the breach. We had a new fleet of sixty pots onboard and would now have ten fleets of this length in the sea, plus the numerous short fleets specifically for wrecks. Eventually I'd come to realise that the pots didn't need to be in the wrecks and that the lobsters would be tempted out of their habitat for the bait if the pots were close alongside the sunken vessels, especially on neap tides. The day was exceptional and brought a huge catch, consisting of about 300 stone of crabs and around 400 pounds of lobsters. The sea was flat calm, the sun still shining and not a breath of wind.

"We could tek this lot to Ostend," Robert suggested. "We'd be there in t' mornin' in this boat."

This suggestion, from someone who hardly spoke a word came as a surprise, so maybe there was some merit in the idea.

I was aware that he and his brother had often landed in this Belgian port and obtained better prices for their produce so this big catch could make the passage worthwhile for us. I checked the distance on the plotter and against a Southern North Sea chart. It was just over 150 miles to the canal entrance. Robert was right; we could be there in time for the morning market in Ostend. We'd give it a go, though we'd have to take on fuel again before leaving Belgium.

Steaming south southeast towards North Norfolk, *Undaunted* was making barely sixteen knots due to our large catch, stacked at the stern of the vessel and causing significant drag. She'd have performed much better if the boxes of shellfish had been stowed further forward to improve her trim, but I was concerned that the heat from the powerful engines directly under this section of deck would affect the vulnerable, live catch.

For the first few hours we cruised along well passing the Haisborough Sands, Winterton Ridges and Sheringham Shoal and were now east of the Cross Sands, passing Great Yarmouth on a flat sea. This extensive sandbar running north to south dried out at low water and had been a major hazard in the days of sail in heavy weather when seas broke across this sandy reef. We played the seawater deck hose on the stacked boxes frequently, the top layer of which were covered with hessian sacking, thus ensuring our catch was kept cool and wet.

With the sea like glass there was even an opportunity for each in turn to have a brief rest below without being bounced about. But then, in the space of half an hour the sky darkened and black clouds developed, quickly engulfing our little craft. Day turned into night. A bolt of lightening, closely followed by its related clap of thunder was immediately followed by a deluge of rain. More flashes of electricity forked from the heavens, turning the premature dark back to daylight with each flash. The violent summer storm that had rent the sky lasted less than an hour before the sky cleared, leaving a balmy summer evening and a steaming deck, but the damage had been done.

The shellfish in the top boxes were mostly dead. Claws on the crabs and in the one container of lobsters accessible, hung lifeless and limp, no longer supported by their inert bodies. The freak electrical storm had wiped out the lot. I could only pray that the creatures in the boxes lower down the pile had survived. I hosed each stack liberally to give any survivors a chance and hopefully to minimise our loss. My heart was in my boots. The euphoria of the big catch had gone. We were half way to the continent with an almost worthless cargo. If we'd headed north instead of south the catch would have been safely ashore now and we'd have avoided this localised phenomena.

Long past midnight and really dark in a clear, moonless sky, a million stars were on display. We were past North Foreland's jutting peninsular that splits the North Sea from the Channel. A line of outward bound shipping heading southwest from the UK and the continent was showing on the radar as we approached the charted separation zone from the north. Starboard and masthead lights of these ships were soon visible as we converged with the procession, as were the stern lights of the ships that had passed ahead of us.

Altering to port we bounced on the invisible bow wave of a large vessel before slipping effortlessly across the stern of the darkened ship and into the gap between the two convoys. Was this how U boat Commanders had operated? On through the dark and heading southeast by south with less than forty miles to run we could see the procession of freighters showing red and white lights coming in the opposite direction. More care would have to be taken with this crossing as these ships were converging from ahead. We passed port to port at less than half a mile with what, judging by the size of the radar target, was a really big vessel. At her stern we passed hard across what turned out to be a huge container ship, her afterdeck illuminated and showing some of her cargo, piled high. She was probably inbound for Rotterdam where the miles of quayside with monstrous steel structures, looking like pre-historic creatures handled these boxes in tens of thousands.

A mile on our starboard bow, the green and red side lights of the next inbound ship were topped by its two white masthead lights one above the other as we crossed her stem. These pinpricks of light the only indication of the vast, bulky merchant ship heading in our direction; literally, ships that pass in the night. Beyond this set of coloured dots another and yet more incoming vessels. There were navigation lights as far as the eye could see. Some would be reaching the end of voyages from all parts of the globe, others on their everyday passages along this busy waterway. I couldn't help thinking how chaotic this, the busiest waterway in the world, must have been in dense fog, prior to the advent of radar and the strict demarcation of this narrow strait. Even now, the scores of cross-channel ferries must have some interesting experiences when constantly cutting these processions at right angles.

I'd briefly forgotten our worthless cargo in the excitement as we crossed these busy shipping lanes. I wondered what the shore stations monitoring vessel movements would make of the little craft flitting between these mammoths. Would they think we were smugglers? Was I supposed to report our movements to someone?

The sun was above the horizon when we reached the coast and the sky was cloudless. It was going to be another hot day. Following Robert's pointing finger we made our way into the lock and canal. It was only a short run from the coast to the fish market where we tied up to the quay. The fish-selling agent, a large barrel-chested man called 'Ferdie' who was known to Robert, came along the wharf as we stepped ashore. A pleasant man with a good command of English, he shook my hand. The big man said he'd been a skipper out of Grimsby many years ago. I realised I'd spoken to him several times on the VHF in those days when I'd fished off the Lincolnshire coast in my first boat, *Pioneer*.

Not feeling particularly chatty, I explained to the salesman that we'd encountered a thunderstorm en route and I thought most of our catch was now dead.

"They will be worth something if they have recently died," Ferdie said. "The merchants will cook them quickly. Our beam trawlers land lots of crab claws. Do you have your T2M, skipper?"

I was about to say something about the unsavoury practise of retaining crab claws when I realised he'd made a request.

"T2M?" I muttered, looking at the man vacantly. "What's a T2M?" I was already tired and warm and now felt sweat running down my back. This had turned into the trip from hell.

"It's your customs form. You cannot land your catch without a T2M," the agent stated.

Hot, frustrated and now angry, I turned to Robert. "Yer didn't fuckin' tell me ah needed a customs form before we could land 'ere," I challenged. "Ah wouldn't 'ave bloody come."

The man just looked at me with his usual inane countenance before saying, "ah thought yer knew."

I regretted my outburst immediately. The situation was of my own making. I shouldn't have listened to him in the first place and certainly not relied on his knowledge.

"We will get your agent to fax one on this occasion. It will be OK," the salesmen said, saving the situation. "You must bring a book of T2M's another time."

"There isn't gonna be another time," I said to myself.

The pair onboard began to throw the boxes of crabs ashore and two men from the shore company tipped each in turn into plastic cases marked, 'Port of Ostend' before associates dragged each box into the auction hall. The crabs were now on their backs and normally legs would be thrashing wildly and claws grabbing anything in range. Nothing in the boxes moved.

As the lower boxes from the stacks came ashore I couldn't help noticing the backs of the crabs in these containers were dry, despite the constant dowsing they'd received. The realisation hit me like another thunderclap. These stacking boxes were designed to drain externally. Any water I'd directed on the top containers had been diverted from the bottom of the box externally, out between the stacks. All the lower boxes had remained dry.

A few of the lobsters had a spark of life remaining, but the majority were dead. I insisted that these were transferred individually and gently to ensure those still living didn't expire. When everything was ashore and decanted I walked up the sloping market to look at the catch. What would have been a superb landing was mostly a pile of dead stock. I felt thoroughly dejected.

"Zees are yours?" an elderly gentleman with the appearance of a retired fisherman asked.

I nodded glumly.

"Zen you should be punished," he snarled angrily before ambling off shaking his head.

"Oh, fuckin' great," I said to myself. "As if I didn't feel bad enough."

I couldn't bear to watch the auction and wouldn't have understood it, so waited for Ferdie to come along with the result.

"Have we earned enough t' fill up wi' fuel?" I asked dejectedly.

The man nodded and told me an amount, which sounded a fortune, but this was in Belgian francs and when converted into pounds sterling amounted to about a third of what the live catch would have made at home, but this was more than I'd expected. We could bunker and there'd be something left over to be sent home.

"I'll arrange for your fuel to be delivered," the big friendly chap said with a smile. He'd also organised a small supply of food for our breakfast and passage home. It was gone noon by the time the boat and crew were refuelled and we couldn't get out of the dock till 1600 hours so there was time for a nap. Dave and I went below into the little cabin and crashed out onto the two bunks. Robert, rather than lie on the comfortable cushioned seat locker in the wheelhouse decided to go ashore.

We were rudely woken at about three o'clock by a man shouting, "ello" into the cabin. On seeing life, the red faced van driver clad in a brown overall beamed and said, "I 'ave some beer for you."

Still very dopey and slightly confused I replied, "I 'aven't ordered any beer."

"Ah, eet is for Robert. 'E always gets beer from my company when 'e comes to Ostend." The man stepped ashore and began handing cases of Belgian beer to me, six cases in all.

I was asked to sign for the delivery, but would only scribble my initials on the document after being assured the consignment was paid for. "The crafty bugger," I said to Dave. "'E never told us anythin' about gettin' this lot. It'll be duty free. 'E must 'ave 'ad Belgian francs in 'is wallet."

Fifteen minutes before we were due to sail Robert arrived back at the boat carrying a large, white plastic bag. His usual grin in place. "Aven't yer got any Belgian chocolates?" He asked, raising the bag. "Ah've got three boxes."

"That'll be one each then," I replied quickly, and meant it. I took the bag from unresisting hands then said, "no wonder yer wanted t' come 'ere. Throw t' ropes off, we're goin' 'ome."

The passage back through the shipping lanes in daylight was less dramatic, though the variety of shipping was amazing. Container ships, gas tankers, bulk carriers, old general cargo vessels and even a warship were identified. We were averaging nearly eighteen knots and once clear of the separation zones each managed a few hours sleep. Not long after midnight we were in the region of our pots but I didn't want to hang around till daylight so continued on course directly for home. The sun was rising to starboard as we passed Filey Brigg on the last leg of our trek. It was hard to believe this time yesterday we were going into Ostend. It had been a horrendous experience and one I'd never repeat. We'd sail again the next day but would be bringing our catch home.

The trip to the continent wasn't a totally wasted voyage. Dotty was delighted with her box of delicious but very, very expensive chocolates.

* * * * * *

It's Bill Sheader's funeral. The tall, tough coble fisherman who'd been Coxswain of the lifeboat in my younger days and whom I'd occasionally been a volunteer crewman with, has gone. It's been really sad during these past few years to watch the great man deteriorate with Parkinsons Disease. St Mary's Church will be packed to the doors as his many friends and admirers turn out to pay their respects.

Having no children, Bill has lived alone since the death of his wife Julie, though he had no shortage of friends and was extremely hospitable to his visitors. His measures of rum and whisky were liberal and few left his house sober. Now Bill Sheader had gone to the great fishing grounds in the sky. Bill's humour was legendary and even during his remaining days when in hospital and deteriorating he'd found his wit, though the poignancy had brought floods of tears to those present. A group of lady friends had gone to visit Bill and the occasion was extremely moving. One of the number, wet-eyed and staunching a sob, reached into her bag for a handkerchief.

"Ah don't know what you're roarin' fo'." Bill uttered. "It's me that's dyin'."

It was a sombre, frustrated crowd that left the church to mill around outside following the funeral. The vicar taking the service was not a local and obviously didn't know Bill, so had not depicted the big man or given him the send off he so richly deserved.

"Someone should write about these people," I said to Dotty. "All t' old characters that ah remember as a lad are dyin' off. If nobody records 'em they'll 'ave lived an' died, an' nobody will remember 'em."

With her usual brevity Dotty said, "well get on with it then."

A little seed was sewn.

* * * * * *

The manager of Yorkshire Dry Dock on the River Hull had rung, asking if I was interested in towing a part-completed vessel up to the Scottish northeast port of Macduff for completion by another shipyard. I'd successfully delivered craft constructed in the dock to shipyards in Fraserburgh and Buckie with *Emulator* for this company in the past and been paid for the work. As Sean was now skipper it was up to him to do the delivery, but I'd help him manoeuvre the high-floating hulk from the narrow river out into the Humber with *Undaunted*.

We'd been in Hull at the shipyard on the previous day to rig a towing bridle and secure a floating line ready to deploy from the stern. *Emulator* was to carry a small inflatable raft in case the tow parted and had to be re-established, though with the heavy duty chain and shackles we'd used and the boat's 18 millimetre trawl warp, this was highly unlikely.

At high water the dock was allowed to flood and the heavy gates were drawn open. The new vessel, floating for the first time was slowly pulled from her place of construction with her stern pointing upstream.

It was difficult to believe that the River Hull, this little tributary flowing into the Humber was the foundation for the fine city of Hull, named Kingston upon Hull by decree of King Richard III.

By the time *Emulator's* warp had been connected to the bridle and *Undaunted's* head rope looped around a point on the hulk's stern, allowing the line to be released without boarding, the ebb tide was running. Traffic crossing the busy Myton Street Bridge came to a standstill as the bridge was raised to allow Sean to haul his charge towards the conflux. *Undaunted*, her engines going slowly astern acted as a brake to slow and control the procession.

As soon as our column was clear of the little river and with our engines in neutral, one end of the attached line was released. This loose end pleasingly ran out clear towards the towed vessel. Passing freely around the strong point on the hulk, the end dropped clear into the river to be quickly hauled in while *Undaunted* was stopped in the water. We were free of the tow. Engaging the engines again at less than half speed we soon caught up with the tug and its charge and escorted the pair down river with the following tide.

An hour into the passage and in the buoyed channel a North Sea Ferry came into sight coming in the opposite direction at a rate of knots. At the same time the officer on watch called on the river's VHF working channel, "vessel towing downstream towards the Clay Huts Buoy, are you on this channel please?"

Sean acknowledged the caller, giving his vessel's name and confirming he was towing the unmanned craft.

"Can we pass port to port please skipper?" came the request from the bridge of the passenger vessel.

This seemed a strange request as the converging parties were at present on a starboard to starboard heading and this would mean the tow crossing the ferry's head.

Sean, thinking the officer was in full command of the situation dutifully put his helm hard to starboard to comply with the request.

Shortly after this manoeuvre had been enacted the watch-keeper, now realising the convergence was happening faster than he'd anticipated and with panic in his voice called out, "sorry sir, can we make that starboard to starboard?"

Without a reply *Emulator* went hard to port, dragging her charge round, preventing the hulk crossing the bows of the charging ferry. Unfortunately he and his tow were now across the tide and a starboard-hand navigation marker was anchored downstream from the pair. The racing ebb tide was driving both craft towards this solid, moored buoy.

Listening to the radio traffic between the ferry and Sean and watching the drama unfold, my mind raced ahead and I could visualise the towrope snagging the top of buoy and *Emulator* and her charge being forced downstream either side of the green-painted marker before slamming alongside each other as they met involuntarily.

I watched, open-mouthed and helpless as the towrope passed clear over the top of the buoy and the pair passed unscathed either side of the fixed position. I must have been holding my breath for I let out a large, audible gasp.

Reaching for the VHF handset I was about to give the officer of the watch a mouthful of abuse for almost causing a catastrophe but his transmission came first. "I bet you couldn't do that again," he called out with a nervous chuckle.

The wind completely taken from my sails at his comment and probably with great relief all I could say was, "you cheeky bastard."

We stayed with the tow as far as Spurn, though it had already been proved that unattached, we were of little use. Rounding the long, narrow spit, and bidding Sean a safe passage I pointed *Undaunted* in the direction of Flamborough Head. We'd be home in a couple of hours. *Emulator* would take the best part of two days to take her charge to the Scottish destination, but would arrive unscathed.

Our passage home was not to be as simple as expected. Twenty miles from Flamborough the yellow search and rescue helicopter from RAF Leconfield came from the shore, heading in our direction. Hovering on our stern as we headed north the pilot called on the VHF radio, "SH 271, SH 271, this is rescue helicopter 128, we'd like to put an officer on board if possible, sir."

"128, receiving you sir. This is *Undaunted*, bound for Scarborough. You're welcome to try, but we're doing eighteen knots, do you want me to ease down?"

"No thank you sir. If you could maintain your course and speed that would be fine."

That suited us. We could continue our passage while still assisting the RAF, though I was doubtful they could manage to achieve their objective. I was soon proved wrong. Within a couple of minutes an officer in khaki overalls and flying helmet was dangling from the chopper and being lowered towards the sea while slowly moving in our direction. Ten feet from the surface, in answer to a hand signal from the man on the wire the winch stopped. Now horizontal, the arm directed the aircraft in our direction. With a minimum of fuss the flying officer, dropped to the deck and instantly released his harness, signalling the helicopter away.

Removing his helmet the pleasant young chap gave a huge grin and said, "hi, good afternoon. Thanks for the exercise." He chatted easily and with confidence.

I couldn't believe how young the chap was. It wasn't just policemen that were looking younger. We had nothing to offer the visitor but a cup of tea or coffee; an offer declined and so mission accomplished and helmet back in place, in answer to a terse radio call, the chopper returned and plucked the 'flying' officer from our deck. Not for the first time I commented how fortunate mariners around the UK were to have such a fantastic rescue service.

* * * * * *

It was a wild, wet night when Dotty and I hurried towards the Newcastle Packet. We'd decided to have a change of scenery from our usual haunt but would have stayed at home had we checked the weather outdoors before getting ready. Shaking the rain from our coats we entered the old pub.

There was only one customer in the establishment, old 'Denk' Mainprize, sitting on his usual stool at the end of the bar. Now a widower in his late eighties and retired, Denk had been a successful skipper all his life and was a pioneer of post-war trawling in keelboats. His two sons, Larry and Bobby were both skippers of 'green' boats. All Denk's boats had been painted green since his coble, *Rachel,* which was built soon after the war.

After ordering drinks from Kath, the landlady, I looked around the pub. The place was much bigger now than when I first began drinking here, having undergone several modernisations. A stage and separate upstairs area for playing pool had recently been added. The walls were adorned with nautical memorabilia and photographs of boats, historic and modern. More recently a gallery of some of the harbour's characters had begun to appear around the walls.

Turning to the old fisherman I commented, "it's an 'orrible night Denk. What are yer doin' out? Yer'd be better off at 'ome, 'avin' a night in for a change."

"Ah'll be gettin' plenty o' nights in before o'er long," he replied, quite cheerfully.

"Ah'd rather be in 'ere wi' company than sat at 'ome on me own."

"There's plenty o' life left in you, Tommy Denk," the landlady chipped in and she was right. The old boy was in good health for his advanced years.

We chatted to Denk and Kath for a while then a few more customers began to drift in. The rain had eased off so we decided to make for the Britannia, universally known as the 'Brit'.

This place was livelier and it quickly became obvious why. It was old Bob Kitto's 70th birthday and his family and friends had arranged and prepared a surprise party for him.

Bob had been drinking in the Brit for years and was well known and loved by everyone who knew him. The old boy had been a fisherman all his life apart from war service and had recently spent his time baiting lines and making crab pots since coming ashore. A man without malice, his dry humour was understated and Bob amused everyone with little effort. Today he was regaling the regulars with a tale about a captain from his navy days. The master had been a stickler for cleanliness on his weekly rounds and was obsessed with finding fault. Fed up with always being guilty of minor infringements, Bob and his mates had decided to give their tormentor something to really complain about. The messmates had melted a little chocolate onto a toilet seat in the crew's heads prior to the officers' visit. The captain and his first lieutenant, wearing white gloves, had gone to the fo'c'sle for their Sunday morning inspection, quickly spying the offending stain.

"What's that?" the master had asked, eyes bulging with indignation.

Bob had dipped his finger into the sticky substance, put the browned digit in his mouth and without blinking reported, "it's shit, sir."

No one heard the remainder of the story for laughter.

This evening Eddie and Rosemary who managed the pub had put a list behind the bar and the locals had been asked to contribute to Bob's present. The target was 70 pints of beer, one for each year of the old salt's life.

The gentle old soul had tears in his usually twinkling eyes, which he dabbed with his handkerchief when the goal was achieved. This was done with much enthusiasm and not too much effort, lead very generously by the landlord's twenty-pint contribution. The beer credits wouldn't last more than a few weeks, as the old boy would give as much ale away as he supped himself.

Next day, half way through hauling our newest fleet of gear, very strangely with only thirty pots on board, we pulled a broken end of the main rope onboard. If the gear had been shot through a wreck and we'd heaved strongly on the line this would have been understandable but there'd been no tension on the rope to part it. Making our way to the other end, the buoy was grabbed and hauling commenced once more. It wouldn't matter that we were hauling with the tide, as there was nothing in the vicinity to snag the line. With a further twenty pots aboard we arrived at another bare end. Ten new pots were missing from the middle of the fleet. The line hadn't been cut. Both ends had been strained to breaking point. I could only think a Dutch or Belgian beam-trawler had towed through the middle of the fleet. We would never find out or ever get the pots back. The long hours of making the pots had been wasted. We'd only had the pleasure of hauling them a couple of times.

There was compensation of sorts the following day when, out of the blue a trio of men appeared on the pier. Two were representatives from a commercial advertising unit and were wearing ski jackets and trainers. Both these men had expensive looking cameras strung around their necks. The third person, sporting a smart suit and three-quarter-length topcoat and shiny dress shoes was an executive from a well-known national fish processing company. The group were looking to take action shots of a trawler, hauling and shooting its nets, material for a brochure the fish merchant had commissioned. The harbour was almost empty and the men were looking quite despondent.

The boss approached, handing me a business card and asked if we did any trawling, which gave an indication of how little fishing knowledge he had. Not wanting to pass the opportunity of a charter, I explained that *Undaunted* was not capable of trawling but I was aware that *Our Pride* was fishing at Flamborough Head only an hour's passage away. Some skippers have an unerring ability to catch fish and Col was one of these. (Mickey, a boat owner and occasional sufferer at the hands of clumsy skippers reckoned there were those who couldn't catch a goldfish in a bowl unless they smashed the bowl first.)

At the leader of the group's request I called Col on the radio, asking when he was due to haul.

"In about three-quarters of an hour," came back the prompt reply. "Why?"

"Can yer tow a bit longer?" I asked. "I've got some folks 'ere who want t' tek some photos of yer 'aulin' yer net."

"Ah don't want t' go much longer," he countered. "It's 'ard ground just 'ere. Don't be too long," then added, "an' I want copies of t' photo's they tek."

I couldn't blame him for this. *Our Pride* was a fine craft and this would be an unusual perspective of her working. I quickly consulted with the spokesman for the group. "If we go now we can be alongside 'im in just over an hour. My pal expects copies of yer shots."

This was agreed, along with a fee and I fired up the engines and pulled in the ropes, holding the boat alongside with a short strop. A couple of aluminium boxes of photographic equipment, then the cameras were carefully lowered by light line. The trio gingerly followed down the ladder. I couldn't help noticing a streak of slime from the harbour wall on the boss's coat. He wasn't dressed for the occasion.

It wouldn't take long to get to Flamborough, there was a fresh northwest wind about force six blowing. It would be all down hill. I hadn't mentioned the weather to the party or that it would be a horrible passage back to Scarborough. They'd find out soon enough.

"We're on our way," I called to Col as we rounded the pier.

"Aye OK. We'll be somewhere near t' 'Gun House Packet' by t' time yer get 'ere," came back the reply. The Gun House Packet was a wreck two miles east of the promontory and was so called as its transit coincided with the foghorn building (Gun House) on the cliff face and the lighthouse building set back some considerable distance from the edge.

We were zipping along at seventeen knots, the visibility was good and the passengers seemed to be enjoying the cruise. The northwester showed none of its effects for the first couple of miles but a following swell soon began to form that pushed us along even faster. We rushed close past Filey Bell buoy and opened up the huge expanse of sandy bay where the cliffs began to grow as we moved southeast towards Bempton. This coastline is spectacular and was appreciated by the party, as were the mugs of coffee, which I'd produced while leaving *Undaunted* on autopilot.

Our Pride was visible on the radar for a while before she came into view and we headed in her direction. The swell was quite deep, though not breaking as we surged along towards the green-painted vessel. On sighting *Undaunted* Col had begun hauling. Our cameramen had equipment prepared as we slowed then stopped close to the fine craft, though not ready for the extremely lively platform that they were to work from. We lay up wind from the trawler and I could hear the camera motors clicking away as we rose and fell on the swell. At least some of the shots would be usable. Water was splashing through *Undaunted's* scuppers and crossing the decks in small wavelets, one of which caught the boss, filling his shoes. He wasn't happy with wet socks but would be very annoyed when his highly polished footwear dried white from the saline content of the seawater.

The steel doors came out of the water with a rush, banging loudly on the ironclad hull of the wooden vessel. Though knowing what to expect, it was interesting watching the process from this perspective. The crew quickly unclipped the doors and began to heave on the sweeps. The floats of the trawl appeared on the surface and soon the quarter-ropes were under tension as the heavy ground rope was dragged up the ship's side. I was bereft to see the middle part of the net was damaged.

"Bloody belly's out," my friend needlessly reported over the radio.

I knew I'd get the blame for this. Col had towed half an hour longer than he'd wanted at my request. I said a silent prayer, hoping this damage was recent and that there were some fish in the net, captured prior to the damage. There certainly wouldn't have been anything caught since.

The codend floated to the surface not far from our vessel and I was relieved to see the haul of cod and whiting didn't look too bad. The crew pulled in the net, drawing the thicker green section holding the catch nearer the ship's side as she rolled steadily, broadside to the six to eight foot swell.

"It's not a blank," the skipper conceded.

The photographers, oblivious to the damage, continued to snap away and one efficiently changed a film in his camera, depositing the roll of thirty-six exposures into the small plastic container that had held the new film.

The bag of fish, three-quarters full was drawn up the vessel's side and dropped inside the shelter-deck to be released. There was nothing left for us to see. The fish, hidden within the deck housing would be left while the crew either mended the damaged net or quickly cobbled the sides of the split together to get the trawl back down. This lacing could be chopped out later when a proper mend would be carried out.

The clients seemed pleased with their results as I turned *Undaunted* slowly into the wind and waves to head back for home.

"Thanks Col," I called on the radio. "I owe yer a beer."

"Aye, all right," he replied. "Ah'll go an' 'elp 'em mend up. Don't forget me photos'."

I confirmed that I'd get him copies and looked through the windscreen at the swell, now showing bits of white on the tops, indicating the wind had increased slightly. *Undaunted* was lifting her head gently to the waves before cresting and dipping into the troughs. The passengers looked surprised at the change of motion. "We're 'ead t' wind now," I said. "It'll be a bit more lively goin' this way."

I gradually increased the throttle to find a relatively comfortable speed that wouldn't throw us about too much, but we were only making nine knots. "We might get a lee closer in," I suggested and altered the autopilot to head west towards the cliff, soon discovering that this move only accentuated the size of the swell as the increased weight of the new ebb tide pushed up to the wave heights. Half a mile from the steep, chalky cliff and realising there was no shelter to be gained I turned *Undaunted* northwest again.

The trio were looking a little worried so to relieve their anxiety I said, "does anyone fancy a cup o' coffee?"

There was a nodded affirmation so leaving the boat on autopilot I quickly dropped down the little stairwell to the cabin. Filling the aluminium kettle and replacing the 'whistle' top as the boat moved about wasn't easy but achieved. I placed the little container on the stove and screwed the fiddle to hold it in place. Lighting the gas with one of the disposable lighters kept handy, I hurried back to the helmsman's seat. The operation had taken less that a minute. My passengers, sitting on the cushioned seating on the portside of the wheelhouse were still apprehensive. Though the swell was deep there was nothing to worry about. The boat was lively but she was coping with the conditions with no problem.

The whistle sounded and I went below again to make the drinks. Turning off the gas to kill the sound I put four mugs in the sink then spooned coffee grains into the mugs, spilling much into the sink. Reaching for the steaming kettle I removed the top and picked each mug up in turn, gingerly pouring the scalding water. As I made the fourth drink an extra large sea launched *Undaunted* skywards and I cringed, knowing what was coming. She plunged downwards at speed, nose-diving headlong into the trough, forcing the mugs to jump from the sink and spraying steaming coffee around the cabin. With a spine-jarring crash she hit the next wall of water and along with the falling mugs I was forced to the floor with the inertia. The kettle dropped from my hand, but luckily was almost empty.

The impact had also unshipped *Undaunted's* compass from its bracket, causing the autopilot to go haywire and the boat to lurch hard to port, turning in a tight circle at speed. Shouts of panic and consternation came from the wheelhouse and I picked myself up, clambering up the stairs to reach the throttles and ease back the levers to dead slow. Switching the autopilot to 'off' I pulled the boat up into the wind with the wooden steering wheel.

The vessel was immediately under control and I looked at the trio to my left. There was a look of sheer horror on their faces. "Coffee's off for now," I announced grimly. Re-seating the compass I engaged the autopilot once more then nudged the throttle up slowly. The weather was reasonable again and we encountered no more rogue seas but the damage was done. My passengers were unhappy.

"Don't you have any lifejackets?" the leader asked.

"Of course we have," I replied and this time, before going below I eased the engine down. Lifting the seat-locker, I revealed several black, plastic bags, each containing a new, orange-coloured jacket. I took three bags from the storage space, throwing each in turn into the cockpit before replacing the seating. We were underway again in no time.

The group looked very strange sitting side by side in the warm wheelhouse wearing life preservers, especially the man in the suit, but I didn't say anything.

Once clear of the tideway at Flamborough we were able to follow the coast into Filey Bay where there was a degree of shelter from the swell. As we followed the sweep of the shoreline, the weather improved and I was able to open the throttles more. There were a few moderate seas to slow our passage as we rounded the Filey Bell Buoy to head northwest again, but we now had only six miles to run and with home in sight, the atmosphere lightened. The trio's life expectancy had suddenly extended.

"You didn't tell us it was going to be like that," the boss said, removing his lifejacket and attempting to wipe a dirty mark from his sleeve.

"If ah'd told yer it was goin' t' be poor weather, yer wouldn't 'ave gone," I countered. "It wasn't too bad. Ah suppose ah could 'ave took yer into Brid. Yer could 'ave got a taxi back t' Scarborough from there."

"That would have been helpful," one of the cameramen quipped.

"It's no use telling us now," said the other.

We lost the swell in the final couple of miles of the run and were soon tied alongside the quay. I hitched *Undaunted* to the ladders. We'd been at sea for just over three hours though I suspect it seemed longer to the passengers. We had no trouble passing the gear ashore but as I followed the boss up the metal rungs I couldn't help noticing the bedraggled state of his suit trousers.

Receiving my fee, I turned to the photographers who were ready to depart. "What about Col's photo's? Will yer send 'em t' me please? Ah'll make sure 'e gets 'em." I handed the nearest of the pair a slip of paper with my address on.

Reluctantly he took the sheet, casually crumpling the piece and stuffing it in his pocket. As an afterthought he fished in his wallet and handed me a promotional flyer with the company's contact details. " If I forget, give me a ring," he said, not making eye contact.

This was ominous. I knew then in my heart the photographs were not going to be forthcoming.

Though they'd gained satisfactory results, the trio that walked from the quay to their vehicle were lacklustre in appearance. The shine had gone from their day. It had also gone from the boss's shoes.

Despite several requests from Col, equalled by the number of phone calls from me to the advertising company and subsequent promises, the photos never arrived.

A few weeks later a huge spring tide coincided with a northerly gale, bringing floods all along the east coast. The narrow isthmus to Spurn Point was breached, briefly forming 'Spurn Island' but was later repaired. This causeway is the lifeline for the inhabitants of the little enclave, mostly RNLI crew and their families.

I feared for my gear following this tidal surge. More than six hundred pots were in relatively shallow water off the Humber and the flowing tide would have been astronomic. Though anchored at each end I was concerned that the single, four-pronged grapnels would be insufficient to hold the weight of the pots in the tideway.

My fears were fully justified a couple of days later when we arrived back at our gear. The weather was fine now and the swell had almost abated. At the location of the first fleet I was dismayed to find that the two buoys, which had been two-thirds of a mile apart when deployed were now almost side by side in the lazy swell. We were going to have a mammoth task on our hands if all our gear was like this fleet.

Taking hold of the first buoy we began to haul on the end tow. Normally we would feel a small lurch as the anchor was freed from its hold, but not on this occasion. An intense weight was soon obvious on the 1-ton hauler and we eased the load up gingerly, knowing a giant ball of pots and at least one anchor were being drawn to the surface. Undaunted was heeling to starboard under the load, which though a little worrying was also helpful, as the list helped us to reach into the water and grab any pot near the surface that was visible and accessible. The ones that could be untied from the tangled rope were released and pulled on board; others were cut free and recovered. These would have new strops fastened in place later before being reattached to the main line.

The load gradually lightened by degrees and after three hours of intense, backbreaking labour the remaining half dozen pots were hauled aboard in a heap. It took more than an hour before the fleet was reassembled and reshot. We had another nine fleets yet to address and I prayed they wouldn't all be like this one. My crew were not happy.

The next fleet, in slightly deeper water wasn't as bad. The first seven or eight pots came up together with the anchor tangled in the middle of the heap but then the remainder were clear. These too were shot back. Time was moving on and we'd only hauled two sets.

Heading to the next position I sighed with dismay when seeing the next two buoys were together. This was going to be another marathon tussle. By the time this tangle had been cleared we'd all had enough for the day. When we next came to the gear we would be able to haul the three clear fleets first then tackle the remainder by degrees until they were back in good order. This of course would affect our earnings.

The reinstatement of the gear took two weeks in total and we had been lucky, though the pair on board wouldn't agree. Some boats had been completely wiped out or lost most of their gear in the rogue tidal surge.

Though I hadn't realised it, my health was beginning to suffer with the tough regime I'd imposed on myself with the potting project. I'd lost a considerable amount of weight, which on its own was not too bad, but people were asking if I was feeling OK and Dotty was expressing concern for my welfare. My wife said I appeared preoccupied and not fully focused. For a few weeks I merely replied in the affirmative when asked, but then realised so many people were saying the same thing that maybe there was something wrong with me. I did feel constantly weary but that was understandable. I was only getting a full night of sleep every second night and wasn't recovering fully. For the past couple of decades I'd been used to a trawling routine where catnapping was a way of life and even on long spells awake I spent a fair amount of time sitting in a comfy chair, despite occasional coarse weather.

It was time for a re-think. I needed a change of direction. This decision coincided with a chance meeting on a train between Danny, now travelling to nautical college, and a former hull trawler-man looking for a new diversion in his career. The man sailed with us for a few trips to get a grasp of the work then sailed without my help. For the first time in many years I didn't have a boat to sail in. I was on the beach.

CHAPTER 17

ON THE BEACH

Lying in bed next morning I heard *Undaunted*'s throaty engines powering her from the harbour on her passage towards Flamborough. Half an hour later I could still hear the rumbling of the huge exhausts. Dotty and others had often mentioned the recurring engine noise heard on fine, still days and now, for the first time I could experience the sound for myself. Gradually the sound faded until there was only an occasional hum. Looking at the clock I realised it was almost an hour since the boat had sailed. She would be off Flamborough Head now and I'd just lost the sound. A slight feeling of guilt came over me as I wondered how many people I'd kept awake during the past year or so.

I was hopeful that the new, younger crew would be able to make *Undaunted* work. I would drive them to and from Grimsby when required and continue to make pots and buoys when needed and for a while the plan worked, but then began to unravel.

The skipper began landing the lobsters to a Grimsby merchant, claiming the prices were better than in Scarborough. He and his crew were paid their wages on the better price but then Alliance was unable to recover the funds due from the merchant, which created problems. The relationship became unpleasant and eventually the skipper and his crew quit.

The following day I boarded *Undaunted* to make sure the vessel was in order and all seemed well until I looked for the cards recording the positions of the fleets of pots. The box was empty. How could this be when the door had been locked?

The ex-skipper denied taking the cards and though the door had been locked, I had no way of proving otherwise. Not long after, the rumour mill was buzzing with word that a Bridlington skipper had the cards and was now in possession of my gear. Though initially denying this, on issuing a County Court summons against the man, I received a token payment for the pots he'd acquired.

Now left with a boat and no gear there was no alternative but to sell *Undaunted* and she was sold at a huge loss, though some of the shortfall was made up with the separate sale of her license. The potting venture was finished, though others realised the potential of fishing this unexploited area with fast boats located nearer the grounds and the gap was soon filled.

* * * * * *

The European Commissioner, Señor Manuel Marin from Spain called for the EU fleet to be cut by at least forty percent and finally, years too late but no less welcome, the UK government announced there was to be a decommissioning scheme. This followed persistent lobbying by the fishing organisations north and south of the border on behalf of their members. These representatives pleaded that it was impossible for men to make a living without breaking the law. Within a given time frame, owners were now able to have their vessels broken up and to surrender their fishing licence's in exchange for a decommissioning grant. Quota could be retained and sold separately by those not replacing their craft. On the downside, anything received would be liable to tax, which could create further problems in the year to come for those in debt and for the less prudent.

This was to be the first of several rounds of decommissioning that would take out two-thirds of the UK fleet and take the heart out of many fishing communities. The regulation stated that the vessels must be destroyed. Some first class vessels would be broken up. These unviable craft would have enabled many people in less developed parts of the world to make a living, rather than depend on foreign financial aid but the faceless bureaucrats in Brussels would not allow this.

The scrapping scheme was over subscribed and a waiting list compiled. There were many fishermen around the country who could no longer face running the daily gauntlet and being compelled to break the law. Some would take the money and downsize into smaller boats, fishing outside the quota system while others would leave the sea. For those wishing to stay in the industry there now was an opportunity to purchase the freed up quota in an attempt to remain legal.

Good crew were becoming harder to find as there were plenty of well paid jobs ashore and the expanding offshore oil industry was able to take all the available fishermen, knowing their capacity to work was astonishing compared with men from alternative sources of employment.

It wasn't only Great Britain that was decommissioning vessels. In the Netherlands and Denmark fine ships were being broken up for lack of fishing opportunities, just as the fleets from Hull and Grimsby has been eradicated in recent years. The difference was that we were being denied access to our own stocks, in UK waters, not those of Iceland. What wouldn't become clear for many years was that when Señor Marin was calling for forty percent of the EU fleet to be decommissioned, he didn't mean Spanish vessels, which were not subject to quota restrictions.

Following the many rounds of decommissioning, fish stocks recovered rapidly but those expecting quotas to remain static or increase were to be disappointed. Year on year fishermen still faced cut after cut. Large, good quality marketable fish were being dumped overboard dead for lack of quota and worse was to follow.

When the EU Commission realised 'declining stocks' alone could no longer be used as an excuse to reduce fishing opportunities for vessels, a 'days at sea' limit was introduced. The 'days at sea' tool, along with stringent quotas would combine to further reduce the fleet and make the surviving boats unviable. In the mixed fishery of the North Sea the varied species are caught in different seasons. Cod and whiting are caught in spring and autumn. Plaice and haddock are thin and in poor condition until late spring. Dover sole are mostly taken in summer and autumn. The limited number of days and shortage of quota are no longer sufficient to allow men to fish throughout the year and they are now part-time fishermen with full time mortgages on their vessels and homes.

Fishermen are being cynically starved out of existence in a sea of plenty and our civil servants are more concerned that they don't upset the European Commission rather than assist the UK fishing industry to survive.

Politicians continue to point at 'science' as the basis for further quota cuts but the science is flawed. The stock assessments are based on two main factors, firstly the results from a huge research vessel which is not fit for purpose as the ship cannot trawl slow enough to herd fish. She uses inappropriate gear that no self-respecting fisherman would consider. Secondly, the assessment is based on vessels' landing information. But with only twenty percent of the fleet remaining and so little quota, fishermen are avoiding the areas of high abundance and are dumping over quota species. This obscene practise serves no purpose. The wastage is not recorded or fully taken into account in the statistics; all this in the limited time men are permitted to go to sea.

When this flawed information is collated it takes the scientists nearly two years to work up the stock assessment with computer modelling, then present their advice to the EU commission. If incorrect information is fed into the programme, the correct results cannot be derived. Even IF the assessment is correct, the information never reflects the real mass of fish on the grounds, as it is two years out of date.

In recent years English scientific observers have sailed on fishing vessels and seen firsthand, some of the wastage. Funds have been found for fishing/science partnership voyages and time series data are starting to develop, though this information does not feature highly in the inputs yet. It is only when fishermen do the research that the findings will be believed.

There are dozens of environmental groups, some well meaning, some vindictive, all with never-ending demands and access to governments wanting to show green credentials. Academics with no knowledge of catching fish or what happens onboard boats, but completely sure in their beliefs, influence decision makers, despite having never been to sea. These people never cease churning out their propaganda from slick PR departments. If they did, the public would stop funding their organizations.

The latest serious situation to hit the remaining vessels has come in the form of an agreement, signed by some unknown, uninformed representative of the UK government. With no consultation, they have committed the British fishing industry to the 'Johannesburg Agreement'. This states that from 2011 fishermen will have to conform to 'maximum sustainable yield' (MSY). This scheme cannot work in a mixed fishery. When the prescribed amount of any single species is caught, no more can be taken, regardless of any shortfall in un-caught stocks. If this plan is followed rigidly, the fleet will finally be tied up and the removal of the Northern fleets will be complete. Who will fish the North Sea then?

Not long ago fishermen thought there was light at the end of the long, dark tunnel. Was it a train coming the other way?

The following are the keelboats and their skippers, mostly trawling, from the three Yorkshire ports, Scarborough, Bridlington and Whitby between 1980 and 1990. The 2010 boats names are listed as a comparison. 20 years have passed and the European Commission still insist there are too many boats chasing too few fish.

Scarborough 1980 - 90

Vessel name	Registration	Skipper
Alexander Woods	GY	Bill Elliott
Allegiance	SH 90	Tom Sheader
Blenheim	BF 4	Tom Pashby
Brilliant Star	SH 117	George Scales
Burton Lonsdale	H 343	John Swift
Carol Anne	SH 175	Larry Mainprize
Caro Sal	H 424	Raymond Trotter
Cassamanda	SH 128	Dave Bevan
Challenge	OB 280	Brian Cox
Christiana S	SH 225	Ron Cappleman
Crystal Sea	H 102	Herbert Nicholson
Crystal W	SH 15	Michael Watts
Elizabeth	SH 191	Phil Lawrence
Emulator	FR 500	Fred Normandale
Faith	SH 21	Lawrence Watson
Faithful R	GY 362	John Reeveley
Floreat	SH 6	John Normandale
Good Intent	FR 47	Tom Mainprize
Jann Denise	FR 80	Bob Walker
Janorus	HL 1	Mick Brookes
June Anne*	SH 108	Bill Messruther
Magdalene Ann	CT 33	Brian Nicholson
Maggie M	SH 170	Robert Mainprize
Margaret Jane	FR 297	Robert Mainprize
Mary Allison	SH 163	Jim Sheader

Nicola Suzanne	FR 141	Michael Anderson
Onward Star	SH 165	Jim Mason
Optimistic	H 417	Thomas Williamson
Our Heritage	FR 237	William Jenkinson
Our Janet	GY 315	Mick Bayes
Our Margaret	SH 137	Tom Rowley
Our Pride	SH 77	Colin Jenkinson
Our Rachel	FR 79	Roy Jenkinson
Pathfinder	FR 172	Robert Mainprize
Pioneer	LH 397	Jim Whitlow
Pride of Redcar	HL 70	Ian Firman
Progressive	SH 28	Martin Douglas
Prospector P	SH 2	Richard Pashby
Silver Line	SH 52	Peter Watkinson
Sincere	CK 97	Terry Hunter
Soolee	H 402	Alan Jagger
Summer Rose	WY 234	Ken Fishburn
Tim Winsor	SH 45	Frank Taal
Willemina	GY 198	Jim Lawrence later Len Price
Valiant	BF 54	Bill Pashby
Vigilantes	GY 179	Ken Luntley

2010

Carousel	SH 298	Derek Tye
Challenge*	SU 513	Jamie Cox
CJ Lewis*	RX 408	Ronnie Ford
Eagernoon	GY 92	John Edmund
Emulator	FR 500	Sean Crowe
Independence	FR 196	Mark Cappleman
Maire Kelly*	OB 2	Colin Jenkinson
Provider*	E 87	Malcolm Ward & Tom Sheader

* *Under 10 metre vessels*

Bridlington 1980 – 90

Acorn	BRD 32	Ernie Buttle
Anmara	H 91	Dave Barratt
Betty	FR 68	Ted Jones
Charlotte May	H 6	Harvey Holbrook
Christel Star	H 56	Gary Lee
Contester	PD 192	Dave Purvis
Crusader	SH 173	Tom Cowling, later Roy Leng
Diana	SY 86	John Collinson
Dominant	H 170	Dave Crawford
Eagernoon	GY 92	Pete Thundercliff
Ejlena	GY 455	Brian Carr
Enchanter	FR 408	Frank Powell
Flamborough Light	H 392	Jim Buckingham
Galatea	H 82	Roy Artley
Glenda	GY 304	Colin Newby
Grenaa Way	GY 1375	Mark Freeman
Guide Us	H 46	Norman Redhead
Industry	H 443	Alwyn Emmerson
Karianda	H 359	Robert Quinn
Madalia	SH 1	Steve Emmerson
My Rose-Anne	H 87	Neil Murray
Janet M	H 491	George, then Chris Traves
Lois Anne	KY 40	Peter Ibbottson
Margaret H	INS 279	David Holbrook
Ocean Contender	H 340	Alan Coates
Ocean Reward	FR 28	Jack, then Andrew Sanderson
Onward Star	SH 165	Pip Sayers
Pamela S	FR 38	Jim, then Paul Scotter

Pickering	H 484	Derek Gates
Pilot Us	H 45	Alan Kirby
Q Varl	H 1	Robert Quinn
Radiant Trust	H 256	Mike Coates
Regal Star	H 273	Peter Carr
Sarb J	H 446	Brian Taylor
Sea Hunter	FR 414	Mick Laws
St Andrew	H 12	Willie Baxter
St Amant	SH 38	Derek Gates
St Keverne	H 340	Alan Kirby
Sunningdale	GY 1388	Roger Newby
Three Fevers	H 103	Graham Young
Tradition	H 232	Dennis Jewitt
Ubique	KY 28	Bill Edmonds
Valmont	GY 254	Walt Lewis
Wayfinder	SH 76	Peter Ibbottson
Wayside Flower	H 65	Pip Sayers

There are no trawlers fishing from Bridlington in 2010, the boats have gone. A healthy fleet of shellfish vessels still exploit the shallow grounds from the east to south of Flamborough Head.

Whitby 1980 - 90

Achieve	WY 155	Eric Young
Ard Adhm	WY 135	George Storr
Arrivain	WY 170	Richard Brewer
Border Maid	AH 117	Mike Smith
CKS	KY 47	Billy Storr
Emulate	WY 41	Howard Locker
Endeavour	WY 1	Matt Hutcheson
Eskglen	A 187	Robert Peart
Falcon	WY 162	T Durrant
Fertile	LK 317	

Gemma Fidelis	GY 419	John Hall
George Wetherill	OB 200	Dave Locker
Golden Fleece	FH 208	Harry Smith
Golden Hope	WY 141	Ron Frampton then David Frampton
Heather Belle	LH 257	Richard Brewer
Ina B	WY 219	Tex Hansell
Jaqueline Stuart	LH 159	Arnold Locker
Jasper	PD 174	Richard Brewer
Kristanjo	WY 211	James Leadley Jnr
Lead Us	KY 46	Raymond Storr (Red Ned)
Lead Us Forth	WY 264	Andrew Storr
Ocean Charm	PD 127	Richard Brewer
Ocean Herald		Tal Bennison
Ocean Venture	KY 209	Jack Hebden (Bant)
Our Samaria	WY 347	Robert Cole
Palmire	WY 302	Jim Leadley Snr
Press On		Robert Cole
Provider	AH 71	Arthur Storr
Radiant Morn	FR 141	Pete Hansell
Sardia Louise	WY 335	William Hall
Scoresby	WY 12	Ian Brittan
Semper Cresendo		
Shulamit	BH 21	Richard Brewer
Stella Maris	WY 42	Ian Davis
Success	WY 212	Peter Leadley
Venus	FR 79	James Cole
Wakeful	KY 261	Tony Price
Wellspring	BA 337	Tony Young
Whitby Light	WY 170	William Hall

2010

Abbie Lee	WY 211	John Hall
Copious	WY 170	Richard Brewer
Defiant	WY 219	David Frampton
		sank October 2010
Emulate II	WY 110	Howard Locker
Good Intent	WY 79	James Cole

These lists are not definitive but indicative. Not all the boats were in the ports for the full decade. Some skippers changed vessels during the period. There were also many cobles fishing from the three ports with two or three men on board, working with lines for cod and haddock in winter and shellfish in summer.

All these vessels made a living for their crews prior to the stranglehold of the EU. Can the science possibly be correct when these few remaining boats are still starved of fish and of days to catch their meager quotas?

This scenario is not limited to the Yorkshire Coast. The sad affair is reflected throughout the United Kingdom.

Gone but not forgotten

Chris 'Stoff' Arnold

Alan England (Mansfield diver)

Bill Colling

Mick 'Lager Legs' Bayes

Jackie Clark

Dave 'Injection' Allison

Marjorie 'Madge' Plummer

Walter 'Rall' Crawford (my Uncle Walt)

Harry Messruther

Bob Cammish

Paul Lever

Eddie Morris

George Brockwell (Brocky) Junior

Bill Brown

Margaret Temple (wife of Eddie)

Dot Clutterbuck nee Eves

David Elliott (son of Dick)

Herbert Nicholson Junior (Herby)

Len 'Ikey' Price

Stanislaw 'Stan' Zajac

Colin Bell (Sub Aqua diver) The first casualty of the club in its 49-year existence.

Bernie Luntley

Jack Dalton

Mavis Clayton

Barry Jenkinson
Margaret Turnell (Mum's sister)
Bill Scales
John Oliver, Parkol Marine Whitby
Dennis 'Wacker' Walker
Eric Dalton
Jilly Swales, Leeds Arms barmaid, friend and proofreader.
Jonty Rhodes (Brother in Law)
Chris Coole

The majority of this volume has been written on trains, planes and in hotel rooms while attending meetings with politicians, mostly futile encounters. In writing this book the author intended to give his readers an insight into the way of life in the 1980s and early 1990s as seen through his eyes. It is acknowledged that certain events may not be in chronological order. Some characters depicted are fictitious. The opinions and comments relating to the politics and regulations of the following two decades, 1990 -2010 are those of the author.

Slack Water

Fred Normandale

First of the Flood

Fred Normandale

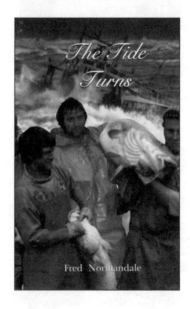

The Tide Turns

Fred Normandale